STEAM LOCOMOTIVES COMPARED

TERRY ESSERY

TRANSPORT
Atlantic
PUBLISHERS

The 1950s were the last decade when steam reigned supreme on British railways. Many of the older types, though much reduced in numbers, were still running lighter passenger trains and even piloting heavy expresses. The Compound on the far left was one of many of its type still in use while the Stanier 'Jubilee' class dominated mainline trains. The 'Scots', by now all rebuilt with tapered boilers, claimed the heavy expresses. Stanier Pacifics kept very much to the west coast mainline. Tucked in behind 45594 'Bhopal' can be seen one of the new BR standard 4-6-0s which at the time seemed secondary to the more common 'Black 5'. The time was a unique period of change when the many designs of locomotive, old and new, could be compared.

STEAM LOCOMOTIVES COMPARED

TERRY ESSERY

Atlantic

IT WAS my original intention to dedicate this book to all those who are besotted with railways in general and steam locomotives in particular.

However, since completing the manuscript it has been pointed out that much of the text could well serve as a reference guide to aspiring loco crews on preserved railways. In all honesty this had not been my intention, but should it prove to be so, then I shall be doubly delighted since it is not only essential to preserve steam engines but also the skills to operate them.

With regard to the work itself, my sincere thanks to David Jenkinson for supplying most of the illustration and to him and David Joy for having the confidence to publish it, to Bob Essery for his support and encourgement, and to my wife Hazel for the blood, sweat, toil and tears shed over a hot typewriter.

Prepared and produced by the Pendragon Partnership
on behalf of Atlantic Transport Publishers
Trevithick House, West End, Penryn, Cornwall TR10 8HE

© Terry Essery, Pendragon Partnership and
Atlantic Transport Publishers 1996

ISBN: 0 906899 65 6

Layout and Design by Barry C. Lane, Sutton-in-Craven

Phototypeset by Royd Typesetting, Silsden, West Yorkshire

Printed by Redwood Books, Trowbridge

British Cataloguing in Publication Data
A catalogue record for this book is available
from the British Library

CONTENTS

INTRODUCTION

THE NEED to make comparisons would seem to be a deeply engrained facet of the human psyche. It is understandable that this should be so because without making comparisons we would not be able to select that which is most suited to our particular individual requirements. Fortunately, not only our requirements differ widely but also our ideas on how best to translate these into the designs and usable artefacts which do so much to enrich life's experiences.

Few discoveries have had such a significant impact on mankind as steam power, particularly in relationship to rail transport and it is here that professionals and enthusiasts alike can revel in a veritable plethora of variety.

During the Golden Years of the 1950s the new family of BR Standard locomotives started to mingle with not only those designs of the 'Big Four' but also the hosts of familiar old faithfuls, many emanating from the previous century, which had served the companies of the pre-grouping era so well. Obviously with so many contenders to perform a specific task, comparisons were bound to be made by enthusiasts and locomen, both

often becoming extremely partisan over their preferences to the extent that they closed their minds to the possibility of other designs having any merit whatsoever.

I was fortunate that my footplate career encompassed those buoyant and innovative years when, although steam had enjoyed a long and rich lineage, it still appeared to have quite a future. Obviously we locomen daily discussed the merits of engines, equipment and indeed everything which affected our working lives. Needless to say our opinions were sought by all those with an interest in railway matters and it is still so, well over 25 years after the withdrawal of steam from BR (written in 1995).

Because of the probability that in a further 25 years I will not be in a position to pass opinions of any sort, I was persuaded to record these personal impressions. However I must emphasise that my comments are purely personal and because I have included only locomotives on which I have actually worked, they are not based on hearsay; this of course leaves many omissions for which I apologise.

Viewed from any angle, Jubilees certainly looked the part and were the very epitome of an express passenger locomotive. Graceful, well balanced lines atop traditional large diameter coupled wheels truly gave an impression of speed, an impression which remained until the end of the steam era.

Also it must be born in mind that my remarks will be coloured by the needs of a working footplateman and therefore biased towards the practical rather than the aesthetic which after all is in the eye of the beholder. Be that as it may, there is much to be said for the old adage: 'If it looks right, then generally it is right'.

Soon after the decision of placing these opinions of certain steam locomotives on record was made, it was pointed out that while a number of enthusiasts had a good understanding of locomotives and how they function, there were also many whose knowledge was less comprehensive. Furthermore, even those falling into the former category would be doubtless interested in learning more of the footplateman's techniques and modus operandi.

It is therefore my intention firstly (in Part I) briefly to cover the basic principles of steam locomotives and their more important components together with working methods. The rest of the book will be devoted to personal impressions of locomotives on which I have worked.

Many are probably aware that no two locomotives, even of the same class, were exactly alike. One might suppose that in the latter days of steam when mass production techniques were used as much as possible, these variations would not occur. However, if one considers the multitude of components involved and that even in those last days, most still needed to be assembled by skilled fitters, this possibility becomes more understandable. As with the majority of engineering operations, work was permitted to vary between certain predetermined tolerances which gave an acceptable average; and most locomotives fell into this category. Occasionally an engine was turned out which seemed to be assembled from all the lowest tolerance parts. The aggravation and resentment this caused the fitters was possibly imprinted on the whole assembly because these locomotives never ran quite up to standard and were often a source of recurrent problems. On the other hand there were odd times when the opposite happened and all the pluses came together to produce an exceptional engine which performed far beyond expectation.

Many other facts could affect the day to day performance of locomotives, be they hauling passengers, fitted, or loose coupled trains, and so a particular engine working the same booked train would not necessarily respond in exactly the same way on consecutive days, viz:-

> The use of a different grade of fuel.
> The fire may not have been cleaned properly.
> Scamped preparation.
> Defective brick arch or Baffle plate.
> High Scale concentration of impurities in the boiler water and therefore in need of a washout.
> Strong winds – which can help, but usually hinder progress.
> Very low outside temperatures causing extra drag in axleboxes. (Quite a number of greasebox wagons were still in use during the 50s).
> Minor anomalies with the continuous brake on fitted trains causing increased drag etc.

These are quite apart from any mechanical problems which may develop on the locomotive itself, which could range from jammed cylinder drain cocks, through blowing piston glands to leaking superheater elements. However, unless recurrent, mechanical defects would not influence the assessment of a locomotives performance.

With the possibility of so much variation, it would be unwise to judge a particular locomotive let alone a whole class on a single trip. To obtain a true impression one really had to sample the greatest number of individual engines covering the widest range of duties over the longest possible period and unfortunately this was not always practical. Therefore whilst my experience with some classes of locomotive was quite comprehensive, with others it was rather brief, but this will be stated in the notes.

T.E.
Stoke-on-Trent
1995

Chapter 1
Basic Principles

WHEN AN IDEA is correct in principle, the basic concept changes little over the years and nowhere is this more apparent than in steam locomotives. The basic concept which the Stephensons incorporated into *Rocket* was perpetuated right through to Riddles magnificent 9Fs. Admittedly, those engines were the culmination of 130 years of steady development in every aspect of engineering but a description of the working principles of a 9F would be almost equally applicable to its early ancestor.

Let us look for a moment at these logical design features in *Rocket* which gave the steam locomotive such a long term future. None of them were completely new but they all came together for the first time in *Rocket* thereby ensuring its outstanding success. So,. before examining in greater detail the various components that make up a steam locomotive, it may be helpful to touch very briefly on what part these components play.

It used a multi-firetube boiler which allowed a much larger heating surface than the original single flue type. This necessitated a separate water jacketed firebox to contain the grate and its burning fuel; being part of the pressure vessel, the firebox was stayed accordingly. Inclined outside cylinders drove directly on to crankpins in the wheels which permitted the driving axle to be provided with springs, while the valves controlling admission of steam to the cylinders were driven by eccentrics rather than the earlier tappet arrangements. Exhaust steam was directed into the chimney so as to ensure a good draught upon the fire which at the same time overcame the objection of exhausting directly to atmosphere.

Fuel burned on a grate in the firebox supplies heat in the form of radiation and hot gases to water contained in the boiler. Adequate draught to the fire is ensured by the action of exhaust steam from the cylinders emerging from the blast pipe and passing up the chimney. This causes a partial vacuum in the smokebox thus drawing hot gases through the firetubes and air via the ashpan to the underside of the grate. Steam raised in the boiler is collected from its highest point and passes through a regulator valve controlled from the cab. It then travels along the main steam pipe to the superheater elements (if fitted) and then to the steam chests. Here it is distributed to the cylinders by the action of valves operated by eccentrics and levers which are under the control of the reversing mechanism. Steam expanding in the cylinders exerts pressure on the pistons which is then transferred via the connecting rods to the driving wheel cranks.

Most locomotives and tenders are equipped with some form of steam brake which via cranks, pull rods and hangers, clamps blocks directly on to the wheel tyres. Normally only driving and tender wheels are braked and since a locomotive needs to be secure when stationary, a hand brake is also fitted. When used on trains equipped with vacuum brakes, the required vacuum is created by means of ejectors and/or pumps and the brakes are applied by means of a brake valve which is often combined with the steam brake valve.

Boiler water level is maintained usually by two injectors and registered in gauge glasses equipped with protectors. Other gauges in the cab show Boiler steam pressure, Vacuum pressure, Carriage Warming Apparatus steam pressure and in certain classes, Steam Chest pressure and a speedometer.

In order to maintain an adequate draught on the fire when stationary, a blower in the form of a perforated pipe usually surrounding the top of the blast pipe is fitted. The blower, which takes steam direct from the boiler, serves to create a draught in lieu of exhaust steam and is controlled from a valve in the cab.

These then are the principal features we shall be examining and since the heart of a steam locomotive is its boiler we can do no better than start with this.

The Boiler

From the earliest days the locomotive boiler was set a number of severe tasks. It had to be as compact and as light as possible yet produce high volumes of steam in relation to its size. It had to be strong enough to withstand considerable stresses of both mechanical and thermal origin and it had to tolerate water-level and furnace heat fluctuations while also being able to meet excessive demands over short periods.

The Stephensons, in particular George's son, Robert (who was the real brains behind *Rocket*) showed the way and the most successful subsequent developments right up to the final days of the steam era were based on the multi-firetube principle. Experiments with other types of boilers had previously and have subsequently been made over the years, but none were able to meet the above requirements with reliability nor were they to prove so adaptable.

SECTIONAL VIEW OF BOILER

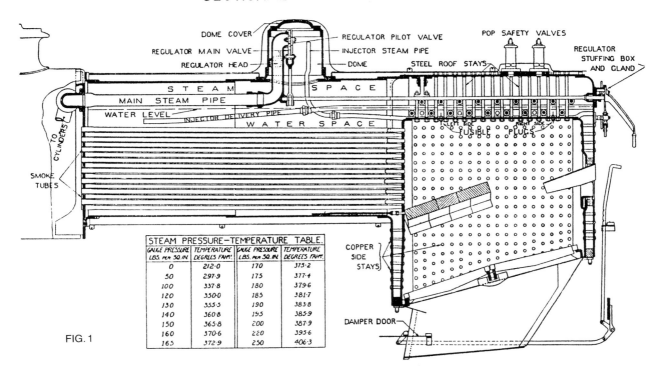

FIG. 1

STEAM PRESSURE—TEMPERATURE TABLE.			
GAUGE PRESSURE LBS. PER SQ.IN.	TEMPERATURE DEGREES FAHT.	GAUGE PRESSURE LBS. PER SQ. IN.	TEMPERATURE DEGREES FAHT.
0	212·0	170	375·2
50	297·9	175	377·4
100	337·8	180	379·6
120	350·0	185	381·7
130	355·5	190	383·8
140	360·8	195	385·9
150	365·8	200	387·9
160	370·6	220	395·6
165	372·9	250	406·3

The locomotive boiler's shape is basically a horizonal cylinder with a downward extending firebox at one end. This shape, together with its innate strength, made it a suitable foundation for driven machinery such as traction engines, steam rollers and even some early locomotives.

The barrel of the boiler was first made as cylindrical as possible although a certain amount of taper could occur by the need to lap the joints of rings of plates from which it was made. Before larger plates became available, boilers were often made from three rings with the central one being smaller in diameter than the other two so that it could fit inside them for riveting. Later on with shorter boiler barrels at least, only two rings were necessary but it will be seen that the position of the dome for example was dictated more by engineering expedience than a whim of the designers.

Reference should be made to Fig. 1 and Fig. 2 which show sectional views of parallel and tapered boilers.

It will be seen that the firebox tube plate needs to be the same size as the smokebox tube plate, but whereas the latter is a flat plate, in effect closing the front of the barrel and needing only to be large enough to allow adequate circulation around the tubes, the firebox end of the barrel has to encompass that extra width of the water space surrounding the inner firebox. These water legs being at least 3 inches wide means that the firebox outer wrapper is somewhat wider than the front of the barrel. One way of achieving this difference in width is simply by tapering the boiler.

Tapered boiler barrels with conically rolled rings appeared quite early in America and usually took the form of one tapered ring just ahead of the firebox. G.J. Churchward, whose initial designs for the GWR were apparently influenced by American practice adopted this same layout although later the whole barrel was tapered on some examples. This style was also adopted by Stanier for his LMS locomotives and perpetuated on the BR Standard locomotives. Theoretically, the principal virtues of the taper boiler are to give a large steam space over the firebox, improved water circulation around the firebox tubeplate and a significant weight saving at the smokebox end, this last consideration being especially useful when designing locomotives with restricted axle loads. However, taper boilers are more complex to manufacture and therefore add to the initial cost.

Whether tapered or parallel the principal parts of a boiler may be said to consist of a steel shell (which includes the boiler barrel, firebox wrapper plates and

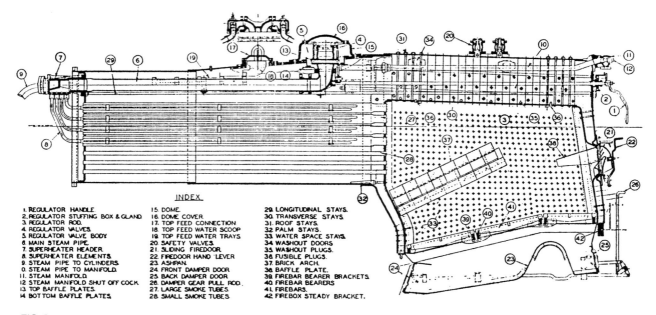

FIG. 2

smokebox tube plate), the inner firebox (generally made of copper) and the firetubes leading from the inner firebox to the smokebox tube plate within the barrel. The inner firebox is secured to the wrapper plates by numerous stays passing through the water spaces which surround the inner firebox on all sides except the bottom which is closed by a foundation ring.

When a superheater is fitted, this is made up of a number of large flue tubes placed above the ordinary fire tubes within the boiler barrel, these flues house the superheater element tubes through which steam has to pass on its way from the regulator valve via the main steam pipe to the steam chest.

Boilers are designed to work at a certain pressure and this registered working pressure should be indicated by a metal tablet secured to the firebox backplate and also by a red line on the face of the steam pressure gauge. Compliance to the working pressure is ensured by safety valves which are usually mounted over the firebox crown where the bulk of the steam is generated and should lift within plus or minus 5lbs of the registered pressure.

In order to ascertain the water level in the boiler, water gauges in the form of glass tubes are fitted to the boiler back plate inside the cab. As an additional safety measure and to reduce possible damage to the firebox crown sheets should the water level become too low, fusible lead plugs are located in the firebox crown.

Overheating in this area causes them to fuse allowing steam to fill the firebox and to smother the fire.

Water is supplied to the boiler by means of two injectors which are often mounted behind the cab footsteps. These draw the steam needed to operate them from the highest point of the boiler and deliver water by means of an internal pipe either directly or via distributor trays to the front (coolest) end of the boiler.

The regulator valve is also generally fitted inside the boiler at the highest point and when there is a steam dome it will be mounted within this. Sometimes the regulator is located in the smokebox, in which case steam is led to it by an internal pipe running from the highest point inside the boiler shell where steam is driest.

On older engines, separate pipes drawing live steam from the boiler led to the steam brake, vacuum ejectors, blower, steam sanders, whistle, carriage warming apparatus and possibly one or more sight feed displacement type lubricator. On later designs, steam for these auxiliary fittings (with the exception of the blower) is supplied from a steam manifold mounted on the back of the firebox. The manifold casting, taking steam from the highest point of the boiler through a single pipe, can be isolated by a plug in the centre.

Whenever water is evaporated, any salts dissolved in that water will remain behind, consequently there is a steady build up of scale forming salts. Water supplies were chemically treated so as to minimise these effects but even so it was necessary to withdraw locomotives from service every 7-14 days or so for periodic boiler washouts. To facilitate this, boilers are fitted with a number of Washout Plugs and Mud Doors, the former being a simple removable plug, the latter an oval cover secured by a nut and bridge piece over a rather larger opening. Loose scale and precipitated salts often referred to as mud or sludge, are washed from these openings by forcing clean water through the boiler barrel. Also, to extend the periods between washouts a continuous blowdown valve was fitted to many locomotives. This valve was mounted on the boiler backplate operating only when the regulator was open and allowed a small measured quantity of water to pass out of the boiler, thereby reducing the concentration of scale forming salts. Fig. 3.

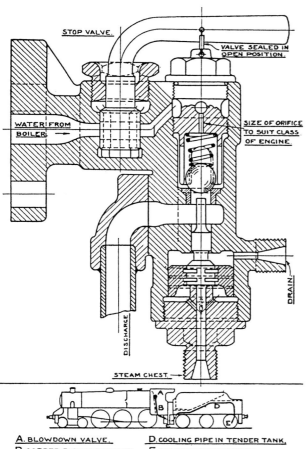

A. BLOWDOWN VALVE.
B. COPPER DISCHARGE PIPE.
C. FLEXIBLE CONNECTION BETWEEN ENGINE & TENDER.
D. COOLING PIPE IN TENDER TANK.
E. DISCHARGE TO TRACK.

FIG. 3

The Firebox

For various reasons fireboxes have enjoyed a rather wider variety of shapes than boiler barrels. In *Rocket* it was a water jacketed box attached to the rear of the barrel and linked to its water circulation system by large diameter copper pipes. However, within a year or two of this, the firebox was incorporated within the boiler barrel using a foundation ring to separate the inner and outer firebox plates, thus forming water walls on three sides of the firebox. This practice has been the basis of construction ever since.

At the front, the inner firebox wall rose from the foundation ring to become the tubeplate, while at the back, the firehole joined inner and outer boxes with firehole rings. The inner box had a more or less flat top, called the crown, about three quarters of the height of the barrel. The tops of the tubes being somewhat lower and the minimum water level rather higher than this crown.

Some early locomlotives, notably those designed by Bury in England and Norris in America, had fireboxes which were circular in plan except for a flattened front where the tube plate was situated. This circular form extended upwards beyond the boiler barrel to form a steam dome the full diameter of the firebox. When in later engines the plan become square, the dome followed suit giving rise to the so called 'Haystack' firebox. However, firebox shapes were often dictated by the wheel arrangement, type of fuel burned and the method used in constructing the frames.

During the early 1860s boilers with square topped fireboxes made their appearance. The design is usually attributed to Alfred Belpaire of the Belgian Railways where coal of low calorific value and high ash content led to a requirement for relatively large fireboxes. This layout enlarged the steam space over the crown sheet and also simplified the arrangement of internal stays to support what in effect was now two parallel surfaces. Although adopted by many railways, Belpaire fireboxes were not universally accepted and examples of round-topped types could be seen in service to the end of the steam era.

While locomotives were still quite small, fireboxes in this country were often fitted between axles within the plate frames used by most manufacturers. They were deep and narrow, usually with horizontal grates, but despite the size limitations imposed by their location, they performed well on the high grade coal then generally available. As the need arose for larger grate arears, so grates became somewhat higher and were frequently sloped upwards towards the back in order to clear the rear axle.

One advantage of this type of firebox is that it allowed the highest possible adhesive weight to be carried by the coupled wheels which could be of large diameter.

In countries where only poor grade fuel was in use, large grate areas were needed, particularly for the more powerful locomotives. Obviously there is a limit to the length at which firebox can be manually fired, so wide boxes evolved to give the necessary grate area. Even when bar frames, which are somewhat lower than plate frames, are used, these wide boxes could not fit between them. The usual wide firebox therefore, sloped slightly towards the front and its ashpan was arranged to clear any trailing wheels needed to support it at the rear. Because the grate could not be low down, such boxes tended to have a low volume in relation to grate area, a situation not conducive to full and efficient combustion. This was overcome by providing a forward extension of the inner box into the barrel, known as the combustion chamber, instead of allowing the tube plate to rise vertically from the foundation ring or the top of the inner throat plate. This solution also reduced the length of the tubes which could be an advantage in a large locomotive with a long barrel.

Fireboxes, therefore, fall into two basic categories – deep narrow grates and wide shallow grates, the latter being used principally on larger types.

Even in Britain, early steam locomotives burned coke or wood but after the middle of the 19th century coke had been replaced by coal. However, the burning of coal presented problems because it gave off large quantities of hydrocarbons which, if left unburned, was emitted as smoke. Charles Markham and Mathew Kirtley of the Midland Railway solved this by devising the brick arch coupled with an improved secondary air supply via the firehole door. This brick arch extends from the tube plate just below the bottom row of tubes, backwards and upwards towards the rear of the box angled to a line above the firehole. Supported by rails on each side, it stops short of the back of the box by an amount between a half and a third of the box length. The purpose of the brick arch will be dealt with in greater detail in the section under combustion but briefly it served to lengthen the 'path' taken by the firebox gases before entering the fire tubes themselves.

The Smokebox

The smokebox is usually described as a chamber forming an extension at the front end of the boiler barrel. Initially the important contribution which this chamber, or rather what it housed, made to the overall performance of a locomotive was not fully appreciated.

However, realisation gradually dawned that it was not just a bin in which to collect char, or keep the blast pipe out of sight. The degree of blast or volume of air drawn through a fire affects its brightness and ultimately the steaming properties of the boiler. This draught is proportional to the amount of vacuum that can be induced in the smokebox by the action of exhaust steam from the cylinders passing through the blast pipe and chimney. Over the years, much work had been done in an effort to improve the draughting on locomotives for it was not simply a question of trying to obtain the greatest possible blast for a specific working condition. As always there were many conflicting requirements and the solution was only found in a carefully balanced compromise.

The fire needed to burn well, whether the locomotive was working hard and using much steam or running easily and using little. Ideally it should cope with a wide range of fuel grades and not be too demanding on the fireman's skill – or his back muscles! It should provide adequate blast for a thick fire and yet not tear a thinner fire into holes nor throw an excessive amount of cinders out through the chimney. The blast should be evenly distributed over the entire grate area but it should achieve all the above objectives without creating too much back pressure on the pistons and thus compromising the free running of the locomotive.

Many different approaches were made to overcome these draughting problems, much coming from continental Europe. Koechlin in France devised a movable internal cone for the blast pipe which reduced the orifice as it rose. The Macallen cap also featured on a number of French locomotives early this century. This was a supplementary nozzle fitted with hinged vanes which could be lowered over the blast pipe and controlled by the driver.

In order to cope with the problem of large steam flow within a restricted height, Legein of the Belgium State Railways improved the performance of some large Pacifics by fitting a double chimney and blastpipe in the early 1920s.

Kylala of Finland split the exhaust steam jet into four streams which filled an enlarged circular chimney. However, Chapelon improved this with specially designed intermediate petticoat pipes arranged to increase the entraining efficiency and draw in furnace gases at several levels and across a greater width of the tube plate. This 'Kylchap' exhaust, commonly fitted in double form, proved very popular and was adopted for the LNER A4 Pacific *Mallard*.

Lemaître used a ring of nozzles, while more recently the Austrian Dr. Giesl-Gieslingen invented an oblong

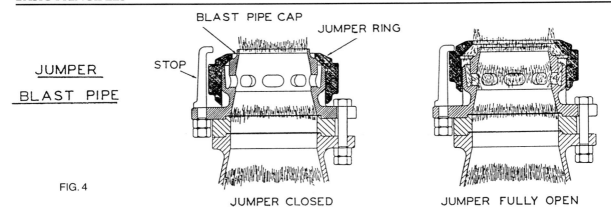

JUMPER
BLAST PIPE

BLAST PIPE CAP

JUMPER RING

STOP

FIG. 4

JUMPER CLOSED   JUMPER FULLY OPEN

ejector in which a row of nozzles set longdituinally in the smokebox, discharged upwards through a long narrow chimney.

In this country developments were somewhat more conservative although even from very early days, drivers used simple mechanical devices for splitting the exhaust jet in order to improve steaming. These 'jimmies' took many forms, but could be quickly fitted – and just as quickly removed, for they were not approved of by the authorities since any improvement in steaming was thought to be at the cost of increased coal consumption.

The Jumper blast pipe cap was a device developed by the GWR and perpetuated by Stanier on some of his earlier LMS locomotives. The blast pipe cap (see Fig. 4) is fitted with a jumper ring which lifts when the exhaust steam pressure rises, thereby exposing an annular opening surrounding the normal blast pipe nozzle. The additional opening provided in this way when the jumper lifts is equal to 50% of the normal blast pipe orifice and serves to cut down the sharp blast which is usually obtained when engines are worked heavily and the tendency to lift the fire is reduced. This of course was the opposite effect to what many others were trying to achieve but now it will be appreciated that so many factors are involved that to be efficient, the draughting arrangements need to be designed from chimney to ashpan as an integrated whole.

Also, on some Stanier locomotives, baffle plates were fitted in the smokebox in front of the tubes and below the top of the blast pipe. The purpose of these was to even up the effect of the blast over the whole tube plate and to cut down excessive loss of fuel in the form of cinders thrown up the chimney.

With the installation of these baffle plates, what was once a fairly empty chamber was now becoming rather well filled, since also housed there would be the super-heater header, the main steam pipes, the blower, the exhaust pipe from the ejectors and in some instances, the regulator valve. All these fittings impeded the daily

work of cleaning out smokeboxes and made an already onerous task even more difficult, but then came an invention which filled it altogether.

During the late 1940s, self-cleaning smokeboxes were introduced on the LMS by H.G. Ivatt. The self cleaning action was achieved by an arrangement of baffle plates and wire sieves which directed the gases downwards scouring char collected in the bottom of the smokebox. Any cinders too large to initially pass through the mesh were bounced and pulverised by the action of the blast until they were small enough to be ejected through the chimney. At the same time, these mesh sieves served as spark arrestors since particles capable of causing fires were both reduced in size and cooled by the process. It was a wonderful labour saving device much appreciated by footplate crews engaged in disposal work (see Fig. 5).

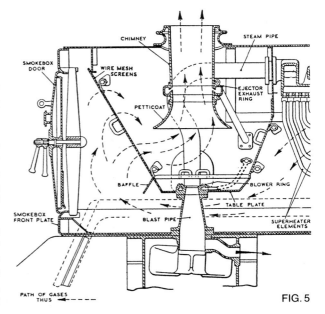

CHIMNEY   STEAM PIPE

SMOKEBOX
DOOR

WIRE MESH
SCREENS

EJECTOR
EXHAUST
RING

PETTICOAT

BAFFLE   BLOWER RING

TABLE PLATE

SMOKEBOX
FRONT PLATE   BLAST PIPE   SUPERHEATER
ELEMENTS

PATH OF GASES
THUS   FIG. 5

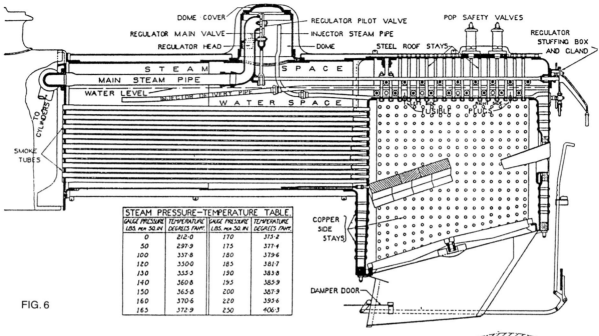

FIG. 6

STEAM PRESSURE—TEMPERATURE TABLE.			
GAUGE PRESSURE LBS. per SQ. IN.	TEMPERATURE DEGREES FAHT.	GAUGE PRESSURE LBS. per SQ. IN.	TEMPERATURE DEGREES FAHT.
0	212·0	170	375·2
50	297·9	175	377·4
100	337·8	180	379·6
120	350·0	185	381·7
130	355·5	190	383·8
140	360·8	195	385·9
150	365·8	200	387·9
160	370·6	220	395·6
165	372·9	250	406·3

Regulators

The two most common types of regulator valves used on the LMS were the vertical slide valve pattern fitted to older standard engines (see Fig. 6) and the horizontal slide valve regulator as used on taper boiler locomotives (see Fig. 7).

The vertical slide valve regulator is so called because the valve face is arranged vertically. Usually the face has four ports, two small ones for starting purposes and two large ports for normal running. Resting on the valve face is the main valve which has four ports cut in it and the starting or pilot valve rests in turn on top of the main valve. The pilot valve usually has two ports which are used for starting purposes.

Operating the regulator brings about the following sequence:-

First movement of the regulator handle lifts the pilot valve till the two small starting ports are open. Further movement of the handle then moves both the pilot valve and main valve together, the action of which opens the large ports in the main valve and closes the starting ports. During closing, the pilot valve is first moved down over the main valve into its normal position and then both valves are brought back together to their original location, closing the main steam ports as they move down.

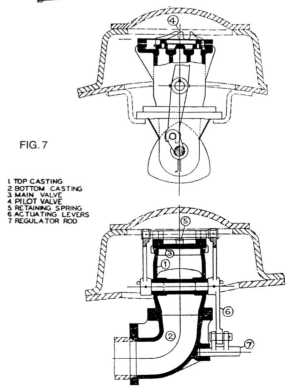

FIG. 7

1 TOP CASTING
2 BOTTOM CASTING
3 MAIN VALVE
4 PILOT VALVE
5 RETAINING SPRING
6 ACTUATING LEVERS
7 REGULATOR ROD

REGULATOR ARRANGEMENT — HORIZONTAL DOME TYPE

FIG. 8

STANDARD COMPOUND REGULATOR

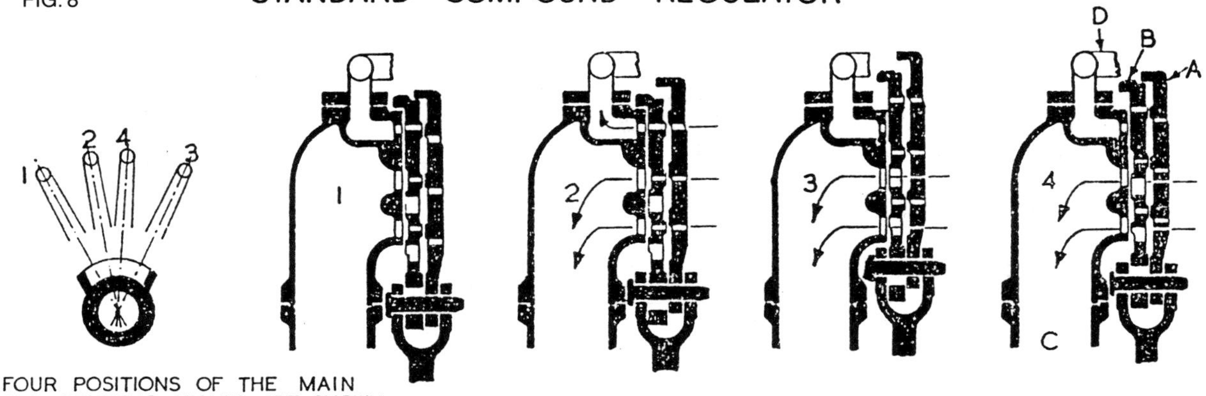

FOUR POSITIONS OF THE MAIN
AND STARTING VALVES ARE SHOWN
FOR CORRESPONDING POSITIONS
OF THE REGULATOR HANDLE

1 REGULATOR CLOSED.
2 REGULATOR 1/3 RD. OPEN. ENGINE
  WORKING SIMPLE.
3 REGULATOR FULLY OPEN. FULL
  COMPOUND WORKING.
4 REGULATOR PARTLY CLOSED.
  ENGINE CONTINUES COMPOUNDING.

A. STARTING OR PILOT VALVE.
B. MAIN VALVE.
C. MAIN STEAM PIPE
D. AUXILIARY STEAM PIPE.

The independent movement of the pilot valve is obtained by the use of a circular fitted hole for the operating pin in the pilot valve and an elongated hole or slot in the main valve, the result being that the latter does not move till the pin has travelled a distance corresponding to the clearance in the slotted hole, an amount which is made equal to the lap and port opening of the pilot valve.

The principle of the horizontal slide type regulator is exactly the same as the vertical pattern, the only difference being of arrangement to suit the horizontal mounting.

A main and pilot valve are employed, but the operating pin in this case engages with slots formed in the raised sides of the valves, the slots in the main valve being wider than the diameter of the pin by an amount equal to the lap and port opening of the pilot valves.

There was one other type of regulator valve to be found on the LMS and this was the special one fitted to Standard Compounds which is known as the Deeley Regulator. This regulator permits the engine to start away from rest as a simple engine on the two low pressure cylinders working with saturated steam at slightly reduced pressure. At the same time the high pressure piston is kept in equilibrium by steam at equal pressure in the front and rear. A further single movement of the regulator handle effects the change over to full compound working and a single movement back across the quadrant from any position will close it.

This regulator (see Fig. 8) is of the vertical slide valve type, the main face of which carries three ports, namely a starting port at the top and two main ports beneath. The starting port communicates with a separate chamber in the regulator head which is connected with the low pressure receiver via the 1½ inch diameter auxiliary steam pipe. The two main ports lead via the main steam pipe and superheater to the high pressure steam chest.

The main valve of this regulator rests directly on the valve face and carries five ports, three for starting purposes and two for the main steam supply, the starting valve has two ports. The starting valve rides on top of the main valve as in the case of an ordinary slide regulator and movement of the valves is controlled from the regulator handle and rod by the usual pin and slot arrangement.

Movement of the regulator handle up to about one third of the way across the quadrant opens the starting ports which supply the low pressure receiver with saturated steam via the auxiliary steam pipe and at the same time allows a small quantity of steam to enter the main steam pipe and to flow to the high pressure piston valve and cylinder to assist in balancing the high pressure piston.

Further movement of the regulator handle closes the starting port and opens the two large ports in the main valve so that the engine now works in full compound. Drawing the handle slowly back from the full open position will gradually close the main steam ports but will maintain proper compound working until the regulator closes altogether.

Injectors

Originally feed water was delivered to the boiler by means of a pump, but around the middle of the 19th Century Henry Giffard developed a device known as an injector. This proved so successful that it rapidly displaced the less efficient and more troublesome pumps and was eventually almost universally adopted.

All locomotives were equipped with two injectors, either two live steam or one live steam and one exhaust steam injector. The basic principle is the same in both types although different in detail (see Fig. 9).

A jet of steam emerging at high velocity from the steam cone is brought into contact with the cold feed water which is admitted around the tip of the steam cone. Partial condensation of the steam jet takes place, a partial vacuum is formed and water is drawn forward at considerable speed into the wide end of the converging combining cone.

Passage through this cone completes condensation of the steam producing a high vacuum and the water emerges from the small end of the cone at greatly increased velocity. The water jet then jumps the overflow gap and enters a diverging cone known as the delivery cone.

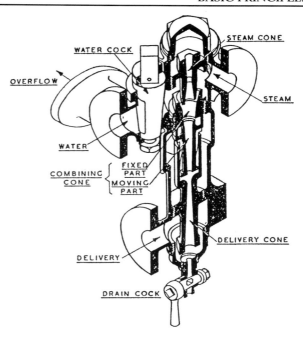

FIG. 9   STANDARD INJECTOR

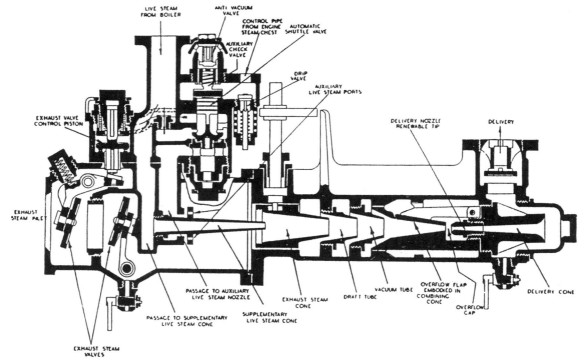

FIG. 10   EXHAUST INJECTOR
                   CLASS 'H'

The shape of this cone causes the speed of flow to be quickly and considerably reduced, which process converts the energy of motion in the water jet into pressure energy at the outlet end of the delivery cone.

The pressure developed in this way at the delivery end of the injector exceeds the boiler pressure sufficiently to enable the feed water to lift the clack against steam pressure and enter the boiler. The vacuum developed in the combining cone when the injector is working is used to hold a movable section of the cone up against the front portion giving the effect of a continuous cone. If the action of the injector is interrupted or the water jet upset, the vacuum in the cone is replaced by pressure, the moving section is forced away from its seating and any surplus steam and water escapes through the gap so formed to the overflow outlet. When the pressure has been relieved the working vacuum rapidly re-establishes itself and the injectors will then start again.

In some types of injector the moving cone is replaced by a hinged flap forming one side of the combining cone. In this case the flap is forced open when the injector flies off.

Injectors incorporating such devices are known as automatic restarting injectors.

The object of exhaust injectors is to provide an economical method of injecting water into the boiler by utilising exhaust steam from the cylinders for the purpose. Exhaust steam also heats the feed water, so a very hot feed is obtained. The exhaust injector is far more complex since a greater number of cones are required and also provision has to be made to ensure an automatic change over to live steam. They should not be used during shunting operations for example, when the engine regulator is continually being opened and closed, as this causes undue wear on the shuttle valve. For best results the injector should always be at work when the engine regulator is open, the feed being regulated by the handle on the fireman's side of the cab. The hottest feed is obtained with this handle in the minimum position. Exhaust injectors were therefore best suited to continuous running conditions.

The basic working principle however was similar to that of the live steam injector although more complex – see Fig. 10 which shows the class H exhaust injector.

With the regulator open, the exhaust injector works with exhaust steam together with a small supply of supplementary live steam. With the engine regulator shut, auxiliary live steam replaces the exhaust steam, the supply of supplementary live steam continuing. The change over from exhaust steam to auxiliary live steam is controlled automatically by a shuttle valve operated by steam pressure from the steam chest.

Generally speaking, injectors were quite reliable if regularly maintained although overall efficiency depended principally on original design. However, this will be discussed in the sections dealing with individual locomotives.

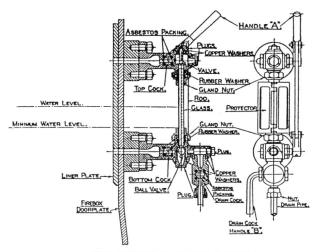

TO TEST GAUGE COCKS.

1. SHUT TOP AND BOTTOM COCKS BY PULLING HANDLE 'A' UNTIL IT IS POINTING DOWNWARDS HALFWAY BETWEEN THE HORIZONTAL AND VERTICAL.
2. OPEN DRAIN COCK BY PULLING HANDLE 'B' UPWARDS UNTIL HORIZONTAL, AND WATER SHOULD DISAPPEAR.
3. OPEN TOP AND BOTTOM COCKS BY RAISING HANDLE 'A' SLOWLY UNTIL IT IS POINTING UPWARDS HALF WAY BETWEEN THE HORIZONTAL AND VERTICAL IN ORDER TO BLOW THROUGH, AND CLOSE AGAIN.
4. SHUT DRAIN COCK BY TURNING HANDLE 'B' DOWNWARDS.
5. OPEN TOP AND BOTTOM COCKS WITH HANDLE 'A' UNTIL IT IS POINTING UPWARDS HALF WAY BETWEEN THE HORIZONTAL AND VERTICAL AND WATER SHOULD RISE TO LEVEL.

WATER GAUGE COCKS.

FIG. 11

Water Gauges

LMS and BR Standard locomotives were equipped with two water gauges mounted on the boiler back plate in such a position that even when water was only just visible in the bottom of the glass, a safe depth still covered the inner firebox crown.

Two patterns were used on LMS engines but the basic principles were the same, the obvious difference being that on the type fitted to more modern designs both top and bottom cocks could be closed with one movement of a single handle since they were coupled together by means of a rod. Heavy, hinged brass protectors, glazed

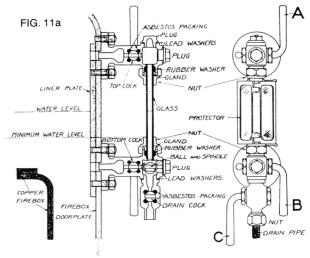

FIG. 11a

TO TEST GAUGE COCKS

1. Shut top cock and bottom cock by pulling handles 'A' and 'B' backwards until horizontal.
2. Open drain cock by pulling handle 'C' backwards until horizontal and water should disappear.
3. Blow through top cock by opening with handle 'A' and close again.
4. Blow through bottom cock by opening with handle 'B' and close again.
5. Shut drain cock with handle 'C'.
6. Open top cock and bottom cock with handles 'A' and 'B' and water should rise to level.

on three sides and with a perforated plate on the fourth side secured by a vertical pin contributed to overall safety on both versions.

Obviously, the modern pattern was more convenient to use and could be shut off very quickly in the event of an emergency (see Figs. 11 & 11a).

Because of the importance of being constantly aware of boiler water level, these gauges were the only ones to be provided with dedicated illumination. This took the form of a simple rape oil lamp which was no more than a small rectangular box with a hinged door in one side and a glazed window in another. Protruding vertically down from the base was a short spigot designed to locate in a holding bracket mounted adjacent to the gauges.

Being in such close proximity to the boiler back plate, the lamp was constantly subjected to relatively high temperatures, which precluded paraffin as a fuel. Rape oil, having a much higher boiling point was used in these gauge lamps, although it must be said that the light produced was rather feeble, unstable and at times smoky. Frequently the glass window was missing which meant that if anything more than a gentle breeze entered the cab the lamp was extinguished. It was therefore a sensible precaution to carry an electric torch particularly if tender first running was contemplated.

Safety Valves

Although a few examples of Ramsbottom valves could still be occasionally seen on older engines in the 1950s, all modern locomotives were fitted with Ross 'pop' valves. Not only did these occupy considerably less space, they were more reliable and the pressure difference between lifting and closing was around 1 to 2 psi against the Ramsbottom's 5 psi or more.

The number of safety valves employed is to some extent influenced by the boiler capacity. Beyer Garratts had four but generally two sufficed and these were normally mounted over the firebox. However on some larger locomotives where lack of space was a consideration, the valves were located on the boiler barrel.

The Ross valve uses a helical spring in compression and is designed so that when it lifts the area subjected to pressure is considerably increased and the valve rapidly opens to allow ample release of steam (see Fig. 12).

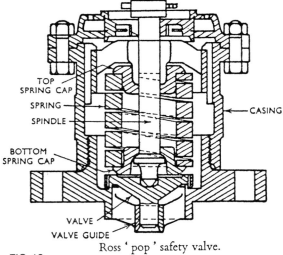

Ross ' pop ' safety valve.

FIG. 12

Carriage Warming Apparatus

The need to provide some form of carriage heating for the passengers comfort was realised from very early days, but not until reliable flexible pressure hoses and couplings were developed was it possible to tap into the steam available in the locomotive boiler. However, since it was neither necessary nor desirable to use full boiler pressure for this purpose, carriage warming reducing valves were fitted which allowed a steady suitable pressure. Fig. 13 shows a section view of the valve with the working parts in the normal or closed position.

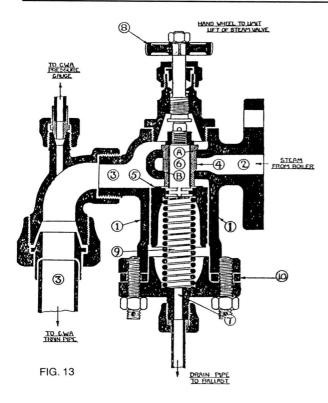

FIG. 13

This is similar but somewhat simpler than the earlier Venturi pattern since it employs no Venturi tube or attachment.

Regulation of pressure is effected by the control piston (5) and coil spring (9) supplemented when required for use with short trains by screwing down the hand wheel (8) which limits the stroke of the piston (5) and the lift of the steam valve (4).

The valve body (1) has the steam inlet and delivery ports (2) and (3) arranged on each side of the upper portion and the double seated steam admission valve (4) centrally situated between them. In the lower part of the body is the cylinder housing the control piston (5) with its spring (9) in compression acting on the under side. Firmly secured to the crown of the control piston is the spindle (6) by which attachment is made to the steam valve (4). The under side of the control piston (5) is permanently open to atmosphere via the drain port (7) which allows steam and condensate which may leak past the piston to escape freely.

When putting the valve into operation the handwheel (8) should be unscrewed to allow ample lift on the steam valve (4) and control piston, but it may be screwed down later if it is found that the delivery pressure is being maintained at too high a value.

Although the hand wheel will shut the valve off if screwed right down, it was not intended to be used as a stopcock. When it is necessary to shut the valve down altogether the independent stop plug must be used.

The cycle of events which control the reduction of boiler steam pressure suitable for the carriage warming system is therefore as follows:-

Steam from the boiler enters the valve by the passage (2) and flows through the top and bottom seatings (A & B) in the valve (4) into the space (3) where it exerts a pressure on the comparatively large area of the top of the piston (5). It will be seen that if no spring were provided under the piston the steam pressure acting on the top space would tend to force the piston in a downward direction, thereby closing the valve (4).

The desired carriage warming pressure is therefore controlled by the amount of lift of the valve (4) which is governed by the relationship of the downward course of the piston and the upward force of the spring (9).

In working these reducing valves, enginemen should aim at maintaining the full 50lbs pressure in the warming pipe on main line trains of more than ten bogie vehicles. On main line trains of ten bogie vehicles and under it was recommended that 50lbs should be maintained for the first half hour and afterwards reduced to 30lbs for the remainder of the journey, while local and motor trains should only be supplied at 30 psi. Judgment as to exact pressures used was obviously influenced by outside ambient temperatures and the general condition of the warming pipes and their couplings.

Vacuum and Steam Brakes

Over the years, the automatic vacuum brake had been developed to a high level of reliability and was the most common system to be used in this country right up to the end of the steam era.

It may be described as a brake which under certain conditions is self-acting and which utilises the pressure of atmospheric air to operate the brake piston. Vacuum does not operate the brake since brake power is applied by the pressure of the atmosphere trying to destroy a partial vacuum created on one side of the brake pistons by ejectors on the engine.

A full power application of this brake would take place if the train became divided causing the train pipe to be broken. Similarly it would go on if any key part of the apparatus became broken or damaged so that outside air could gain access to these parts of the apparatus in which a vacuum must normally be retained in order to maintain the brake in the off position, i.e. the train pipe and connections, vacuum reservoirs and on both sides of all brake pistons throughout the train.

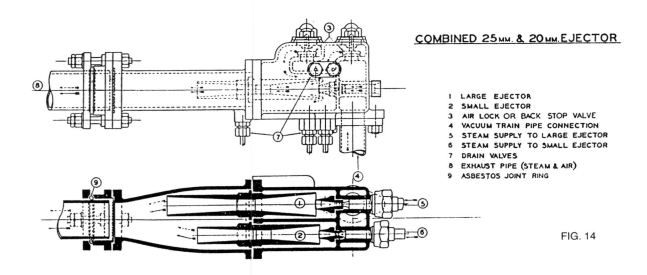

COMBINED 25mm. & 20mm. EJECTOR

1   LARGE EJECTOR
2   SMALL EJECTOR
3   AIR LOCK OR BACK STOP VALVE
4   VACUUM TRAIN PIPE CONNECTION
5   STEAM SUPPLY TO LARGE EJECTOR
6   STEAM SUPPLY TO SMALL EJECTOR
7   DRAIN VALVES
8   EXHAUST PIPE (STEAM & AIR)
9   ASBESTOS JOINT RING

FIG. 14

In a normal application of the brake the driver admits the desired quantity of air to the train pipe by way of the ports in his disc valve and the quantity of air admitted regulates braking power. Full power is reached when all vacuum in the train pipe is destroyed.

Vacuum is measured in inches of mercury and gauges on engines and brake vans were graduated in this manner. A perfect vacuum corresponds to approximately thirty inches of mercury. However on LMS & BR brake systems a partial vacuum of twenty one inches was the regulation value, but even this gave in effect 10½lbs per square inch pressure on the brake piston.

With the common size nineteen inch diameter brake cylinder which has a piston area of two hundred and eighty five square inches, a pull of two thousand, nine hundred and ninety two pounds or rather more than one and a quarter tons would be produced on the brake piston rod.

Although vacuum pumps were used for a period on a number of LMS locomotives to maintain train pipe vacuum, they tended to be less efficient and require more maintenance than ejectors. It was, therefore, decided in 1938 to remove these pumps where feasible and replace them with combination ejectors which, as the name implies, housed two ejectors, a large and a small.

Because of their basic simplicity and lack of moving parts ejectors generally were very reliable, requiring only the minimum of attention in service. Fig. 14 shows the layout of a combination ejector and reference to this will assist in understanding its working principles.

A jet of steam emerging at high velocity from a specially shaped cone within the ejector draws surrounding air forward by friction and carries it through a second larger cone, known as the air cone, to exhaust in the smokebox. This removal of air from the space in the immediate vicinity of the steam jet sets up a partial vacuum inside the ejector, to fill which, air flows past the two back stop valves from the train pipe and other parts of the brake system connected to it.

In this way it is possible to maintain the desired amount of vacuum in the train pipe so long as the ejector is kept at work and the brake is not applied. As previously indicated, the combination ejector contains two separate ejectors each one independent of the other and possessing its own set of two back stop valves. Usually the large ejector has a steam cone about 25mm in diameter and the small ejector about 20mm in diameter. Whilst the large ejector can create a vacuum quickly it also uses a large quantity of steam, therefore a small ejector is provided to maintain the vacuum more economically once created.

The two back stop valves and air lock chamber are for the purpose of preventing loss of vacuum through the ejector cones when the ejector is shut down and also to guard against steam and smokebox gases being drawn into the train pipe and connections.

A vacuum relief valve is provided in order to prevent the vacuum rising above the regulation twenty one inches. This consists of a spring loaded valve which can be adjusted so that it will open and admit air to the train pipe as soon as twenty one inches is exceeded.

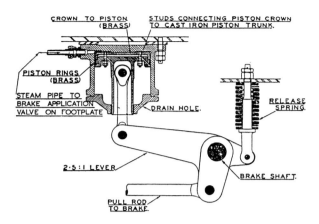

ENGINE STEAM BRAKE CYLINDER

FIG. 15

This relief valve is protected by a fine gauze filter to prevent entry of dust and dirt into the train pipe and this requires periodic cleaning because should it become clogged, free passage of air to the relief valve is prevented and trouble may occur due to an excessive amount of vacuum being created in the train pipe. As previously explained, to release the brake, the vacuum on the train pipe and reservoir sides of all the brake pistons must be equalised.

If more than twenty one inches is created in the reservoirs of the train, any other engine having a relief valve operating at normal pressure coupled to these vehicles will be unable to equalise the brake pistons and consequently the brakes will not release properly.

LMS locomotives were equipped with a steam brake which acted on both engine and tender (when fitted) and in most cases this was operated by a vacuum controlled valve. This valve was arranged to admit live steam to the brake cylinder(s) as the train pipe vacuum was destroyed and to release steam pressure from the brake cylinder as the train pipe vacuum was restored. The steam brake cylinder (Fig. 15) contains a piston fitted with wedge shaped rings which are forced outwards against the cylinder walls by steam pressure acting on the piston crown, thereby rendering the piston steam tight while the brake is applied. When the brake is released, steam escapes back up the pipe to the application valve and thence via the exhaust pipe into the ashpan. The wedge rings on the piston contract so allowing the release spring to return the piston to the top of the cylinder, at the same time any condensed water can escape past the piston to drain holes in the base of the cylinder. The thrust of the brake piston rod is transmitted to the brake blocks by way of the brake rigging in which provision is made for adjustment to take up wear in the brake blocks.

The driver's combined automatic steam and vacuum brake valve is shown in Fig. 16 and automatically applies both the steam brake on the engine and the vacuum brakes on the train.

BR Standard locomotives were fitted with a Graduable Automatic steam brake valve which applied the steam brake on the engine under the control of the vacuum brake on the train and proportional to it. Unlike the LMS design, two separate driver's valves allowed independent manual operation of the locomotive steam brake by means of a hand lever and notched quadrant, while a combined vacuum plus steam brake application was made by using a horizontal handle mounted on the pedestal in front of the driver.

In practice this North Eastern derived system was not only more convenient to use but was also more economical on steam since there was no need to use the small ejector when running light engine or with a loose coupled train. Also, being able to hold a train secure on the steam brake while creating vacuum was a distinct advantage particularly when operating stopping passenger duties.

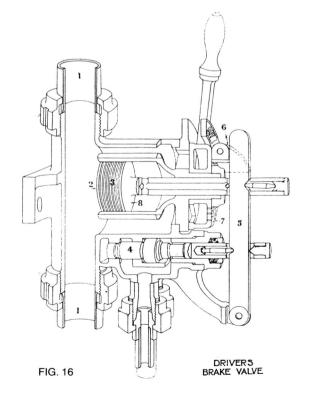

FIG. 16   DRIVERS
                                    BRAKE VALVE

Operation of LMS Combined Automatic Steam & Vacuum Brake Valve

Movement of the driver's handle to the 'on' position admits air into the train pipe (1) and thus also to the inner side (2) of a piston (3) which is connected to the steam brake supply plug (4) by means of a lever (5). A cam (6) which is part of the application valve disc (7) ensures the outward movement of the lever (5) which opens the steam supply plug (4) and admits steam to the engine steam brake cylinder. The effective action of the steam brake on the engine is automatically retarded to allow time for the braking effect to come into action on the train.

Moving the brake valve handle back to the 'off' position causes the creation of vacuum in the train pipe and also on the inner side (2) of the piston (3) and as the opposite side (8) of this piston is under atmospheric pressure, the piston (3) moves inwards and by means of the connecting lever (5) closes the steam brake supply plug (4).

To avoid using the small ejector for maintaining a vacuum in the train pipe when the engine is standing, a hook is provided to hold the lever (5) in this inward position. The steam to the brake cylinder is thus shut off preventing unnecessary wastage of steam.

Although not actually part of a locomotive, some knowledge of the working principles of vacuum brake equipment fitted to passenger and freight vehicles was an essential aprt of footplate crew training. Fig. 17 illustrates a typical vacuum brake cylinder.

It consists of a vacuum reservoir and cylinder combined, the cylinder proper being open at the top and enclosed within the reservoir. The brake piston is of fairly deep section and it is kept airtight within the cylinder by a rubber rolling ring nipped between the piston head and cylinder wall. The piston rod passes through the bottom of the cylinder and is kept airtight by a gland.

The brake cylinder is connected to the train pipe by a small flexibile hose attached to the ball valve housing at the base of the vacuum chamber. The purpose of this ball valve is to control movement of the brake piston in accordance with the variations in train pipe vacuum and also to provide a means for releasing the brake by hand when necessary. It can close the vacuum chamber port, or it can place the lower side of the brake piston and vacuum chamber in communication with each other and with the train pipe when it drops off its seating.

Running with the brake off, the ball valve is unseated, leaving the train pipe in communication with both sides

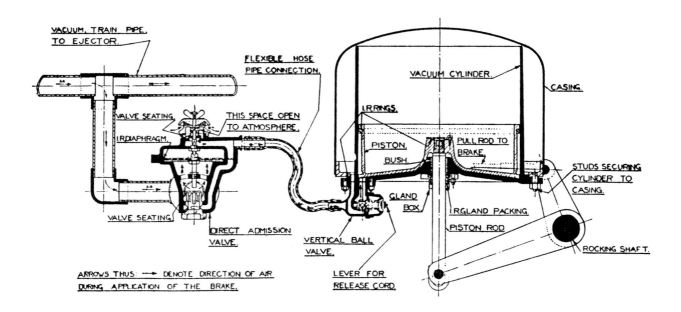

VACUUM BRAKE CYLINDER & D.A. VALVE WITH
CONNECTION TO TRAIN PIPE.

FIG. 17

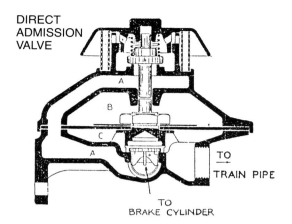

DIRECT
ADMISSION
VALVE

TO
TRAIN PIPE

TO
BRAKE CYLINDER

FIG. 18

of the piston, which will then be in equilibrium and resting by its own weight at the bottom of the cylinder. Immediately air is admitted to the train pipe it passes up the connecting pipe and forces the ball valve over till it seats on the port leading to the vacuum chamber, thereby retaining the vacuum on the top side of the piston. The port to the underside of the piston is, however, left open and air accordingly flows into the bottom of the cylinder, lifts the piston and applies the brake. Restoration of the train pipe vacuum extracts air from below the piston till the vacuum below equals that in the chamber above, after which the piston being equalised, will sink once more allowing the brake to release. At the same time the ball valve will drop away from its seating on the vacuum chamber port, leaving the whole cylinder in its original condition ready for the next application.

The hand release arrangement is effected by enclosing the ball valve inside a sliding cage connected to an external lever, as shown in the drawing. When the cord is pulled, the cage is displaced, forcing the ball valve away from the vacuum chamber port, thereby placing both sides of the vacuum piston in communication with the train pipe.

Direct Admission Valves were designed to give greater efficiency and flexibility especially on longer fitted trains. Fig. 18 illustrates the Gresham D.A. valve which operates as follows:-

Working vacuum is created through the train pipe in the usual way, the cylinder being exhausted past non-return valve (a). The same degree of vacuum is also produced in chamber (B) by way of the clearance between the stem of the valve (b) and the body of the valve so that diaphragm (c) remains in equilibrium and valve (b) closed as shown.

When air is admitted to the train pipe to apply the brakes it is prevented from passing to the cylinders and chambers (A) and (B) by non-return valve (a) and in consequence pressure builds up under diaphragm (c). Owing to the relatively large area of this diaphragm a very small reduction of vacuum in the train pipe enables it to lift and open valve (b). Air at atmospheric pressure then passes direct to the underside of the brake cylinder pistons through filter (d) port (e) and passage (4) and at the same time to chamber (B) past the stem of valve (b).

This reduction of vacuum in chamber (B) corresponds with the initial train pipe reduction made by the driver, when the diaphragm is again balanced and falls to the lower position, allowing valve (b) to close. In this way the degree of brake application in each cylinder follows exactly the fall of vacuum in the train pipe so that the driver retains the same complete control of graduation as with standard equipment.

When a full application of the brakes is made the air admitted through the driver's brake valve has only to destroy the vacuum in the relatively small volume of the train pipe and this is effected very rapidly, even on the longest trains. Brake pressure then builds up evenly in all the brake cylinders of the train at a rate controlled by the size of port (e) in the cap.

This port is proportioned to suit the size of brake cylinder so as to give a full brake application on the longest train within five seconds, which is the minimum filling time experience has shown to be desirable if undue shocks are to be avoided when emergency applications are made from comparatively low speeds.

Passenger vehicles are fitted with a communication cord which operates an alarm signal to the driver in order to stop the train in case of emergency. This consists of a chain passing through each compartment of the coach and connected at the end of the vehicle to the passengers alarm valve and indicating disc. When operated by the chain being pulled, this alarm valve opens and allows air to enter the train pipe causing a reduction in vacuum of five to ten inches which is sufficient to apply the brake with moderate force and to attract the driver's attention.

The indicating discs at the end of the coach normally lie in a horizontal position but when the communication cord is pulled they will be turned to the verticle thus indicating the coach from which the alarm was given.

In order to keep the train pipe as free as possible from water of condensation it is usual to provide at every downward bend a 'drip-trap' fitted with the usual ball valve. One such valve is always placed on the train pipe at the bottom of the down pipe from the ejectors and its action may be taken as typical of the remainder.

The ball valve is held in position by a small perforated nut fitted to the end of the pipe. When the vacuum in the train pipe is destroyed, the pressure of the air displaces the ball and any water of condensation which may have collected in the pipe is thus allowed to escape. The valve, of course, closes again as soon as vacuum begins to be restored.

Knowing what takes place throughout the train when the brake valve is applied obviously helps the driver develop his technique to ensure smooth and effective progression in all conditions.

Valves and Pistons

For a steam locomotive to function, the energy produced in the boiler needs to be converted to effort developed between wheels and rail and this is done in the cylinder. No matter how large and efficient a boiler may be, the overall performance of a locomotive would be quite mediocre unless equipped with equally efficient valves, valve gear, cylinders and accompanying steam passages.

Slide valves were developed early in the history of steam engines, being used almost exclusively during the 19th Century and indeed right until the end of the steam era on certain types of small non-superheated locomotives. Their basic simplicity can be seen illustrated in Fig. 19.

It will be recalled that steam from the boiler travels to the steam chest via the regulator and main steam pipe. The steam chest is a chamber in the cylinder casting containing the valves and portfaces. From here, steam is admitted to each end of the cylinders in turn by the valves as they move to and fro across the portfaces, opening the cylinder ports alternately to the steam chest and to the exhaust cavity which in turn leads to atmosphere via the blast pipe.

On a few designs the slide valves were placed on top, but usually they were located back to back between the cylinders and sharing a common steam chest. The portfaces in this case would be flat surfaces formed on the sides of the steam chest. Each portface carries three rectangular openings or ports, the central one being the exhaust port leading to the blast pipe while the other two are the steam ports to the front and back end of each cylinder. The exhaust ports are usually made about three times the width of steam ports.

The slide or 'D' valve itself is an oblong and shallow dish shaped casting which rests open side towards the portface. The flanges of the valve are bedded down to the portface making a steam tight fit with it to prevent direct leakage of live steam into the valve cavity. The overall width of the slide valve is rather more than the

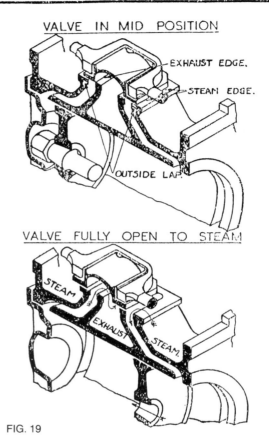

FIG. 19

distance between the outer edges of the two cylinder steam ports, which enables it to close both these ports when in the central position.

The width of the valve cavity is made to equal the distance between the outside edge of either cylinder steam port and the opposite edge of the central exhaust port, which enables the cavity to place either steam port at a time in communication with the exhaust port according to whether the valve is forward or in rear of its central position. Therefore when the valve uncovers a steam port to admit steam to the cylinder, the steam port at the other end is connected to the exhaust port by the cavity of the valve and so there is steam at one end of the cylinder and exhaust taking place at the other.

The steam edges of a valve are the edges which control the admission and cut off of live steam to the cylinder ports, while the exhaust edges are those which control the escape of exhaust steam from the cylinder ports. In the case of a slide valve, the steam edges are the extreme outside edges of the valve flanges and the exhaust edges are the front and back edges of the central cavity.

Lap is the amount by which the steam edges of a valve overlap the outside edges of the cylinder steam ports when the valve is in its central position. The purpose of lap is to obtain a rather earlier cut off than could be obtained without its use, thereby taking better advantage of steam's expansive powers. The amount of lap given to the valve is generally sufficient to provide a cut off at about 75% of the stroke in full gear. Lead is provided to ensure that the full steam pressure is built up in the steam port and clearance space between the cylinder covers and piston right at the commencement of the stroke, an important factor for high speed running with heavy loads. Lead is the amount or width of steam port opening when the piston is at the extreme ends of the cylinder. The lead steam also serves to cushion the

pistons and attached moving parts at the ends of the stroke thereby reducing the tendency to knock in the big and little ends as well as the axle boxes.

The sequence of events within a cylinder during a single revolution of the driving wheels is therefore:-

Admission, Expansion, Exhaust, Compression.

Admission and Expansion take place during the outward stroke of the piston, whilst Exhaust and Compression occur during the return stroke, all of course in the same end of the cylinder. At the other end, the Exhaust and Compression periods would occur during the outward stroke and Expansion during the return stroke.

Necessity is the mother of invention and although experiments had been conducted with piston valves quite early in railway history, it was not until the development of superheating at the end of the 19th century that sufficient impetus was generated to perfect the system.

One major problem with slide valves is that the live steam pressure acting on the back of the valve presses it against the portface with a force of several tons, which produces considerable friction and waste of power in moving the valve. Whilst non superheated or 'wet' steam is quite a good lubricant for the flat sliding surfaces of 'D' valves, superheated or dry steam is not and consequently rapid wear took place.

In order to minimise these difficulties, simple slide valves were made much shorter than the length of the cylinder but this then created the further problem of long and tortuous steam passages.

The piston valve largely overcame these objections since the valve events are controlled by two pistons mounted on a rod or spindle. With steam pressure acting in equal and opposite directions on the valve heads, the valve is balanced and therefore independent of steam pressure. Also they are far easier to lubricate than slide valves. Fig. 20 shows how these piston heads slide inside cylindrical sleeves or liners pressed into the steam chest casting. The cylilnder ports lead from a series of openings cut around the circumference of the valve liners in such positions that the valve heads will cover and uncover them as the valve and spindle is moved to and fro.

There are two kinds of piston valve in general use, known respectively as the inside and outside admission types.

In the former case live steam is fed to the central part of the steam chest between the two valve heads whilst the exhaust is led away from the two ends. In the latter case, steam is fed to the two ends of the steam chest and the exhaust is collected from the centre.

PISTON VALVE AND STEAM CHEST

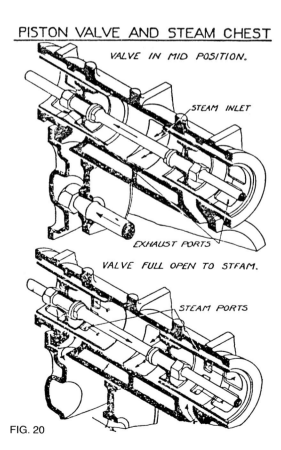

VALVE IN MID POSITION.

STEAM INLET

EXHAUST PORTS

VALVE FULL OPEN TO STEAM.

STEAM PORTS

FIG. 20

All LMS and BR Standard engines with the exception of Compounds and Class 2ps were fitted with piston valves of the inside admission type since there are marked advantages with layout. For example the valve spindle glands which prevent the escape of steam from the sliding surfaces where the valve spindle enters the cylinder assembly has to withstand only exhaust pressure. Also the high pressure pipework both inside the smokebox and externally is less complicated giving rise to more efficient steam flow.

A variation of the piston valve was developed to overcome certain shortcomings found with short lap, short travel valves which restricted port openings when a cut off of less than about 30% was used.

In Germany Dr. Schmidt adapted an earlier idea of Joseph Trick's and designed a valve fitted with an internal passage which allowed supplementary live steam to enter the valve ports through circumferential slots cut in the single broad piston ring. However, it did nothing to assist the release of any extra steam admitted and so produced high back pressures and consequent noisy exhaust. For a period these Trick valves were used extensively on the LNWR.

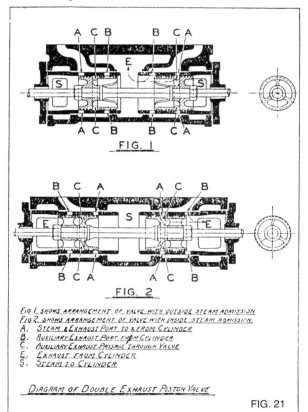

FIG. I

FIG. 2

Fig 1 shows arrangement of valve with outside steam admission
Fig 2 shows arrangement of valve with inside steam admission
A. Steam & Exhaust Port to & from Cylinder
B. Auxiliary Exhaust Port from Cylinder
C. Auxiliary Exhaust Passage through Valve
E. Exhaust from Cylinder
S. Steam to Cylinder

Diagram of Double Exhaust Piston Valve

FIG. 21

In 1927 on the LMS, D.W. Sandford reversed Schmidt's design so to speak and produced what was known as double exhaust valves. The objective here was to provide a larger port opening to exhaust steam than for admission in order to reduce back pressure at the shorter cut offs. As can be seen in Fig. 21 it employed two additional heads on each spindle. The purpose of these heads is to open auxiliary exhaust ports in the liners during the exhaust stroke. The width of these heads is sufficient to keep the auxiliary ports closed during the admission and expansion periods of the steam cycle.

These double exhaust valves were fitted to 2P 4-4-0s, 3P 2-6-2Ts and Garretts where they showed on the latter an economy in coal consumption of some 11% compared to the original locomotives fitted with single valves.

An entirely different type of valve is the Rotary Cam Poppet Valve Gear, of which the best known makes are Caprotti and Lentz. The theoretical advantage of poppet valves being the separation of admission and exhaust events since their timing is dependent upon individual cam profiles as is the case in internal combustion engines.

This should lead to improved exhaust port openings, less back pressure and consequent free running at high speed. Also, because the valves dropped from their seats when steam was shut off, a by-pass was created between the ends of the cylinder eliminating the pumping action of the pistons and the possibility of drawing in furnace gases.

During the 1920s and 30s a number of experiments were conducted with poppet valves, the LMS equipping ten Claughtons with Caprotti and five Crabs with Lentz gear. The latter's main drawback was that the cut-off could only be altered in a number of finite steps; however a new camshaft mechanism devised by Reidinger was fitted in 1953 which allowed a continuously variable cut-off. Although both types of poppet valves showed some savings in coal consumed, service and repair costs were considerably lower, indeed mileage between piston and valve examinations increased by a third. In addition, the amount of work involved was less than with a normal piston valve locomotives.

With so much post war emphasis on low maintenance and accessibility, poppet valves were re-examined in a more favourable light particularly in view of progressive improvements in design. H.G. Ivatt, actively pursuing this course, arranged for twenty Class 5 4-6-0s to be constructed (along with other variants) fitted with Caprotti gear. How they performed will be discussed in a later chapter, but their success became evident when

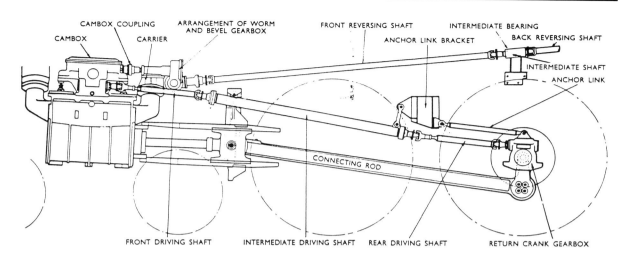

FIG. 21a   **GENERAL ARRANGEMENT OF BRITISH CAPROTTI VALVE GEAR,
OUTSIDE DRIVE**

BR built not only two more Black 5s with further improved gear but also thirty new Standard 5s and the one Class 8 4-6-2 using this latest Caprotti equipment. In the description of poppet valves, mention was made of benefits gained because of the by pass effect established by these valves dropping off their seats when coasting. It may therefore be helpful to examine what takes place when coasting with a piston valve engine.

The movement of valves and pistons causes the cylinders to act like a large pump tending to draw air continuously from the steam chest, which action rapidly produces a partial vacuum inside the steam chest and cylinder. As the valves alternately uncover the cylinder ports to exhaust, air rushes back down the blast pipe to destroy the vacuum in the cylinders carrying with it hot gases and possibly cinders from the smokebox, a most undesirable state of affairs.

The heat and vacuum inside the cylinders cause lubricating oil to decompose into light vapours and sticky deposits, whilst the grit produces wear on the working parts. In order to counteract these effects, air or anti-vacuum valves are fitted to the steam chest which lift and admit air immediately the pressure within falls below that of the atmosphere outside. The vacuum is therefore partially destroyed and its unwanted effects largely removed when running with steam off.

A further improvement is obtained particularly on more modern engines with large ports and long travel valve gear if the gear is left partially notched up, usually about 45% when coasting and a breath of steam supplied to the steam chest by slightly opening the

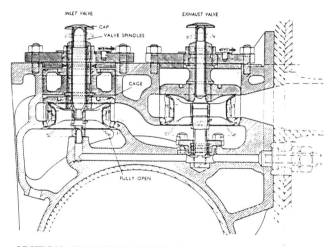

SECTION THROUGH INLET AND EXHAUST VALVES

regulator. The letter 'D' marked on the cut off scale donating this 'drift' position.

The steam supply destroys the vacuum inside the cylinders and steam chest and excludes all traces of air so that the oil retains its lubricating properties whilst the shortened valve travel also tends to reduce excessive wear on the piston valve rings and liners.

This of course does not apply to engines fitted with slide valves since when steam is shut off the valves fall away from the faces so that a by pass effect is produced as is the case with poppet valves. With slide valve engines therefore, it is best to drop down into full gear and keep the regulator closed when coasting.

So far we have only discussed simple expansion engines which are those where boiler steam is allowed to expand and do work only once in the cylinders before being exhausted into the atmosphere. Compound engines, on the other hand, make the boiler steam expand in two stages successively in two or more cylinders before being exhausted to atmosphere.

Over the years compound engines, good, bad and indifferent have made their appearance with perhaps the 4-4-0 Midland Compound and its LMS derivative being the most well known in Britain. A description of these famous locomotives will be given in the chapter dealing specifically with them.

It is useful to remember, though, that with the advent of long lap, long travel piston valves with generous ports and streamlined steam passages, simple engines so equipped, out-performed contemporary compounds in the UK. It took some years before this realisation eventually dawned and became universally accepted since for maximum efficiency it needed to be coupled to high degree superheating. However, once these principles were established, compounding with its additional costs and complications were no longer pursued here, although in France under the genius of Chapelon, compounds were taken to a very high level of development.

Valve Gears

Valves of whatever type are driven by the valve gear which also incorporates an arrangement for regulating the valve travel and for reversing the engine by changing the valve's position on the portface in relation to the piston. Of the many designs developed during the steam era, we shall only consider the two most common.

Stephenson's Link Motion and Walschaert's Valve Gear. First though, a quick reminder as to what an eccentric is in the context of valve gear.

An eccentric is a form of auxiliary crank frequently used in valve gears to obtain a reciprocating movement for the valves from the crank axle or other rotating part. It consists of a circular disk called the 'sheave' which is securely fixed to the axle so that it will rotate with it. The centre of the sheave does not coincide with the centre of the axle and the distance separating the sheave centre from the axle centre is called the 'throw' of the eccentric, in exactly the same way as the distance between the crank pin centre and the axle centre is the 'throw' of an ordinary crank.

The 'throw' of the sheave causes it to describe a circular path about the axle centre so that the eccentric strap, which encircles the sheave is forced to follow the same circular path, producing a reciprocating movement at the front of the eccentric rod which is bolted to the strap.

The other point to bear in mind is that with inside admission valves the eccentric lags 90° behind the main crank whereas with outside admission it leads by 90°.

Stephenson's Link Motion (See Figs. 22 & 23)

This type of motion employs two eccentrics for each valve, one being used for forward and the other for backward running.

The eccentric rods are connected respectively to the top and bottom of a curved expansion link, which is supported by the lifting link from the reversing shaft. The link and forward ends of the eccentric rods can be raised or lowered by means of the reversing lever in the cab for regulating valve travel and reversing the engine.

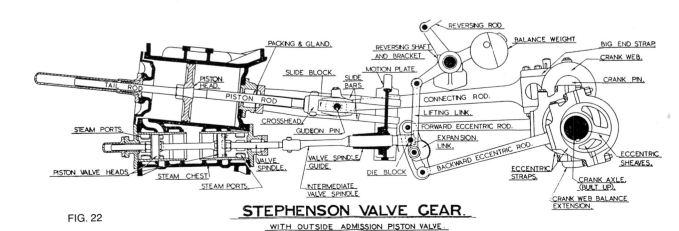

FIG. 22

STEPHENSON VALVE GEAR.
WITH OUTSIDE ADMISSION PISTON VALVE.

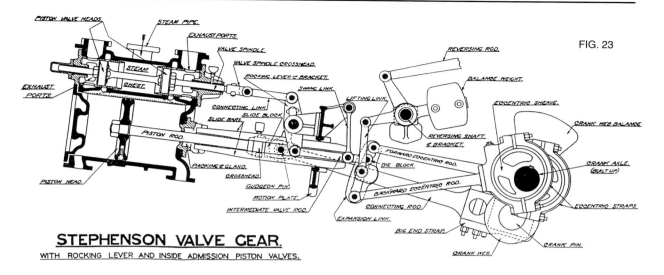

STEPHENSON VALVE GEAR.
WITH ROCKING LEVER AND INSIDE ADMISSION PISTON VALVES.

The expansion link contains a die block which is coupled via the valve spindle guide to the valve spindle but on engines having inside admission valves, drive from the die block is conveyed to the valve spindle through a rocking lever which alters the direction of valve movement in relation to the die block and thereby avoids the necessity to change the setting of the eccentrics or to employ crossed eccentric rods.

The forward and backward eccentrics are each mounted on the axle in the correct position to drive the valve for the corresponding direction of running, the usual setting being 90° in advance of the crank (outside admission) to give the necessary port opening plus a further angle of advance equal to 15° or 16° to give the required lap and lead on the valve. The total angular advance of each eccentric is therefore from 105° to 106° in front of the crank.

In operating the gear, the expansion link is raised or lowered in order to bring the die block in line with, or closer to the backward or forward eccentric rod according to the desired direction or travel and the cut off required. In full gear positions the die block will be at either end of the link, in mid gear it will be central, where it is acted upon equally by both eccentrics and thereby has a travel equal only to twice the lap and lead.

It should be noted that the amount of lead given to the valve by Stephenson's Motion is not quite constant for all positions of the gear. In mid gear the lead is increased slightly above the amount obtained in full backward or forward gear Ref: Fig. 24.

The advantage of a variable lead has its advocates but tests with Stanier Black 5 44767 in 1948/9 fitted with Stephenson's gear were rather inconclusive and no further locomotives were so modified.

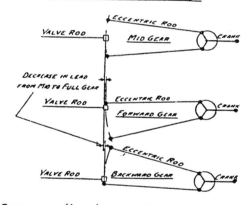

In Stephenson's Gear with Rods as shown in the sketch the Valve Lead gradually increases as the gear is notched up from Full Backward or Full Forward to Midgear and becomes a Maximum in Midgear.

This is owing to the control of the valve by the eccentrics having a varying effect from Midgear to Full Forward or Backward Gear. At Midgear Both eccentrics exercise effect on the movement of the Valves giving Maximum Lead. When Full Forward or Full Backward Gear is approached one eccentric exercises a decreasing control and the other eccentric an increasing control until Full Gear is reached. The forward eccentric has Full Control in Forward Gear and the Backward eccentric Full Control in Back Gear Giving Minimum Lead. See above sketches.

FIG. 24

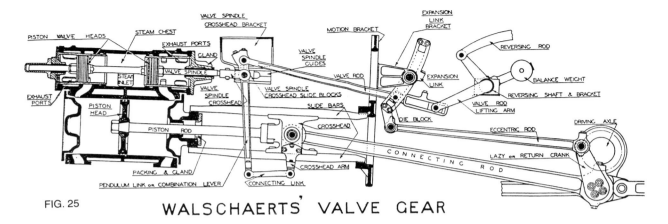

FIG. 25   WALSCHAERTS' VALVE GEAR

Walschaert's Valve Gear

In the Walschaert Motion (see Fig. 25) the valve travel is derived from two separate points. Movement amounting to twice the lap and twice the lead is obtained from the piston rod cross head, giving a constant lead for all positions of the gear. The remainder of the valve travel, amounting to twice the port opening, is obtained from the eccentric or return crank by way of the eccentric rod, expansion link, die block and valve rod.

These two movements are added together at the valve spindle pin in the combining lever, thereby producing the total travel of the valve when the reversing lever is in full gear position.

Adjustment of the valve travel is controlled from the reversing lever by raising and lowering the die block in the expansion link, which regulates the amount of drive passed forward to the valve spindle from the eccentric. When the die block is central in the link, it is in line with the link trunnion pins and consequently no movement is imported to the radius rod, the reversing lever then being in mid gear position. In this case the valve travel is confined to the lap and lead movement obtained from the cross head drive, the ports being opened to the extent of lead only at each end of the cylinder.

Foregear drive for the valve is obtained by lowering the die block in the link and drive for backward gear by raising the die block above the link centre.

The return crank is set at 90° in relation to the main crank though sometimes this is varied by one or two degrees in order to counteract the effects of angularity when the motion rods are short.

As already mentioned, for inside admission valves the eccentric follows the crank and with outside admission valves it will lead the crank by the same amount. This change of position is necessary in order to keep the fore-

gear position of the die block within the lower half of the expansion link. In addition, where outside admission valves are used, the valve spindle will be coupled to the top of the combining lever and the radius rod to the intermediate pin.

Walschaert's motion was certainly favoured by modern locomotive designers for a number of reasons. It could be easily adapted for use with inside cylinders, inside or outside admission valves, it was capable of providing a long valve travel and requiring only one eccentric per cylinder, was not complicated. Being of robust construction, valve events could be accurately set and maintained over long periods.

Lubrication

To effectively lubricate the multitude of moving parts that make up a locomotive has always been a major task for both design engineers and engine crews alike and different requirements produced different solutions.

Pistons and valves are invariably lubricated by Hydrostatic Displacement lubricators or by Mechanical lubricators feeding through Atomisers. Because of the high temperatures involved, special viscous oils which are more stable under these conditions are used.

Other engine parts are lubricated by mechanical or fountain type lubricators, ordinary oil cups and trimmings and in the case of big ends and side rods on modern engines, by felt pads. Here, oil is thrown on to a restrictor plug by the oscillations of the motion and then drips down on to the felt pad which bears on the journal (see Fig. 26). Little ends on Stanier locomotives had a needle oil feed as shown also in Fig. 26.

Grease lubrication was frequently used in many cases to such points as brakes, reversing and motion pins and indeed on Ivatt and BR Standard locomotives, grease was used more intensively, much to the delight of drivers.

The various models of Hydrostatic Displacement lubricators although differing in detail all used the same principle and if properly maintained gave good service. However, they were gradually replaced with Mechanical lubricators and by the late 1950s on the LM Region, only some non-superheated locomotives were still using this equipment.

The principle of the Hydrostatic Displacement lubricator is the utilisation of condensed steam which on entering the oil reservoir displaces oil causing it to overflow into the feed passages. In the case of the Detroit lubricator (see Fig. 27) the oil is then controlled by the oil regulating valve and after passing this point it rises through the water in the sight glass into a delivery tube, where it is caught up by a current of steam and carried to the choke plug which is inserted in the feed pipe near the point of delivery. The choke plug gives a constant resistance to the lubricator and so prevents the feed being affected by variations of pressure in the steam chest etc. Wear on the fine holes on these choke plugs will eventually cause irregular rate of feed and this can usually be rectified by a change of plug.

The lubricator is filled by closing all valves, starting at the oil regulating valve H, then closing the water feed valve E, followed by steam valve C and steam valve from the boiler. Drain off the condensation from the oil chamber by opening drain valve J, remove filler plug B and fill with oil closing drain valve J. If there is a deficiency of oil to fill the reservoir, always top up with water.

To start the lubricator, the boiler steam valve and steam valve C must always be fully open when in use. Open valve E to allow water from the condensation chamber to enter the oil chamber and regulate the rate of feed by each individual oil regulation valve I. It was necessary to open and close valves in the correct sequence in order to ensure the efficient working of this type of lubricator.

Perhaps it is now understandable why Hydrostatic lubricators were superseded by Mechanical ones on modern locomotives. This system of atomiser lubrication for the cylinder and piston valves is shown in Fig. 28.

From the mechanical lubricator, oil is forced to the atomiser C where it is atomised by means of a steam jet

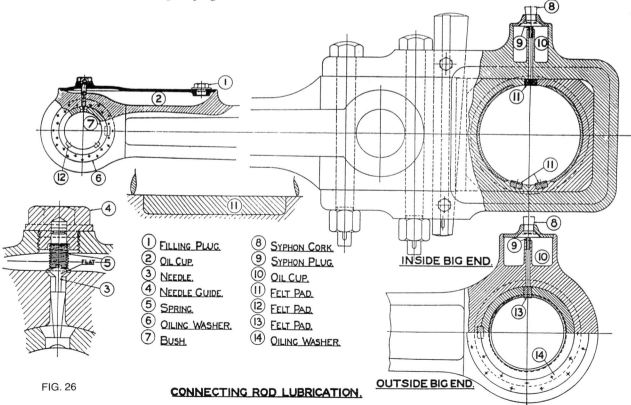

① Filling Plug.
② Oil Cup.
③ Needle.
④ Needle Guide.
⑤ Spring.
⑥ Oiling Washer.
⑦ Bush.
⑧ Syphon Cork.
⑨ Syphon Plug.
⑩ Oil Cup.
⑪ Felt Pad.
⑫ Felt Pad.
⑬ Felt Pad.
⑭ Oiling Washer.

INSIDE BIG END.

OUTSIDE BIG END.

FIG. 26

CONNECTING ROD LUBRICATION.

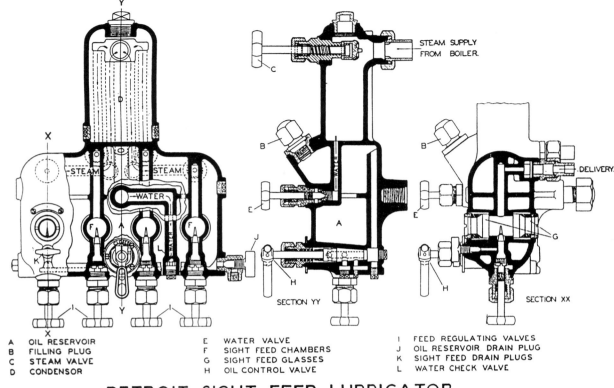

A	OIL RESERVOIR	E	WATER VALVE	I	FEED REGULATING VALVES
B	FILLING PLUG	F	SIGHT FEED CHAMBERS	J	OIL RESERVOIR DRAIN PLUG
C	STEAM VALVE	G	SIGHT FEED GLASSES	K	SIGHT FEED DRAIN PLUGS
D	CONDENSOR	H	OIL CONTROL VALVE	L	WATER CHECK VALVE

DETROIT SIGHT FEED LUBRICATOR

FIG. 27

and then passed to the cylinders and piston valves. The steam for the atomisers is taken from the boiler top at the front end of the left hand side and the same pipe supplies the steam warming coil for the mechanical lubricator. The steam pipe also includes a valve B coupled to the cylinder cock gear, which is shut when the cylinder cocks are open. For this reason it is imperative that the cylinder cocks be left open while the engine is standing.

Mechanical lubricators are usually a series of single acting or double acting pumps, housed in the lubricator body, the pumps being operated by ratchet or friction driven cams receiving the necessary motion from some reciprocating part of the valve gear. With Waschaert's motion it was coupled to the expansion link which gave constant movement in all positions of the reversing gear.

If an engine had been standing for a considerable period it was good policy to give the driving shaft a few turns by hand to ensure that there would be oil in the pipe before starting away.

Mechanical lubricators similar in appearance and principle, except that they were not fitted with atom-isers, also fed the axleboxes of coupled wheels on more modern locomotives. Prior to their introduction, gravity feed axlebox lubricators were much in vogue, the Wakefield Fountain type (see Fig. 29) being a typical example of this interim design.

It consists of a sealed oil reservoir which delivers oil to a feed chamber through the main shut off valve, the level of oil in this feed chamber controls the admission of air to the reservoir and consequently regulates the delivery of oil from it. Regulated by feed needles, oil is fed from the feed chamber through drip nozzles in drops. The drops of oil pass through sight feed glasses into the oil pipes and from there by gravity to the axlebox. To prevent syphoning of oil there is an air inlet situated in the oil pipe above each axlebox.

Worsted trimmings are to be found at a variety of lubrication points on all locomotives both old and modern, where a regular, regulated supply of oil is required.

Plug trimmings are those which only feeds when the engine is running and is used for those rotating or oscillating parts which have sufficient motion to splash

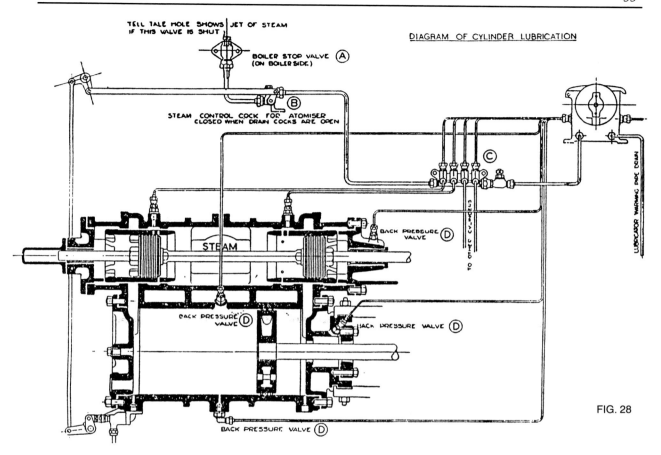

FIG. 28

the oil over the end of the syphon pipe such as big ends, side rods etc.

A plug trimming is made by wrapping several strands of worsted lengthwise over a piece of twisted wire forming a plug which should well fit the syphon pipe and when in use the top of the plug should be a little below the top of the syphon pipe. The plug must be shorter than the syphon pipe to obviate any chance of it touching the bearing. Increasing the number of strands in a plug trimming decreases the flow, since the increased thickness causes restriction in the hole.

Tail trimmings are used for non-rotating parts such as axleboxes, glands, slide bars etc. and they are made from the same material as the plug trimmings, but a few strands of the worsted are left at the top end. These turn over and hang in the oil receptacle, syphoning oil as long as the trimming is clean and in its normal position. For this reason, tail trimmings must be lifted out of the syphon pipes when the engine ceases work.

In the case of tail trimmings an increase in the number of tail strands will increase the feed.

All worsted trimmings were made to the standard patterns shown in Fig. 30 and dimensional details of each type were exhibited in the notice cases at Motive Power Depots.

Tenders

It may not be generally appreciated but the design of a tender greatly influenced not only the use a given locomotive could be put to, but also the engine crew's acceptance of it. To a somewhat lesser degree the same applied to tank locomotives with regard to water capacity and bunkerage.

On long runs over lines where no water troughs existed, rather larger water capacity was desirable so that the minimum of intermediate water stops were necessary. Where troughs were plentiful, smaller tenders with the advantage of lower weight, could aid locomotive performance or emphasis could be slanted to higher coal capacity. There were of course some exceptional runs where both coal and water capacity

INSTRUCTIONS FOR OPERATING THE LUBRICATOR

TO FILL   Set handle "P" in "OFF" position.
Remove filling plug "B" and fill reservoir with clean oil.
Replace filling plug "B" making sure that it is screwed down and air tight.

TO OPERATE   Examine needles "J" to see that they are clean, and that no foreign matter is accumulated around or in the nipples "V."
Then replace needles "J" and move handle "P" to "ON" position.

SPECIAL NOTE   Handle "P" has two positions, "ON" and "OFF." It does not regulate the oil feed. Feed regulation is obtained by varying the size of needle "J."

NO OIL MUST BE POURED INTO CHAMBER "F"

Lid on chamber "F" is for inspection purposes only.
Move handle "P" into "OFF" position when running into terminal stations, or during any lengthy stoppage.
Do not move handle "P" into the "ON" position until the steam regulator is again opened. The small quantity of oil accumulating in each chamber "G" from feed chamber "F" flows quickly down the oil pipes to the journals immediately the Lubricator is set to work again.
When shunting, operate Lubricator at intervals sufficient to maintain an oil film on the journals.
Should an Axle-box heat, remove needle "J" of the Axle-box feed concerned to temporarily increase the oil delivery until conditions improve, then replace needle "J" or fit a smaller size needle.

TO DETECT STOPPAGE IN PIPE LINE   Should oil flood sight glass, it indicates that the feed pipe is choked between the Lubricator and the air inlet in the pipe line.
If oil appears at the air inlet in the pipe line it denotes an obstruction in the pipe between the air inlet and Axle-box.
Air inlets should be periodically examined and kept free from dirt.

HOW IT FUNCTIONS   When handle "P" is in the "ON" position, oil from the reservoir "A" passes through main shut-off valve "C" and along passage "D" into feed chamber "F," where it rises to a level just above top of outlet passage "D" and is fed through the nozzle "L" in drops regulated by the needle "J" fitted in the nipple "V."
As soon as the oil level in chamber "F" drops below top of passage "D," air enters the reservoir "A" through the air tube "T," destroys the partial vacuum, permits the oil to flow through until it again rises to a level above the top of passage "D" and cuts off the air.
This cycle of operations is repeated the whole time the handle "P" is in the "ON" position.
When handle "P" is in the "OFF" position, the main shut-off valve "C" and shut-off valve "K" are closed, and oil in the chamber "F" continues to feed to each auxiliary chamber "G" until the oil level in chamber "F" falls to the level of the top of the nipple "V."
Immediately handle "P" is set in the "ON" position the oil accumulated in each chamber "G" quickly flows down the pipes to the journals, while the cycle of operations between the reservoir "A" and chamber "F" has allowed the level in chamber "F" to rise and feed oil past the needle "J."
The air tube "T" regulates the expansion or contraction, due to variation of temperature in reservoir "A."
By strictly observing the above instructions, an appreciable economy in oil consumption will be effected.

FOUNTAIN TYPE AXLE-BOX LUBRICATOR

DESCRIPTION

A	OIL RESERVOIR	M	SIGHT FEED GLASS
B	FILLING PLUG	N	SIGHT FEED FITTING
C	MAIN OIL SHUT OFF VALVE	O	OIL OUTLET
D	OIL OUTLET FROM RESERVOIR TO FEED CHAMBER	P	OPERATING HANDLE 2 POSITIONS OFF ON
E	BAFFLE	Q	DRAIN PLUGS
F	OIL FEED CHAMBER	R	OIL LEVEL GAUGE GLASS
G	AUXILIARY OIL CHAMBER	S	FILLING LUG
H	AIR VENT	T	AIR INLET TUBE
J	FEED REGULATING NEEDLE	U	WIRE GAUGE STRAINER
K	SHUT OFF VALVE	V	FEED NIPPLE
L	DRIP NOZZLE		

FIG. 29

needed to be as great as possible and one may wonder why the larger tenders required for those were not adopted as standard for general use.

As indicated above the answer lies in the simple fact that 4000 gallons of water weighs nearly 18 tons which together with some 9 tons of coal and its carrying vehicle needs to be accelerated and checked continuously throughout its journey. Obviously this represents a considerable expenditure of energy, the cost of which must be deducted from the revenue earnings of the train.

The efficient working of a loose coupled freight train depended not only on the haulage ability of the locomotive but also on its brake power. Having an additional brake cylinder and all wheels braked, tenders could in some instances provide more braking effort than the engine to which it was attached, particularly in the case of four coupled locomotives. For this reason tank engines of equal tractive effort were always at a disadvantage when hauling unfitted freights.

Many factors affected operating convenience especially with regard to the fireman.

Not only should coal capacity be sufficient for the designated job, but it should also be accessible. So called self-trimming bunkers may work reasonably well with small cobbles but in the days of hand hewn coal, lumps could be as large as coffins and only the first ton or two would drop on to the shovelling plate. It was then a case of going into the tender and dragging the remainder forward as well as breaking up any major obstructions. Modern tenders were fitted with access door which

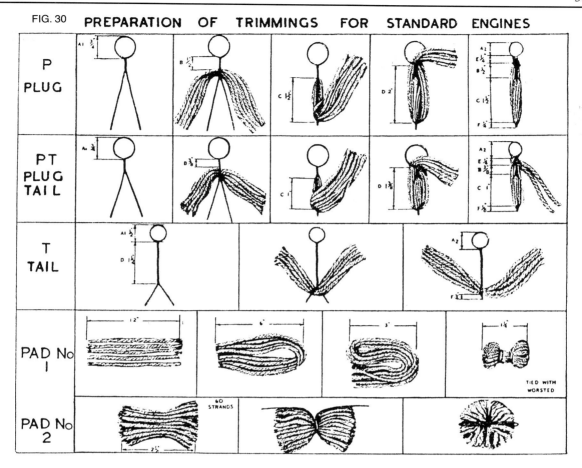

FIG. 30 PREPARATION OF TRIMMINGS FOR STANDARD ENGINES

made the task easier and considerably safer but on some designs the doors themselves could be obstructive when folded back. A convenient storage space for fire irons and indeed personal effects was much appreciated and here once again Stanier's designs showed a significant step forward.

Inset bunkers allowed for better vision when travelling tender first although it carried the penalty of reduced coal space. Ivatt pursued this theme with his Class 2 and Class 4 2-6-0 Moguls which were always envisaged as being involved with a fair proportion of tender first running since they were also equipped with tender cabs. Similar strategy was perpetuated with the range of BR Standard locomotives where considerable radical redesigning of cab and tender layout took place. Initially, the major change was the elimination of the normal fall plate between engine and tender by extending the footplate rearward. This gave the fireman a wonderfully stable platform to work off, but resulted in

drivers complaining of draughts they had never before experienced.

A good compromise was achieved on later versions by slightly reducing the rearward extension and fitting a 'short' fall plate right up against the tender front plate. Since BR Standard locomotives were intended to work in all regions where widely varying operating conditions are found, it is not surprising that some half a dozen different versions of the BR tender were developed with coal capacities ranging from 7 to 9 tons and water from 4250 to 5625 gallons.

This tailoring of tenders to suit specific jobs within the regions was rather a luxury which could only take place on a National Railway operating in the conditions which prevailed in the 1950s. Whatever attributes a tender may possess it was essentially a means of conveying coal and water and the latter sometimes had to be taken on board whilst the engine was in motion. This was accomplished by means of a Water Scoop, the most complex

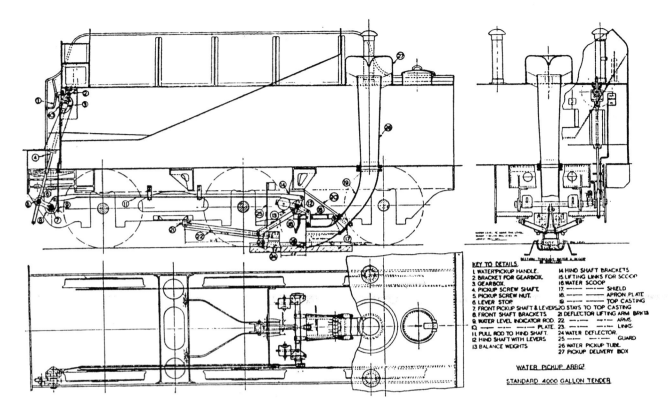

KEY TO DETAILS.
1. WATER PICKUP HANDLE.
2. BRACKET FOR GEARBOX.
3. GEARBOX.
4. PICKUP SCREW SHAFT.
5. PICKUP SCREW NUT.
6. LEVER STOP.
7. FRONT PICKUP SHAFT & LEVERS.
8. FRONT SHAFT BRACKETS.
9. WATER LEVEL INDICATOR ROD.
10. ——— " ——— PLATE.
11. PULL ROD TO HIND SHAFT.
12. HIND SHAFT WITH LEVERS.
13. BALANCE WEIGHTS.
14. HIND SHAFT BRACKETS.
15. LIFTING LINKS FOR SCOOP.
16. WATER SCOOP.
17. ——— " ——— SHIELD.
18. ——— " ——— APRON PLATE.
19. ——— " ——— TOP CASTING.
20. STAYS TO TOP CASTING.
21. DEFLECTOR LIFTING ARM BRKT.
22. ——— " ——— ARMS.
23. ——— " ——— LINKS.
24. WATER DEFLECTOR.
25. ——— " ——— GUARD.
26. WATER PICKUP TUBE.
27. PICKUP DELIVERY BOX

WATER PICKUP ARRG.

STANDARD 4000 GALLON TENDER

FIG. 31

piece of equipment on a tender, and its mechanism is shown in Fig. 31.

A movable scoop is fitted which, by the operation of a hand screw, is caused to swing downwards until its lip is a little below the level of the water in troughs laid between the rails at certain points on the line. The forward movement of the engine then causes water to be forced up the scoop, then up a large pipe leading nearly to the top of the tender tank where it overflows into the tank. The top of this delivery pipe (or water pickup tube) is just above the water level when the tank is full. The flow of water up the scoop was aided by a special deflector plate designed to bank up water in front of the lip of the scoop. It was important to try and anticipate when to start raising the scoop because water pressure increased with speed making the scoop handle very difficult to turn. If the scoop was allowed to remain lowered too long the tank would overflow causing wastage and possible inconvenience to passengers if seated by open windows.

Obviously it was undesirable to lower the scoop too early or allow it to remain lowered after passing the trough as there was grave danger of it catching crossover-roads, wooden crossings etc. which might cause serious damage.

When double heading it was a wise precaution to close everything on the train engine; dampers, firehole door and windows and for the crew to keep their heads well in. It could get very wet. It was also standard practice for the train engine to have 'first dip' so that it could effectively scoop water undisturbed by the Pilot.

Combustion

Important as it was for footplate crews to know the mechanics of their engines, it was equally important for them to be aware of what took place when coal was ignited in the grate and the properties possessed by the steam thus produced.

They were taught the basic principles of combustion and advised on firing methods; but, of course, the application of theory over many years was required before a fireman could be regarded as experienced. As with all other ventures in the University of Life, one learns best from mistakes and with so many variables to contend with, firemen had the opportunity to make them in abundance. However, it is perhaps not out of place to look at these theories once more before discussing enginemen's duties in general. Taken from the LMS Enginemen's Handbook, the following differed little from Midland Railway teaching fifty years earlier:-

"The principal combustible constituent of coal is carbon, but it also contains substances known as Hydrocarbons and traces of sulphur etc. Hydrocarbons are chemical compounds of the gas hydrogen and carbon. In gas coals the hydrocarbons are the chief light producing constituents. When coal burns the carbon and other combustible constituents combine chemically with oxygen from the air, in the process of which a considerable amount of heat is given out. The necessary supply of oxygen to burn coal in a locomotive firebox is obtained from air drawn in through the dampers and the firehole door by the action of the blast in the smokebox. If combustion is complete, a colourless gas called carbon dioxide is formed. Each pound of carbon so burned produces approximately 14,000 BT units of heat. If combustion is not perfect, the whole of the carbon would not be consumed and a colourless and highly poisonous gas called carbon monoxide would be produced.

"Each pound of carbon so imperfectly burned only produces 4,500 BT units of heat. If a further supply of oxygen was then introduced the carbon monoxide gas would ignite and burn with a pale blue flame, giving out a further considerable quantity of heat to form carbon dioxide gas. In the absence of a further supply of oxygen the carbon monoxide gas would escape up the chimney unburned and the available heat in it would be lost. This represents a loss of 69% of the available heat.

"The hydrocarbons in the coal are burned by combining with atmospheric oxygen to form carbon dioxide and water, which the heat of the firebox converts into steam, and which is carried away with the other flue gases up the chimney by draught. If the combustion is not complete due to lack of sufficient oxygen, some of the carbon will be left in a free state and will pass away up the chimney where it will appear in the form of smoke.

"If clinker is allowed to form in large quantities it will block the air spaces in the grate and prevent the air supply admitted via the dampers from passing through the fire which in consequence will become dead, refusing to burn properly, so that the steaming of the boiler will be affected. In this event it will be necessary to break up and dislodge the clinker by using the straight dart to lift it from the firebars and the pricker to clear out the air spaces in the grate. Incorrect firing and mismanagement of the dampers tends to accelerate the formation of clinker. The best safeguard is to spread about half to one bucketful of broken clean firebrick or limestone over the grate before the fire is built up during engine preparation. These materials tend to collect the clinker round themselves as it forms and by so doing preventing it from adhering to the firebars. A large quantity of air is required to ensure proper combustion and as previously stated this is drawn in by the blast and enters the firebox through the dampers, upwards through the firegrate and also through the firehole door, to the top of the fire. Most ex-LMS engines have hollow firehole doors which allows a certain amount of secondary air to be admitted even when the doors are closed.

"It is nearly always necessary to admit air through both the firehole door and the dampers. The air drawn through the firegrate is required to maintain the bed of fire incandescent, whilst the air admitted by the firehole door serves to complete the combustion of the gases liberated from the glowing coal below. However, all air admitted to the firebox over and above the quantity necessary for complete combustion of the coal will pass through the boiler unchanged except that it will become heated in its passage. This means that the surplus air robs useful heat from the fire which could otherwise be used to produce steam and furthermore the loss of this heat from the fire lowers the temperature of the firebox.

"If insufficient air is allowed to enter the firebox, complete combustion of the coal is impossible because there will not be enough oxygen to combine with all the carbon in the fuel and some of the carbon will pass through the tubes unburned to appear at the chimney in the form of smoke. There is also the risk that the carbon consumed will only be burned to carbon monoxide and that the hydrocarbon vapours will also escape unburned from the chimney, giving rise to a serious heat loss in addition to the production of smoke.

"How then is it possible to judge when the correct amount of air is being admitted to the firebox to give correct combustion? One method is to set the dampers and firehole door so that a clear exhaust is obtained but that when the firehole door is closed very slightly, smoke appears at the chimney. Another method is to adjust the dampers and firedoor so that there is just a perceptible discolouration of the exhaust at the chimney. This method has the advantage that there is something visible to watch and there is no chance of admitting excess air. In either case, if combustion is almost perfect, each shovel of coal fired will be accompanied by a dash of smoke from the chimney lasting perhaps one or two seconds.

"However, efficient combustion would not be possible without a brick arch which fortuitously serves several useful purposes. It protects the tubes and tube plate ends from the direct flame of the fire. During intervals of firing when the firebox temperature falls, the brick arch radiates heat which tends to prevent rapid fluctuations in the tube plate temperature. The brick arch also promotes thorough combustion of the gaseous products of the fuel by lengthening their path from the firegrate to the tube plate and at the same time acting in conjunction with the firehole deflector plate it causes these burning gases to be intimately mixed with the supply of top air admitted to the firebox through the firehole door."

It was not possible nor for that matter attempted, to teach firing techniques from books or in the lecture room, although the method known as 'Controlled Firing' was officially encouraged. It took the 'little and often' theme somewhat further by stating how little and how often:-

"Controlled firing can be described as firing at equal time intervals, as it lays down that a definite number of shovels of coal well broken up should be fired at short regular intervals and the time between firings should not be altered by reason of speed or gradient. The actual number of shovels of coal fired will, of course, depend on the work the engine has to do and this will be determined by experience, but as the firing is done on a time basis, variations in speed and gradient will not effect the rate of firing. An engine pulling a train up a bank will burn more coal per mile than on the level but as it travels more slowly uphill, the coal burnt per minute need not vary. Controlled firing saves coal because it is never added at such a rate that the gases it gives off cannot be burnt by the air passing over the fire from the firedoor. It also prevents waste due to excessive firing before or on a rising gradient. It is better to use the coal on the grate as a reservoir of heat to be

COMPLETE COMBUSTION

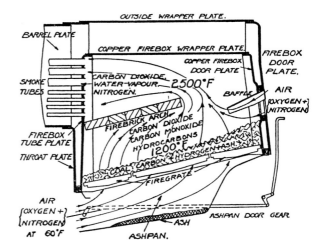

SECTION OF FIREBOX SHOWING THAT GASES ARE FORMED AND THAT TEMPERATURES OF UPWARDS OF 2500°F. ARE OBTAINED DURING THE COMPLETE COMBUSTION OF COAL.

FIG. 32

drawn on when the engine is working hard, than to make a large increase in the rate of firing, bringing down the temperature in the firebox and causing black smoke. In Controlled firing the reservoir is built up again on the down gradient by continuing to add coal at the regular two minute intervals. The number of shovels of coal to be fired will depend upon the work the engine has to do and the fireman's guide to this will be the maintenance of his boiler pressure on the gauge. Controlled firing of course, does not dispense with the fireman's knowledge of the road, when to use the injector and when to cease firing, but it lays down sound principles which, when combined with his road experiences, enables him to fire his engine when running, with efficiency and economy."

This then was the theory, however, there were certain difficulties in practice which require elaboration.

To be properly executed, Controlled Firing required a high degree of skill, knowledge and confidence in oneself, one's driver and the locomotive. As previously mentioned, there were so many variables to be taken into account that even an experienced fireman could get

INCOMPLETE COMBUSTION

FIG. 33

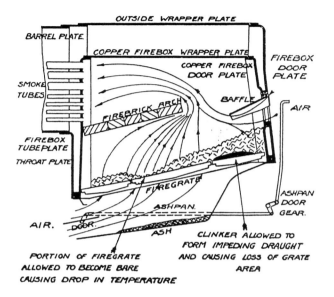

SECTION OF FIREBOX SHOWING EFFECTS OF
MISMANAGEMENT OF FIRE.

in trouble before he realised it. Different engine classes obviously had different characteristics and these had to be learned. To complicate matters, no individual engine in the same class behaved in exactly the same way. Some always seemed to steam, run or pull better than others.

Furthermore the same engine would vary in itself from month to month, week to week, day to day or even hour to hour, depending on its mileage since shopping, quality of current maintenance, whether it needed washing out, the type of coal carried or if the fire needed cleaning.

Apart from the locomotive, train loadings were rarely the same, particularly with freight, and adverse weather could add a considerable burden.

Driver's methods also differed greatly, from perpetual merciless hammering to the opposite extreme of working the engine so lightly that anything but the thinnest of fires never had sufficient blast to burn brightly. The worst were those who drove inconsistently, for it was never possible to anticipate their whims.

Then of course route knowledge was so very important. Knowing just where a maximum effort was needed or when little steam would be required, where the fire

could be cleaned if necessary, where coal could be safely dragged forward from the back of the tender and when to snatch a quick sandwich! It also helped to know when and how other traffic was running since this could either impede or hasten progress.

Controlled Firing therefore, could not always be strictly adhered to since so many other factors over which there was no control could influence matters, but it did provide a sound guide line from which to work. But whether or not Controlled Firing could be faithfully pursued did not detract from the sound advice of 'a little and often'.

It is not difficult to visualise the effect of rapidly firing a large amount of coal on to an incandescent firebed. Opening the firedoor wide immediately allows a high volume of cooling air to rush through the firebox and tubes. Every shovel of coal fired, even if small cobbles, momentarily blocks radiation to the firebox and if large lumps are fired then the blocking can be for quite a long time. In addition, every piece of coal on contact with the hot firebed, instantly generates a stream of hydrocarbon gases which will only burn in an adequate supply of secondary air admitted through the firehole.

If too much coal is applied too quickly, then not only is there insufficient oxygen for complete combustion even with a wide open fire door, but the dense clouds of smoke thus produced blanket heat radiation as effectively as a thunder cloud passing in front of the sun.

The reduction in efficiency therefore stems from three causes: 1. Loss of radiation from screening by unburnt coal on the firebed; 2. The blanket effect of unconsumed smoke; 3. Loss of total calorific value of the fuel by incomplete combustion of the hydrocarbon content.

To make matters worse, at least initially, the inexperienced fireman would often close or partially close the firedoors which further reduced the secondary air supply. This naturally gave rise to even more dense clouds of smoke at the chimney which might look very spectacular in photographs but in reality was a testiment to inept firing with its inevitable waste of coal and damage to the environment. For the above reason advice was also given as to how coal should be put on during firing (see Figs. 32 & 33):-

"This varies with different grates, depending upon the shape and slope etc. but in all cases the person firing must aim to prevent the formation of holes in the fire. Generally it is advisable to maintain the fire thicker at the corners and sides and to avoid placing much coal in the centre which will cause smoke.

"In a sloping grate do not fire much to the front except to prevent the formation of any holes because the coal will shake down forwards and feed the front of the box and it is usually advisable to keep the back corners well filled. It is most important to avoid the formation of holes in the fire because the air naturally tends to pass in at this spot since this is the easiest path for it. The rush of air through the hole will lift particles of glowing fuel, carrying these through the tubes and out of the chimney while the remainder of the fire will become dead and the firebox temperature will fall, due to imperfect combustion. A rapid examination of the state of the fire over the entire grate can be made by resting the shovel blade on the firehole mouthpiece and using it to direct a stream of air on the part of the fire it is desired to examine. By moving the shovel blade, it is possible to direct the air stream to each part of the fire in turn and to examine the whole fire. The fireman should endeavour at all times to avoid the use of fire irons since excessive use of these tends to accelerate the formation of clinker and disturbs the fire.''

The foregoing should only be regarded as basic principles, since to acquire the skills and physical stamina required by a top link fireman involved literally thousands of hours of practical experience with a great variety of engines and conditions. For this reason, fireman progressed through a series of links each which contained duties more taxing than those in the previous one, thus achieving a steady yearly advance in ability. Engine crews were also encouraged to gain some insight into the measurement of heat, the properties of steam and the benefits of superheating.

It was useful to have some idea of the temperatures attained in a locomotive firebox. These could be gauged approximately from its appearance and colour with red, orange and yellow flames indicating temperatures ranging from 1000 to 1200°F. At about 1800°F the fire would be glowing a brilliant red, whilst the fierce white furnace glow under good working conditions indicated temperatures from 2000° to 2500°F.

In case any aspiring fireman had forgotten his basic school physics, it was explained why at these temperatures, which were above the melting points of steel and copper, the firebox plate did not become damaged.

It was of course due to the capacity of water to absorb heat. So long as all the firebox plates and the tubes exposed to radiation from the fire and contact with the hot flue gases are covered on the opposite side with water, the heat passed to the metal is immediately absorbed by that water with the result that the temperature of the plates and tubes remains only a few degrees higher than that of the water inside the boiler.

It would of course be a serious matter if any part of the firebox or tubes were to be uncovered by water for even a few seconds because the plates would become overheated. When this occurs through low water the firebox crown sheet is affected first and the lead plugs fitted to it will fuse, allowing steam to fill the firebox and smother the fire. However, even if the lead plugs fuse, there is still a risk that the firebox crown sheet will be scorched and damaged, therefore to 'drop' a lead plug inevitably results in painful inquisition.

Steam and Superheating

Steam is regarded by many as the visual result of its condensing in air, but steam is really an invisible gas produced by the evaporation of water upon application of heat. When steam is produced in a closed vessel so that it is retained in contact with the water from which it has been generated it is known as saturated steam. If the steam is led away from the water and heated still further at constant pressure in a separate chamber, the steam is then said to be superheated.

Basic Principles

When steam is generated from water in a closed vessel it will accumulate over the water producing a pressure within the vessel and it is found that there is a corresponding temperature for every recorded pressure. As the pressure increases so the temperature of the steam also rises. The object of superheating is to supply it with a greater quantity of energy in the form of heat than it would possess naturally at that particular pressure. Consequently a given weight of superheated steam will be capable of developing more power in the cylinders than the same weight of saturated steam at equal pressure. This application of further heat to the steam during superheating causes it to expand so that less weight of superheated steam is required to fill the cylinders at each working stroke than would be the case if saturated steam at equal pressure was used. Since it takes a pound of water to produce a pound of steam, it follows that if superheating enables the cylinders to do their work on a lower weight of steam, a saving in water and coal will result. A further advantage in favour of superheating is that sufficient heat can be retained in the steam after expansion behind the piston to prevent condensation taking place within the cylinder.

This need to eliminate condensation was appreciated quite early in the development of steam engines but it was not until the middle of the 19th Century that experiments were made which initially, took the form of steam driers such as that fitted to LNWR 2-2-2 locomotives by McConnell in 1852.

Numerous patents were taken out during the next forty years or so, covering designs of superheaters principally located in the smokebox or boiler barrel. None were particularly successful for a variety of reasons, not the least of which, was the difficulty found in adequately lubricating the slide valves then in use. However, in 1897 the Prussian State Railways fitted a firetube superheater developed by Dr. Schmidt to one of their engines. His idea of breaking down the steam flow into series of small tubes or elements in order to present the maximum heater surface in contact with hot flue gases proved to be very successful and in due course was universally adopted. Schmidt, being aware of lubrication problems created by much higher steam temperatures advocated and indeed developed piston valves to be used with his superheaters.

In 1906, Churchward of the GWR fitted the first superheater to a British locomotive. This was a Schmidt type although he eventually designed his own Swindon superheater which aimed at providing dry steam rather than a high degree of superheat. Shortly after, the LYR commenced experiments with superheaters and by 1910, many of the more notable pre-grouping companies had followed suit.

However, it was the LYR which first applied high degree superheat coupled with long travel piston valves to four 4-4-0 locos in 1908. Although these engines performed remarkably well, the system was not pursued because of excessive wear problems in the steam chests. Indeed it was only really when practicable improvements in lubrication and piston valve designs allowed its general adoption in the 1920s. Even then it was not until BR days that the former GWR system finally converted to high degree superheating, bringing their engines up to date with current practice.

Steam has the property of storing up a vast amount of energy in the form of heat and it then does work by giving up this heat as it expands inside the cylinders, a characteristic generally referred to as the expansive property of steam. Therefore, to appreciate how this expansive property is utilised in a locomotive we should look once more at the sequence of events that occur when the regulator is opened.

Steam stored in the boiler at high pressure is admitted to the steam chest by way of the regulator valve, internal steam pipe, superheater and external steam pipe. From the steam chest, distribution to the cylinders is controlled by valves which in turn admit steam to the cylinders, retain it therein and release it to exhaust after it has expended its energy on the pistons. Whilst the steam is enclosed within the cylinder it expands behind the moving piston exerting a gradually diminishing pressure upon it as it does so. This portion of the working cycle in the cylinder is known as the 'expansion period'.

The driver can control the length of the expansion period within limits set by the valve gear by use of the reversing lever. As the lever is 'notched up' toward mid gear the admission period is reduced in length and the expansion period correspondingly increased. This is what is known as 'expansive working' and results in a lower consumption of steam per stroke than would be obtained if live steam were admitted for the entire stroke and the expansive powers of the steam disregarded.

It must also be remembered that the steam ports and passages are of finite size and can only handle a given quantity of steam. Unless residual steam pressure is reduced by shortening cut-off (notching up) as piston speed increases, then that piston speed will be automatically limited by back pressure due to exhaust steam not being able to escape quickly enough. Thus the reversing lever may be likened to the gears of a car. Full gear, approximately 75% cut-off, equals first gear in a car: ideal for starting and maximum pull. Then as the reversing lever is progressively moved towards mid gear the locomotive will pull less strongly but is able to run faster and more economically, just in fact as a car does when in top gear.

Power developed in the cylinders now has to be transferred into work done at the wheels and pull on the drawbar. As a corollary of this, perhaps a look round the wheel and the testing of valves and pistons should now be examined.

The Driving Mechanism

The drive from the piston is conveyed to the wheels by way of the piston rod, crosshead, little end, connecting rod, big end and crank. The connecting rod and crank convert the reciprocating action of the piston into a rotary movement of axle and wheel. In forward gear the pistons push the crank pins under the axle and pull them forward over it, while in back gear the crank pins are pushed over the axle and pulled forward under it. For this reason the thrust of the piston rod crosshead is against the top slide bar when running forwards and against the bottom bar when running backwards.

For convenience, crank positions are discribed at eight points on a circle. The forward and backward crank positions in which the crank webs, connecting rod and piston rod are all in one straight line, are known as the front and back dead centres. When the crank stands vertically upwards or down it is said to be on the top or bottom quarter.

The four intermediate settings which lie midway between the front and back dead centres and the top and bottom quarters are known respectively as the front and back top angles and the front and back bottom angles (see Fig. 34).

By reference to these eight crank positions it is quite easy to visualise the position of the piston within the cylinder. For instance, when the crank is on front or back dead centre the piston will be at the end of its stroke at the front or back of the cylinder. When the crank is on top or bottom quarter the piston will be approximately mid stroke. With the crank on top or bottom front angle, the piston will be rather less than quarter stroke from the front of the cylinder and it will be the same distance from the back cover when the crank is on either of the two back angles.

Events in the steam cycle can be related to the piston position. The duration of the various periods of steam in the cylinder is generally measured in terms of the piston stroke as, for instance, cut-off is referred to as 50% or 75%. It is therefore possible to state where the piston will be when the events of cut-off, release, compression and admission occur. Consequently it is only one step further from this to be able to couple the cylinder events with the crank setting which will enable the valve positions to be judged from the settings of the cranks or side rods. For example, a description of a typical steam cycle in the front end of the cylinder during one revolution of the driving wheels at say 30% cut-off would be as follows:-

Commencing from front dead centre the piston will travel about 30% if its stroke before the valve closes the front port to steam and cut-off occurs. Expansion will occupy a further 45% of travel at which point the exhaust edge of the valve will uncover the front port to exhaust giving the point of release and the piston completes the remaining 25% of the backward stroke with the front port progressively opening to exhaust. The piston will now make about 72% of the return stroke before the exhaust edge of the valve again closes the front port starting the period of compression. This will occupy about 25% of the stroke at which point the steam edge of the valve clears the front port once more, opening it to lead. This is the period of pre-admission which occupies the remaining 3% of the return stroke until the piston reaches front dead centre position in readiness for the commencement of the next cycle.

LEAST EFFORT POSITION OF CRANK

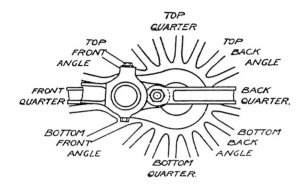

FIG. 34

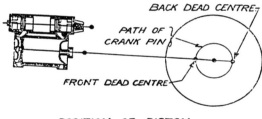

POSITION OF PISTON
WHEN CRANK IS ON FRONT DEAD CENTRE

Meanwhile at the back end of the cylinder during the same period starting from front dead centre, the valve already has the back port open to exhaust, which period continues till the piston has covered about 72% of the backward stroke, when the valve closes the back port and compression starts. This occupies a further 25% of the stroke, when the steam edge of the valve will uncover the back port to lead and the period of pre-admission sets in to occupy the remaining 3% of the backward stroke (see Fig. 35 indicator diagram).

The steam cycle in the cylinder can also be related to the crank positions:-

In forward gear the front side of the piston is exposed to live steam of the admission and expansion periods and the back side is exhausting as the crank moves under the axle from front dead centre to back dead centre. After the crank passes back dead centre position the back of the piston takes admission steam followed by expansion and the front side enters upon the exhaust and compression periods.

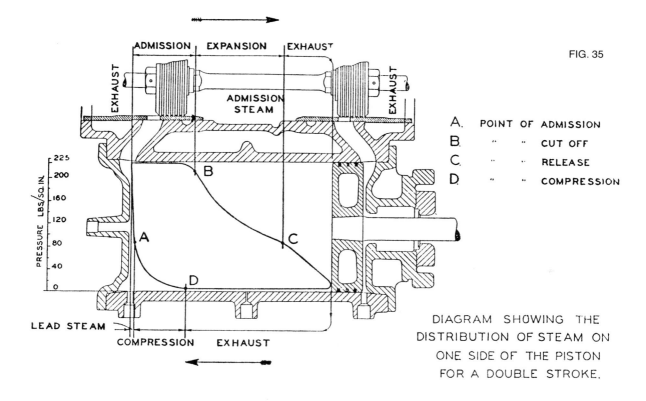

ADMISSION | EXPANSION | EXHAUST

EXHAUST | EXHAUST

ADMISSION STEAM

FIG. 35

A. POINT OF ADMISSION
B.   "   " CUT OFF
C.   "   " RELEASE
D.   "   " COMPRESSION

PRESSURE LBS/SQ.IN.
225
200
160
120
80
40
0

LEAD STEAM

COMPRESSION   EXHAUST

DIAGRAM SHOWING THE
DISTRIBUTION OF STEAM ON
ONE SIDE OF THE PISTON
FOR A DOUBLE STROKE.

The exhaust beat from the front of the cylinder will therefore be heard as the big end passes back dead centre and the exhaust from the back will take place as the big end passes front dead centre.

In backwards gear steam acts in front of the piston as the crank passes back over the axle and behind the piston as it moves forward under it.

As previously mentioned, the driver can effect control over the steam cycle by notching up. This shortens the valve travel which has the effect of shortening the admission and exhaust periods and lengthening the expansion and compression periods.

Earlier it was stated that when the crank is on top or bottom quarter position, the piston would be approximately at mid stroke and not exactly at mid stroke. This effect is produced by the angularity of the connecting rod. Due to this the piston will be at the exact centre of the cylinder barrel only in the two crank positions where the angle made between the centre line of the crank webs and the centre line of the connecting rod is equal to 90° which will occur when the crank is slightly in advance of the top and bottom quarter positions. The extent of this angularity depends upon the length of the connecting rod and the throw of the crank and is

increased when short connecting rods are used. This displacement from the exact centre is expressed as a percentage of the piston stroke, for example at 25% cut-off on a 4F 0-6-0 the displacement is 3.3%. A Class 5 4-6-0 with a longer connecting rod is only 2.0%. Obviously allowance has to be made for this effect when designing valve gear otherwise steam distribution would be adversely affected.

Maximum thrust is obtained when the crank is on top or bottom, quarter positions and minimum thrust when at front or back dead centre. Therefore, in two cylinder engines the cranks are set at 90° and on three cylinder simple engines they would be equally spaced round the axle at 120° apart. Generally the right hand crank leads when in forward gear, but this can be determined by setting the engine with one big end on the top quarter and if the other is then on front dead centre, that one leads, if on the back dead centre it follows.

When oiling an engine, it was useful to set it in the correct position so that this task could be achieved with the minimum effort. Side rods are mounted on the opposite centre to the crank on the same side, so that if one side rod is on the bottom quarter then the big end on that side will be on the top quarter.

Therefore, when positioning for example an inside cylinder 4F 0-6-0, both big ends should ideally be as near the top quarter as possible. Bearing in mind that the left big end follows the right by 90°, setting the right side rod on the bottom back angle will bring both big ends to the top angles which is the best position for access from the running plate.

Testing for Steam Leaks

Knowledge of the valves, piston, crank and side rods relationship is also necessary when testing for internal steam leaks. In order to test for one side, the crank of the cylinder under test should be set on the bottom quarter, the reversing lever placed in mid gear and the regulator opened slightly with the steam brake on and the cylinder cocks closed.

The test is made by moving the reversing lever as required from forward to backward gear and noting the indications given at the front end. If on going into full forward gear a blow is heard from the chimney, which ceases in mid gear and restarts in back gear, a leakage past the piston is indicated. If the blow occurs in fore gear, but not in mid gear or back gear, the front port bar is cracked, similarly if the blow occurs in back gear only, the back port bar is defective. If these indications are obtained on a piston valve engine, a damaged front or back valve liner would be the cause. A continuous blow up the chimney obtained in all positions of the reversing lever would indicate that the valve under test was blowing through, but on two cylinder engines this effect will also be produced by a defective piston on the opposite side. Therefore, if this indication is obtained, the engine should be reset and the other cylinder tested in order to prove the opposite piston before coming to a decision.

If the valves and pistons are in good order when using this test, no blow will be heard from the chimney in any position of the gear, but a single well defined beat will be heard as the lever is pulled over from forward to back gear and vice versa.

A broken valve lap may be found with a crank on quarter setting as described above but the cylinder cocks should be left open. If on moving the lever a short distance towards forward gear, steam blows from the front cock or from the back cock when the lever is moved a short distance towards back gear, this indicates that a portion is broken off the front or back valve lap respectively. In the case of badly damaged laps, a blow from either of the cocks may be obtained with the lever in mid gear according to which lap is affected.

Should an engine be suspected of having a cracked valve cavity or defective piston valve rings causing a bad blow through to exhaust, it would be important to ascertain which valve was at fault. This could be identified by employing the mid stroke test with crank on bottom quarter, but it would be advisable to test both sides. In this test the cylinder cocks should be used and when the defective side is tested steam will issue from both front and back cylinder cocks when the lever is in forward and backward gear. In forward gear a heavy blow will be obtained from the front cock and a light blow from the back, whilst in back gear the back cock will blow heavily and the front one lightly.

A two cylinder engine can also be set to test both sides simultaneously. Provided that the cranks are set on the two front angles, the right hand valve and piston can be tested from the front with the lever in fore gear and the left hand valve and piston can be tested from the front with the lever in back gear.

To test the cylinder from the back, the engine would require to be reset with the cranks on the two back angles, assuming that the right hand crank leads from the left.

It is important to understand the principle of using the front angles for testing. In this position the two crossheads will be dead level in the slide bars and with the reversing lever in mid gear, both front ports will be just covered by the steam edges of the valve whilst the two back ports will be open to exhaust.

In forward gear the right hand valve will uncover the front port to steam and will maintain the back port open to exhaust. The left hand valve will open the front port to exhaust and will close the back port. In backward gear the right hand valve opens the front port to exhaust and closes the back port, whilst the left hand valve will open the front port to steam and the back port to exhaust.

To test an engine by this method it should be set as described above with brakes applied, regulator slightly open, cylinder cocks open and reversing lever in mid gear. A blow up the chimney accompanied by wisps of steam from either of the two back cocks would indicate that the vlave on that side was faulty. In forward gear steam should blow only from the right hand front cylinder cock and in backward gear from the left hand front cock if all is in order.

If steam blows from either of the two front cylinder cocks with the lever in mid gear the front lap of the valve on that side is defective or the engine has not been accurately set for testing. A blow from both right hand cocks in forward gear accompanied by a blow from the chimney indicates that the right hand piston is leaking

The most objectional feature of the original batch of Ivatt 4MTs was without doubt, its horrendous double chimney. Not only did it displease the eye, but it was also very inefficient and the resultant poor draughting soon gained these locomotives an unenviable reputation with regard to steaming. On the other hand, the large cab with angled front windows, fore and aft regulator, external steam manifold and superb injectors mounted together on the fireman's side, were all improvements to be adopted in subsequent BR Standard designs.

past and if the same indications occur on the left side with the lever in back gear then the left hand piston is at fault.

Should there be a heavy blow from the right hand front cock with wisps of steam from the right hand back cock with a blow from the chimney in forward gear then the right hand front port bar is defective. Similar effects on the left hand side with the lever in back gear denote a defect on the left hand port bar.

Steam from the left hand back cock in fore gear and right hand back cock in back gear would indicate a fault on the back lap of the left hand or right hand valve respectively and the engine should therefore be set on the back angles to test the back laps.

With three cylinder simple engines each cylinder should be tested separately by the mid stroke method with the crank on bottom quarter as already described. However, another method is to test each piston separately with its crank on front or back dead centre. By this means a defective piston will be disclosed by a continuous blow up the chimney in all positions of the lever when the regulator is opened because one port will be open to lead and the other to exhaust. If the piston is sound there will, of course, be no blow of any kind.

Whichever method is used, all three pistons must be tested in turn and the results noted before any decision is formed as to where the defect lies, because it is possible to be misled from a single test if defects exist in one or both of the other two cylinders.

In the case of four cylinder simple engines the mid stroke setting with crank on bottom quarter should be used, but it has to be realised that the adjacent inside and outside cylinder will be tested simultaneously due to the fact that their respective cranks are fixed on opposite centres. If any blows from the chimney suggesting defects are obtained, it will be necessary to make use of the cylinder cocks in order to ascertain on which cylinder the defect lies.

HAVING reviewed the working principles, some of the more important components and a few useful tests which apply to steam locomotives, it would now be appropriate to look at a number of basic enginemen's duties in relation to engine preparation and disposal.

After signing on, reading his notices and joining his engine on the shed a fireman's first duty would be to examine and test the water gauges, note the steam pressure and if this is sufficient, at once test both injectors. If there is insufficient pressure he should at once proceed to level the fire in the box and commence to build it up in order to raise steam without delay so that the injectors can be tested as early as possible. If the state of the fire is entirely unsatisfactory or steam pressure and water level excessively low, no time should be lost in notifying the driver and the foreman, who will then, if necessary, be able to provide another engine without incurring any delay.

It should be explained that following disposal, a quantity of fire was retained in the back of the firebox and during the period the engine was stabled on shed this was maintained by steam raisers in order to keep a reasonable head of steam in the boiler. A value of 50 psi and over was considered reasonable, for, at this pressure, most blowers functioned satisfactorily and providing that there was an ample amount of live fire to spread over the grate, pressure could be raised in the time allowed for preparation, i.e. 45 minutes to one hour, depending on the class of locomotive.

If the engine was booked for washout or certain repairs, then the fire would be dropped completely at disposal. It was after such work as this was most of the problems occurred because the engines had to be lit up from cold. Not always did this lighting up proceed as quickly as intended particularly if the boiler had been over filled and the coal was of poor quality.

It was the fireman's duty to draw tools and equipment from the stores, clean, fill and trim the head lamps, gauge lamp and the hand lamp. He must inspect the detonator canister to ascertain whether the lid is properly sealed in position and if not, he should obtain a sealed canister from the stores.

When using a coal of clinkering nature he must obtain a supply of limestone or broken firebrick and spread this evenly over the firebars as early as possible after the fire has been levelled out.

The fireman should also satisfy himself that the smokebox is properly cleared of char, that there are no leaks from the front tube plate and afterwards must see that the smokebox door is securely fastened, taking care to wipe the faces of the door joint clean of char before closing it. He must also be particular to sweep the front platform and foot framing (running plate) clear of all loose char and sand which will be liable to blow about into the motion and in any case, present an untidy and slack appearance.

The sandboxes must be checked and if necessary filled with sand, while it was essential to ensure that coal was safely stacked and the fire irons properly stowed in their correct position.

Special precautions were taken when cleaning the gauge glasses which was inevitably the fireman's first task on joining an engine that had be lit up from cold, since they would be blackened with soot deposits.

It was important not to remove the gauge glass protector before releasing all pressure from the gauge glass and also not to re-apply pressure to the gauge glass before the protector had been properly replaced in position with the perforated brass plate facing the boiler back plate. When opening the gauge frame taps to re-apply pressure to the gauge glass after cleaning they should be only opened very slightly at first with the drain tap still open in order to blow a small quantity of steam through the glass to warm it up. If pressure is applied suddenly to the gauge glass, the rapid heating may fracture it. Gauge glass protectors should always be examined to see that they are in good condition and the catches sound. If the gauge glass is sufficiently dirty as to require a washing, always use a cloth soaked in warm water, a cloth soaked in cold water will probably cause the gauge glass to crack if applied to it.

To prepare the fire on an engine that has been stabled, it is first necessary to spread the live coal heaped in the back of the firebox evenly over the entire grate and then sprinkle a few shovels of small coal around the sides of the box to start the fire burning vigorously. The damper should be opened slightly and the blower applied sufficiently to promote proper combustion. At this stage limestone can be added if required, before putting on any further coal. The lumps of coal should be broken so that the largest put on the grate is about twice the size of a man's closed fist. This exposes to the action of the fire a greater surface than would be exposed if much larger lumps were used.

Now the fire can be built up, putting on a small quantity of coal at a time, firing round the sides of the box, avoiding placing coal in the centre of the grate unless any holes exist in the fire there. If coal is fired to the centre of the grate dense volumes of smoke will be produced and this should be avoided at all times. Firing can thus be continued at intervals, giving each charge of coal time to ignite properly before introducing more until the desired amount of coal is in the firebox and well alight.

The driver would not only sign on but read the current notices and sign for those which required it. He would obtain his job card, any special instructions affecting his workings for the day and oil from the stores. Upon reaching his engine he will see the gauge frames tested and satisfy himself that the lead plugs, stays and tubes are tight, at the same time noting the condition of the fire and the steam pressure.

He should see both injectors tested and himself test the vacuum brake and sanding gear so that if any defects are disclosed he can have them attended to in good time and avoid a late start.

Before leaving the shed, the water scoop should be tested and oiled and great care taken to see that the scoop is in the 'up' position to avoid any damage being done when the engine is moved; and the driver must satisfy himself that the coal and fire irons are properly and safely stored on the tender.

When oiling, the driver should have a definite system in mind and always work to that plan. It is best to commence at the same point, dealing with the various parts methodically and always in the same order, for in this way there is less possibility of overlooking any oiling points. The efficient driver will also be at pains to become acquainted with the differences in layout in the various classes of engines with which he will have to deal in the course of his duties. As he proceeds with his oiling the driver will also check for defects in the same manner as he would carry out an examination at disposal. If the engine is to steam heat the train to be worked, then the flexible hosepipe and connections must be seen to be in good order.

The carriage warming apparatus (CWA) should then be tested by first opening the cock on the tender end (or the cocks at each end of a tank engine) opening the steam valve to blow out all condensed water in the apparatus, close to the cocks and see that the correct steam heating pressure can be obtained (50 psi). Also, when working a passenger train, it was good practice to put a few drops of oil on the tender buffer faces. This prevents chafing of the buffers and lessens the jolts that may be transmitted by the tender to the first coaches of the train.

These were some of the official duties for firemen and drivers when preparing engines.

The 1950s, being the final full decade of the steam era, are regarded by some as the 'Golden Years' of British Railways. Perhaps they had good reason for hope: enthusiasm abounded, new ideas and designs were in abundance, Beeching was in the future and there was more traffic than could be comfortably handled. During this period, congested lines and heavy demands on Motive Power meant that engines were 'turned round' in Depots as quickly as possible. To encourage speed, incentives were instituted for the twin shed duties of preparation and disposal, both turns being just about equally dirty, onerous hard work with little excitement to liven the week. Most large depots offered their shed link disposal crews the option of a quota of six engines per shift and providing the work was performed satisfactorily they would book off with eight hours pay even if the actual time worked was considerably less.

Likewise, shed preparation turns usually required the preparation of six locomotives and once these were completed the crews were allowed to book off. However, a number of factors could delay the progress of preparation crews and they were lucky indeed if they departed in less than six hours. Frequently, suitable engines were not available to prepare much in advance of their booked time, so it was a case of waiting for them to arrive on shed after completing an earlier duty. Because freight trains were often delayed due to heavy congestion caused by the sheer volume of traffic, these arrivals could not even be predicted with any accuracy. It was indeed a shed foreman's nightmare and much juggling was done to cope with contingencies as they arose. Furthermore, even when engines were available tools and equipment were frequently in short supply. Each locomotive required two headlamps, a gauge lamp, a firing shovel of the correct size for that engine, a coal pick, a bucket, four spanners, a canister of detonators and three fire irons. Firing shovels normally came in two sizes, long (36in.) and short (30in.) and it made life very difficult for the fireman if the engine was equipped with the wrong type. As a rough guide, locomotives with long fireboxes and roomy footplates required the 36in. models while for those with short steeply sloping grates, tank engines and more cramped cabs, a 30in. type was preferred.

Fire irons came in a variety of types and sizes which, to be of practical value, should also be matched to the engine. The basic requirement was for a dart, a rake and a clinker shovel and again these could be roughly categorised into long and short models. Darts were designed for breaking up clinker and removing it from the bars which the arrowhead end did very effectively. However, since most locomotives were fired more heavily over the rear half of the grate, this is where the majority of clinker formed. A straight dart could not reach under the firehole or into the back corners, so most short darts were bent through nearly 90°, after which there was no problem in gaining access to these areas. Bent darts were, therefore, equally useful whether the grate be long or short, only the degree and point of bend being varied to suit different engines.

Engine rakes really needed to be as long as the firebox to suit their intended purpose of levelling the fire. The foot of these rakes formed a right angle to the handle and the end of this foot was of fish tail shape which made it ideal for clearing the spaces between fire bars. It was an extremely useful implement and certainly used more frequently than the other two. 'Stop-go' running, poor fuel quality and inadequate firing technique often caused coal to 'set' in the firebox, blocking the passage of air and allowing the fire to become dead. To remedy this, the rake would be drawn through the fire a number of times in order to restore its brightness. Also the rake was very effective in 'lifting' sheets of clinker from the firebars and then manoeuvring them so that they could be removed by means of a short clinker shovel. Even with long grates the combination of long rake and short clinker shovel was the most convenient way of cleaning a fire whilst on the road. Space restrictions, even in large cabs, precluded the efficient handling of a long clinker shovel, so this tool was rarely used.

Because of these cab/tender layout restrictions, fire iron combinations could vary considerably with choice dictated not so much by length of grate but more by what could be wielded comfortably within the limitations of that cab.

A typical set for a Class 5/8F might be a bent dart, a long engine rake and a short clinker shovel, whereas a Class 4F 0-6-0 could have a long or short rake, long or short clinker shovel and of course a bent dart. Choice for

the 4Fs would be to some extent influenced by the model of tender attached, since many different types were used by this class. In order to identify fire irons in the dark each type had a distinctive handle shape which could not be mistaken. Darts were in the form of a flattened elipse, rake handles were triangular, while those of clinker shovels circular – simple, but effective.

Having to forage for all these items of equipment took up a lot of time which had not been allowed for when the original schedules had been calculated. Often it was a case of waiting for incoming engines and then relieving them of some wanted items to complete the required complement. With engines that had been on shed for washout or repairs, the situation was rendered even worse because usually they were bereft of such basic essentials as slaking pipes, driver's platforms and even gauge glass protectors, all of which had to be obtained from other locomotives.

Another onerous duty was the filling of sand boxes. Most depots had one or two sand drying ovens, but it was one of those ironies of life that if an engine had empty sand boxes it was usually stabled at the furthest point possible from one of them. Sand had to be conveyed from the ovens to the engine in sand buckets which in appearance were rather similar to large widenecked watering cans. When filled with sand they weighed about 40lbs each and six empty sand boxes could readily take a dozen buckets, so that by the end of the exercise, the fireman's arms were a trifle stretched and his brow somewhat damp.

With these conditions prevailing throughout the 1950s it can be appreciated that preparation was generally a very strenuous business, at least for the fireman.

With regard to disposal it could be relatively easy or extremely arduous depending on the class of engine involved, how long it had been out in service, how it had been managed and the quantity and quality of fuel consumed. Hardly surprisingly, if a fireman had worked the duty and knew he would be disposing of the engine at the end of it, he would endeavour to arrive on shed with the fire in the best possible condition. On the other hand, when working the quota system, engines had to be taken as they arrived, irrespective of class or condition and inevitably some were in a deplorable state.

Taking the former situation first, the fireman was advised to level the fire in the box towards the end of the run and work it down as much as possible to avoid arriving on shed with a large quantity of unburned coal on the grate. Experience indicated the best time to commence working the fire down but the aim should be to run on to the shed with the fire as low as practicable, a good head of steam and the boiler nearly full of water.

Arriving on the shed at a modernised depot the first duties will be to take on water and then coal from the mechanical coaling plant before proceeding on to the ashpit. On the ashpit the fireman will empty the smoke-box of char and clean or lift out the fire in accordance to his instructions upon the matter. Whilst he is performing these duties the driver will be making his examination of the engine. Finally, the ashpan must be raked out making full use of the slaking pipe and left quite clear of ashes, after which all dampers and the firehole doors are to be tightly closed.

The driver will have ascertained whether the engine is to be turned and where it is to be stabled. The fireman should collect, check and return tools and equipment to the stores. If any item has been lost or damaged he should inform his driver who will report the fact when signing off and the fireman should draw the Storeman's attention to the discrepancy when handing over the equipment. Before leaving the engine inside the shed, the boiler should be filled with water to the height of three quarters of a gauge class. Stress was placed upon the need to close the dampers and firehole door after the fire had been cleaned because if this was not done, cold air would enter the hot firebox and set up severe contraction stresses in the plates, stays and tubes which would then be liable to leakage. For the same reason, the blower jet must not be used if the fire has been lifted and, when necessary to move the engine under its own steam with the fire out, the engine must be worked as lightly as possible to reduce the quantity of cold air which would be drawn through the empty firebox and tubes.

Basic advice was also given with regard to handling some items of machinery used on shed such as the coaling plant and turntables. Persons operating any kind of machinery must take certain elementary precautions in their own interest and that of others in the vicinity. Enginemen should take every opportunity to make themselves familiar with the different types of coaling plants and their controls. During coaling, the crew should stand well clear of the tender and coal chutes and the fireman should on no account get on to the tender to break lumps or clear a jam without first intimating clearly to the person at the controls what his intentions are. Avoid over coaling the tender which leads to excessive spillage and the risk of coal falling off and causing accidents to the staff.

With regard to turntables, it was recommended that enginemen always pushed, not pulled a hand operated table because when pushing, a man operating the table is behind the push bar so that if he should slip or fall the table will move away and leave him clear. On the other hand, if pulling on the bar, a man might be injured by the moving bar passing over him should he fall.

On turntables fitted with vacuum tractor motors, the starting valve must be opened slowly to reduce shock to the gearing. Care must be taken to see that the catches are out before the tractor is started and the table must never be stopped by forcing the catches in. The tractor should be shut down at such a point that the table will roll to a rest in the desired position on its own accord and never stopped by using the tractor in reverse. Finally, always ensure that there is plenty of power available by using the large ejector.

Thus the official instruction manual described disposal procedures in the correct sequence just as it had with preparation but it did not detail exact methods or how to overcome unforeseen problems arising from changed or local conditions. Each class of locomotive required a different method and even the same class would need a change of technique if the fire to be cleaned was in a bad state. It may therefore, perhaps, be instructive at this stage to follow two common, but different classes of locomotives through the disposal process at a modernised depot.

Class 4F 0-6-0

Although a variety of tender types were to be found with these engines, coaling and watering was similar. A competent driver would have his own individual marker at each water column so that irrespective of the class or tender type, he could stop accurately and not waste time drawing up or reversing. Having filled the tank, the engine would be taken under the appropriate chute of the coaling plant. Normally, better quality (passenger) coal was stored in one end and an inferior grade (goods) was contained in the other. Unless advised otherwise by the yard foreman, freight engines received the goods coal; however, if the engine was intended for a particularly arduous freight or even a passenger duty, then the superior coal was specified.

Controls for the delivery chutes were housed in small concrete cabins located at each end of a platform running the full length of the hopper. These were constructed to withstand the impact of even the largest lumps of coal and had windows protected by heavy wire mesh grills. Inside, two large levers mounted in slotted quadrants protruded from the floor. These controlled the angle of the delivery chutes, while mounted on the wall were water valves for the sprinkler system and switch boxes with separate on and off buttons.

The principle was quite straightforward, coal from the hopper fed on to a metal plate which an electric motor drove backwards and forwards like a shuttle when the switch was pressed. Coal dropping over the edge of this moving plate fell on to the chute, which in turn directed it into the tender. The angle of the chute could be altered to distribute the coal more evenly, whilst the sprinkler system was intended to lay the considerable clouds of dust this action generated. There were a number of points to be born in mind when coaling. Always turn on the sprinkler system first, since it took a few moments to become fully effective. Check that the engine is properly positioned and that no one is in the immediate vicinity. Next, be certain which way the chute should be slanted and that the lever is being pulled hard in that direction before releasing the locking catch. The reason for this being that sometimes a large lump of coal would be laying on the chute and its weight could tilt it in the wrong direction.

It was good practice to switch off a little on the light side because a certain amount of coal still drops even when the motor has stopped and in any case more can always be added if necessary. Moreover spillage had to be laboriously collected by the shed staff which wasted time and money.

With tender engines, the usual technique was to stop with the leading end of the tender as near to the chute as possible and then direct the chute towards the rear. This prevented coal from flowing over the shovelling plate and flooding on to the cab floor. It was particularly important to use this method if the tender was fitted with coal doors, since their securing catches could be easily burst open by a sudden avalanche of coal which could then rapidly fill the cab.

After filling the first part to a safe height the engine was moved down and by angling the chute in the opposite direction the rest of the coal space could be topped up to the required level.

It was intended that after coaling, an engine would proceed to the ashpit where the fire, ashpan and smokebox would be cleaned. As the name implies, ashpits were usually brick or concrete lined pits about three feet deep and lay between the tracks. A substantial grid was situated towards one end of the cambered floor and beneath this a tapered chute led down to a chamber where a hopper was located. When full, this hopper was raised by an electric hoist so arranged as to invert the hopper at the end of its travel thus depositing its contents into an adjacent wagon. On either side of the grid and mounted on ball joints in the pit wall were powerful slaking pipes which delivered water in a fan shaped spray. These ashplants were designed so that both clinker from the fire and ash from the ashpan could be deposited down a common chute suitably quenched by the sprinkler systems.

Sadly this rarely worked out at a busy depot, since for long periods the arrival roads were packed with engines awaiting disposal. Therefore fires were cleaned on the approaches to the ashpits and only ashpans raked out in the pit itself. This of course led to the piles of clinker, ash and smokebox char lining both sides of the track between Coal Hopper and Ash Plant which was so much part of the postwar Motive Power Depot scenario.

Unless fitted with a rocking grate it was always advisable to first remove the firehole deflector plate (baffle plate) on any class of locomotive before attempting to clean the fire, otherwise it would obstruct the free movement of fire irons. 4Fs were no exception and once this had been done the next task would be to push any live fire forward from the rear of the grate with either a clinker shovel or engine rake so that it formed a ridge under the brickarch. This served two purposes for it exposed the clinker and ash in the rear half and also provided a barrier half way along the grate against which to shovel. Clinker took many forms, it could be a thin layer of almost metalic quality set on and between the firebars, or possibly several inches of relatively soft ash like material loosely bound together and even sometimes a cocktail of both.

The first type could prove very difficult to break up and lift from the bars and usually required a prolonged assault with first a straight and then a bent dart. Having accomplished this, it could then be quickly removed via the firehole by means of a short clinker shovel. Softer clinker, although often quite deep, could usually be shovelled out without having to be broken up first and a bent dart was only required for access to the back corners of the grate and under the firehole. Whilst this form of clinker was much easier to lift from the bars, its sheer volume necessitated a lot more shovelling and its composition was such that clouds of unpleasant dust were created in large quantities.

Once the rear half of the grate had been cleaned, live fire could be raked back under the firehole and the front section then tackled. Irrespective of clinker type, the front half was somewhat easier in as much that the shovel blade had a flat unobstructed surface to work from. However, this was to some extent negated by the fact that a short clinker shovel would only reach about three quarters of the grate length after which a long version was required. Using this of course increased the difficulty of navigating around all the footplate obstructions and slowed the operation considerably. With the grate duly cleared it was merely a case of dropping some fresh coal under the firehole and returning the baffle plate to its original position. Obviously if the engine was required for washout or repairs then no fire would have been retained.

Whether the smokebox or ashpan were next tackled depended on if the engine could be positioned over the ashpit grid. 4Fs had only a front ashpan door or damper and having ensured that this was fully open it was then necessary to go into the pit beneath the engine. Should the wind be blowing towards the operator it was essential to direct the slaking pipe's spray into the ashpan so as to thoroughly soak its contents before raking commenced. Even then it was prudent to angle the pipe so that a curtain of spray fell in front of the ashpan. Ashpan rakes were some 15 feet in length with a 'T' shaped head which did permit the operator to crouch some distance away but unless time was allowed for the ash to be converted to a slurry it became a very dirty business indeed. With the wind blowing in the other direction it was rather more comfortable; however, liberal use of the slaking pipe was still encouraged in order to reduce the clouds of dust which inevitably settled over the cab and tender. Of all the disposal operations, cleaning out the ashpan was generally considered the dirtiest and wettest, even if not the most physically demanding task.

As with fires and ashpan, smokeboxes could vary from containing just a few inches of char at the bottom to having the blast pipe virtually buried. This of course, depended on how long the engine had been out in service, the type of duty it had been on, quality of coal used and whether it had been properly cleaned out at the previous disposal. 4Fs did not have a very deep framing in front of the smokebox door which was secured by six circumferential lugs or dogs retained by $7/8$in. nuts. The technique was to first slacken all nuts and then release every lug except the one at 10 o'clock which was on the opposite side to the door hinge. Standing clear, a light tap on this would allow the smokebox door to swing open leaving the fireman still on the framing. So as not to be deafened, the blower valve would have been closed down because the in-rush of air it created also caused char to be whipped up in clouds of fine gritty powder which could be most uncomfortable. Otherwise it was just a matter of steady shovelling in the hot, smokey interior and taking care to throw the char, if possible, down wind.

Class 5MT 4-6-0

With a Black 5 or the very similar 8F a rather different method was generally employed.

Having a grate length of nearly nine feet it contained three sets of firebars the rearmost being horizontal and to shovel clinker from the front section with a long shovel was extremely difficult. It was therefore common practice to extract four firebars from the centre of the middle set and drop the fire into the ashpan though the gap thus created. To accomplish this, fire and clinker had to be first removed in order to expose some half dozen firebars and depending on the amount and type of clinker, either an engine rake, short clinker shovel or bent dart was used for this purpose. Occasionally if very rough, all three implements would be required, but having done this the bars could be lifted out on to the footplate. The most convenient way was by using firebar tongs, although these were so heavy and cumbersome that it needed many hours of practice before the art was mastered.

The objective was to clamp the tong's jaws over the rear end of a bar and then squeeze inwards and downwards at the same time. Firebar tongs have handles about 5ft. long and by using the mouthpiece ring as a fulcrum considerable purchase can be gained, but even so, it often required the operator to bounce his full weight on the end of these handles before the first firebar could be prised free. It was then hauled over the slope of fire to the firehole when by means of a complex twisting movement the bar was inverted and dragged out on to the footplate. Usually the following three bars were somewhat easier to prise free but the action of inverting them was the same and it was when so doing that they were most likely to slip into the ashpan or even become lost down the hopper chute.

The gap left by the four extracted firebars enabled entry to be gained to the front compartment of the ashpan which sloped backward and upwards to clear the rear coupled axle. By inserting a long ashpit rake, the contents of this compartment could be pushed out through the open front damper directly into the pit. However, care had to be taken so as not to foul the ashpan bracing stay which was cleverly placed to obstruct such movements and because of this it was expedient to invert the rake so that the blade faced upwards. Once this had been done the fire could be systematically dropped through the gap in small 'parcels' which were then immediately pushed into the pit. By doing a little at a time not only reduced the possibility of a blockage but also safeguarded against burning and distorting the ashpan.

If the engine was not due for washout, then as always, some live fire would be retained in the back corners of the grate. Finally the smaller rear ashpan compartment could be tackled from the trackside using an engine rake.

Cleaning out a full smokebox on a Black 5 could be a long, hot and very dirty operation. Apart from the sheer volume of char it could contain (at 6ft. 8in. length), the fireman had to be well inside before the tube plate could be reached with a firing shovel held at full stretch. To compensate for this though, the platform in front of the smokebox was of very generous proportions and the door, being closed by a central dart, must easier to use.

*   *   *   *

Disposal was therefore, very much a swings and roundabouts situation with some classes having certain advantages over others, but all in all it was generally regarded as the most onerous duty associated with steam locomotives.

Fortunately, H.G. Ivatt was very much aware of the changed conditions of post war railways and of the urgent need to bring down operational costs by simplifying servicing and maintenance procedures. Skilled labour was more expensive and in short supply so many of his innovations were intended to ease these twin problems. Influenced by current American practice he introduced what was perhaps to be the most appreciated of improvements, at least as far as loco crews were concerned. These took the form of self-cleaning smokeboxes, rocking grates and self emptying ashpans and were fitted to Black 5s built from late 1946 onwards.

Disposing one of these locomotives was quick, relatively clean light work which took no more than a few minutes to execute.

Rocking grates were divided into separate front and rear sections which could be operated independently of one another. Each section contained rows of hinged bars which by a system of levers operated from the footplate, could be rotated nearly 90° to drop the fire completely or, through a lesser amount just sufficient to brake up clinker when running (see Fig. 36). Likewise the floor of the self emptying ashpan possessed a number of panels which opened completely, enabling its contents to be dumped in one movement, the most important point being to remember to open these hopper doors before dropping the fire, otherwise a jam would probably occur resulting in a burnt and buckled ashpan.

The detachable operating lever for the ashpan on a Class 5 was secured to the cab side below the fireman's seat by spring clips. Adjacent to the rear coupled wheel

on the driver's side projected a spigot which was attached to the lever system to the hopper doors. This was protected from unintentional movement by a hinged catch held in place by a safety pin chained to the mounting. Having removed the pin and opened the catch, the operating lever could be slipped over the spigot when on rotating through 90° the ashpan would disgorge its contents. Returning to the footplate with the operating lever, attention could now be given to the fire. Live fire would be pushed forward with a clinker shovel to just beyond the half way mark. Two other spigots similar to that of the ashpan's projected from the floor just in front of the firehole, the main difference being that they were fitted with a dual position locking catch. Lifting the outer catch allowed limited movement of the fire bar sections, while unlatching the inner catch enabled the sections to fully open. Applying the operating lever to the right hand spigot with both catches unlocked a few vigorous movements sufficed to break up any clinker and deposit it in the pit below. After closing the grate and securing the catches, live fire could be drawn back under the door in the usual way and then the front half treated in a like manner.

The ashpan doors needed but a quick shake to free any pieces of clinker lodged upon them and after securing this catch the job was completed since the smokebox required no attention whatsoever. Apart from the obvious time saving factor, grates were more effectively cleaned with this system and a further benefit was obtained on the road because the build up of ash and clinker could be kept at bay by regular use of the limited movement facility. This understandably led to more consistent steaming and efficient running. In addition to the 4600 and 4700 series Black 5s, rocking grates were fitted to all Ivatt designs and subsequently to the complete range of BR Standard locomotives.

Following disposal, drivers were required to examine all engines and to execute this efficiently, they were urged to always begin at one particular point, then proceed round the whole engine and tender in a systematic way. Going from one part to another at random would only result in confusion and some important items may be overlooked. For example, if the examination started at the leading end on the driver's side, he would pass down alongside the engine to the rear of the tender, across the back and return to the front end along the fireman's side. He would then go under the engine and proceed right through to the rear of the tender. It facilitated matters considerably if the engine was correctly set for this examination underneath. Engines with two inside cylinders, which, of course, includes

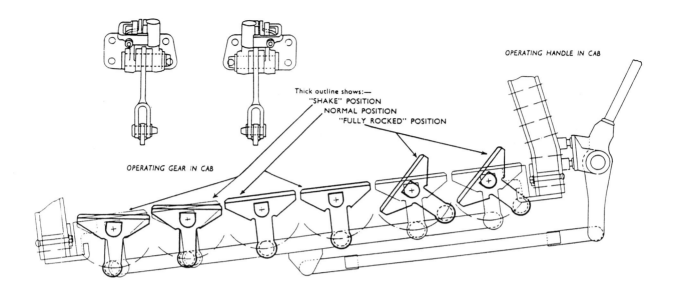

OPERATING HANDLE IN CAB

Thick outline shows:—
"SHAKE" POSITION
NORMAL POSITION
"FULLY ROCKED" POSITION

OPERATING GEAR IN CAB

FIG. 36   **ARRANGEMENT OF ROCKING GRATE**

four cylinder engines, are best set with the inside big ends on the bottom angles and three cylinder engines should be set with the inside big end on the bottom quarter. Special attention was given to the reporting of all blows and the need to ascertain, by test if necessary, their origin. The driver would also note whether valve spindles and piston rods were properly lubricated and not dry, while all slide bar bolts, big and little end cotters would be checked for security.

Any defects noted would then need to be recorded on a Repair Card giving as much detail as possible so that the fitter doing the repair would be able to go straight to the defective part even if the engine was out of steam. If there were no known defects, then a No Repair card had to be made out in order to confirm that the driver had in fact examined the engine.

Although the shed links which incorporated preparation and disposal work were the lowest links in seniority, and therefore the starting point for drivers and firemen alike, their work had a great effect on overall efficiency. Whether a locomotive performed to expectations in service depended as much on how well that locomotive had been disposed of, repaired and prepared, as it did on the skill of its operating crew. Admittedly, experienced and dedicated men would cope more effectively with

adversity but there could be certain problems that, if taken out on the road, would be insurmountable.

For example, the following are preventable causes of engines not steaming properly:- Dirty firebox tube plate, tubes blocked up, leaking joints in smokebox, tubes or superheater elements leaking, blast pipe out of alignment with chimney, smokebox door drawing air (not properly tightened up), defective brick arch, defective dampers, dirty grate, dirty ashpan or a badly fitted or worn baffle plate.

However, even with the most meticulous servicing, things could and did occasionally go wrong in inconvenient places. Driving Inspectors had a list of hypothetical faults with which they quizzed aspiring drivers at their passing out examination. The answers were glibly given, with tongue in cheek I suspect, because the sheer physical difficulty of executing such tasks out in the wilds at dead of night without adequate equipment would have been beyond the capacity of most crews.

One such typical question in this failures and remedies section would be:- How would you deal with a broken piston rod? As can be seen from the following stock answer, it was assumed that there was no such thing as siezed nuts or damaged threads, that all drivers had Herculean physique, that the correct tools and materials were available and that it always happened in broad daylight:-

"In this case it is practically certain that the front cylinder cover and piston will be smashed, but that the piston crosshead connecting rod and valve motion will remain intact.

"If this was so, all that would be necessary would be to disconnect the valve on that side and secure it centrally over the ports of the effected cylinder. This would be done by first disconnecting the drive from the valve spindle which on Walschaert's Motion is accomplished by uncoupling the lower end of the combination lever and taking the eccentric rod down. Next work the valve spindle into position by hand until the end of the valve spindle pin in the combination lever is visible in the centre of the opening in the valve spindle guide casting. This pin is tapped out centrally for a draw bolt and the screwed hole for this will now be in the centre of the opening. A bolt of suitable size should be removed from another part of the engine and screwed into the end of the valve spindle spin.

"Finally, obtain rail keys and insert the necessary amount of wooden packing required to wedge the bolt centrally in the opening of the slipper block guides. Firmly secure the bottom end of the combination lever as far forward as possible to clear the gudgeon pin when running and note that this prevents any further movement of the reversing gear without first freeing the combination lever.

"In the present case it would be unnecessary to disconnect the motion on the affected side from the reversing shaft".

Fortunately drivers were only expected to know what to do and not actually perform the tasks in reality — which was just as well since I've often seen a team of skilled fitters in a fully equipped workshop filling the air with profanities because some item which should come apart easily refused to do so.

However not all questions were of this more theoretical nature and many down to earth, practical remedies were listed for faults which, if not exactly common, could occur from time to time. One of the most popular being "What steps would be taken if one of the top feed clacks sticks up when working a train?"

Unlike the broken piston rod situation, crews could relate to this and would be able to carry out the recommended procedure which was to:- "Immediately put the opposite injector on and then note whether the boiler will supply the demand for steam required to work the train in addition to loss from the sticking clack. If it will not, the train should be stopped at the next point where it can be placed under protection of fixed signals where steps should be taken to reseat the clack. To do this, close the tank or tender feed valve, the blow back steam will then exhaust at the overflow, open the water regulating valve wide, open the injector steam valve fully to expel the blow back steam and to create a partial vacuum in the injector body, open the tank feed quickly and the injector should pick up the water and when regulated, the delivery will disturb the clack which will reseat when the injector is shut off."

This brief glimpse of some facets of the vast amount of knowledge train crews needed to acquire may help in understanding why it took so long for both fireman and drivers to become competent to work in the top links. On these longer distance runs, the former had to gradually develop not only a high degree of technical skill but also great physical stamina, while drivers had the prodigious task of having to memorise virtually every sleeper over a route of perhaps two or three hundred miles. After all they needed to know exactly where they were even in the thickest of fogs.

Having reminded the reader of what makes up a steam locomotive and how some of these parts function we now come to the section dealing with personal impressions of those engines on which I have had sufficient experience to form a balanced judgement.

For convenience, I have chosen to work through the list in roughly power class order but keeping certain groups together where comparisons are relevant.

Chapter 3

0-6-0 Class 2F Freight

The vans behind the tender of 3056 serve to accentuate the diminutive size of this 'modernised' 2F. However, from this angle the excellent all round vision obtained from the cab is very obvious.

THE ORIGINS of these venerable 0-6-0 work-horses are to be found in the series of Johnson single frame goods engines which date back to the 1142 Class built by private contractors for the Midland Railway in 1875. From that date until 1902, no less than seven classes totalling eight hundred and sixty five locomotives which incorporated quite a number of dimensional variations were constructed. A large proportion of these were rebuilt, then at a later stage rebuilt again, some upgraded to Class 3s to be finally rebuilt with G7 Belpaire boilers, while others reverted to Class 2s once again when fitted with G6 Belpaire boilers. Apart from boilers, other variations included 18in. and 18½in. cylinders, 5ft. 3in. and 4ft. 10in. coupled wheels and a number of different cab designs. Tracing the history of individual engines in these classes is quite complex and for those who are interested in such matters they can do no better than refer to 'An Illustrated Review of Midland Locomotives Vol. 4' by R.J. Essery and D. Jenkinson – Wild Swan Publications – ISBN 0 906867 746.

As may be appreciated, footplate crews were not so much interested in historical details but more in how suitable a particular locomotive was for its rostered job on the day in question!

My experience of Class 2F 0-6-0s was limited to the period 1950 to 1952 and indeed my very first firing turn as a Passed Cleaner involved one on what was known as the loco shunt. Because of their age and diminutive size, 2Fs tended to be regarded with some disdain by all concerned and crews worked them with a quite resignation borne from knowledge that nothing else was available for the duty. At this period only three examples were shedded at Saltley (21A) these being 58167, 58230 and 58261, while a further three were stabled at nearby Bournville (21B) 58126, 58138 and 58143.

Nº 2 CLASS GOODS

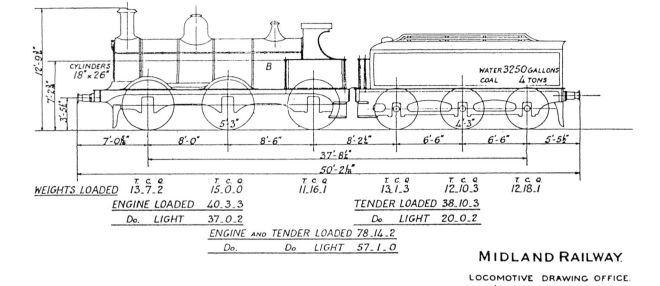

12'-9½"

CYLINDERS
18" × 26"

7'-2½"

B

WATER 3250 GALLONS
COAL   4 TONS

3'-5½"

5'-3"

4'-3"

7'-0½"   8'-0"   8'-6"   8'-2½"   6'-6"   6'-6"   5'-5½"

37'-8½"

50'-2⅛"

	T. C. Q.	T. C. Q.	T. C. Q.	T. C. Q.	T. C. Q.	T. C. Q.
WEIGHTS LOADED	13.7.2	15.0.0	11.16.1	13.1.3	12.10.3	12.18.1

ENGINE LOADED   40.3.3   TENDER LOADED 38.10.3

Do. LIGHT   37.0.2   Do. LIGHT   20.0.2

ENGINE AND TENDER LOADED 78.14.2

Do.   Do.   LIGHT   57.1.0

MIDLAND RAILWAY.

LOCOMOTIVE DRAWING OFFICE.

DERBY.

In all fairness, by 1950 these locomotives, or at least parts of them, had been around for well over half a century so that their design limitations alone restricted them only to the lowliest of duties. Also with labour shortages existing in every department, maintenance tended to be slanted towards keeping more modern locomotives in the best possible condition at the expense of these 'old timers'. That they managed to keep going for so long bears tribute to the basic ruggedness of their construction.

There were, however, a number of local trip jobs around the Saltley area where they could still effectively earn their keep. These involved distributing and collecting (usually light) loads to the numerous small sidings still to be found in the Birmingham conurbation at that time and although the trains were modest, the distances relatively short and the timings generous, the work was important nevertheless, for this traffic had to be assembled daily at the main marshalling yards for long distance trains to convey to all parts of the country.

With a loaded engine weight of only 37½ tons, Class 2Fs were ideally suited to venturing on to some branch lines and sidings where heavier, more powerful loco-

motives were not welcome, although with the passage of ·time, such places were gradually closed down or upgraded which, of course, further accelerated their eventual demise.

To describe a typical 2F is rather difficult in as much that unlike the larger 3Fs they were to be found in many forms. Apart from those already mentioned, other variations could include, dry or steam sanding, whether or not they were fitted with vacuum ejectors and (very occasionally) carriage warming apparatus, while their tender types were legion. Therefore, perhaps the simplest way to help readers compare these two 0-6-0 power classes is to concentrate on one particular 2F stabled at Saltley MPD.

No. 58167 started life as part of a batch of 30 locomotives built by Nielsons in 1876, but like the ''good old axe which has had three heads and seven handles' how much of it was still original after seventy five years would be hard to tell. Although commencing with 17½in. x 26in. cylinders this class was generally upgraded to the later 18in. x 26in. size but wheels remained at 4ft. 10in. In 1927, No. 2994 as it was then numbered, received a Belpaire non-superheated boiler pressed at 160 psi, which gave the engine a tractive effort of 19,417lbs at 85% BP, as against 18,185lbs for its 5ft. 3in. wheel contempories. At the same time a new cab replaced the meagre shelter provided by Johnson and the combined effect smoothed away a few years so that the appearance presented was early Edwardian rather than late Victorian.

By the fifties, engine crews familiar with better more modern machines regarded these antiques with mixed feelings: old drivers misty-eyed with nostalgic memories of working them on crack freights and young firemen even more damp of eye through other reasons, hoping the breakers torch would soon be at work.

As previously stated, by then the 2Fs were gracefully fading into oblivion trying to be useful, pottering about with little jobs considered beneath their younger progeny and going places which some of their successors could not. Occasionally then, I found myself with one of these veteran Class 2Fs working a leisurely local trip duty along one or two of Birmingham's backwaters. In keeping with most young firemen, a certain frustration or even resentment was felt on learning a 2F had been rostered. Apart from a tendency for the young to be impatient and even intolerant of the aged, these engines were so uncomfortable and inconvenient to work on, to say nothing of being downright inefficient, that a certain amount of disdain was bound to creep in.

Perhaps the chief source of annoyance was the inadequacy of its cab which, although considerably better than the original, did not extend far enough back to prevent the fireman getting soaked when carrying out his duties every time it rained. Not that the driver was much better off either when standing 'wrong road to the weather' or travelling tender first. Admittedly, storm sheets could be rigged, but these were inconvenient since they obstructed rearward vision and entry into the tender when getting coal forward or using fire-irons. Another source of discomfort was the absence of proper seats and whilst this may have been more acceptable on through freight work when the opportunity to be seated was limited, trip turns involved a high percentage of static waiting. Blocks of wood placed against the cab side did not prove an ideal alternative and in any case often went missing.

Keeping a clean and tidy footplate was almost a fetish of mine and since no slaking pipe was fitted on these engines I felt very deprived indeed and we all ended the day much dirtier than normal. Nor was there a clean and dry locker in which to keep personal effects, because although tenders could vary, No. 58167 possessed a 3,250 gallon version without a coal bulkhead. Mounted on its leading end was a curved topped 'trunk' intended

to serve the purpose but its hinged lid was sensitive to abuse and consequently permitted a plentiful ingress of coal dust and water. So, having discussed its habitability or rather lack of it, we can now look at how effective it was as a locomotive.

Despite the Belpaire firebox and rounded eaves cab, its small smokebox, slender, low pitched boiler, tall chimney and high dome were illustrative of what it really was, – a little old engine. Providing the engine was standing over a pit, oiling did not pose too many problems, although being devoid of mechanical lubricators meant that axle boxes demanded extra time and attention. Inside cylinders and motion equate with a slow dirty, tedious task and whereas big ends and eccentrics were quite accessible from below, little ends, spindle guides and slide bar cups had to be tackled from above. Unfortunately, the low-pitched boiler allowed meagre space when working from the foot framing and short, rotund drivers experienced much difficulty in reaching these parts.

With such a small engine, firemen, on the other hand, had a relatively easy time when preparing. Having no front step meant of course that access to foot framing had to be made via the cab, but this did not prove much of an additional burden and the sand boxes could be filled from ground level if so desired. Unfortunately, dry sanding was still fitted to No. 58167 and its functioning was erratic to say the least.

It applied sand only to the front of the leading wheels when running forwards and to the rear of the trailing wheels in reverse. The principle was sound in theory, since all coupled wheels received the benefit of a sanded rail. But, as the name implies, the system preferred dry sand, a condition difficult to maintain in our British climate and consequently they became clogged around the top of the delivery tube which was an area difficult to reach. Furthermore, the mechanical operating mechanism seemed to receive little attention, so that the resultant free play which developed made any precise setting impossible. If it worked at all it was a case of all or nothing being either wide open or closed and when flowing, it dumped a veritable torrent of sand towards the rails. Regrettably, misaligned delivery pipes, vibration and cross winds all combined to ensure that little arrived under the wheels, so it must be regarded as a very wasteful method. Steam sanding could also have its problems but on the whole it was much more efficient and economical.

Since there were no rear steps, it was necessary (when watering) for firemen to scramble over the coal in order to reach the tank filler, but once there, they felt quite secure in the shallow footwell. Normally, fire-irons were kept here when not in use if the tender was well coaled, otherwise they would lay alongside the coal rails.

So diminutive was the boiler that forward vision through the four spectacle glasses was really excellent and quite the best of any locomotive I have worked upon. Provided that the coal was correctly trimmed and there was no storm sheet in place the low tender also permitted a first class rear view.

With no ejectors, vacuum controlled steam brake, vacuum gauge, carriage warming apparatus and associated gauge, the boiler face seemed quite bare. In pride of place top centre, was a short handled upper quadrant regulator and below this the brass wheel of the steam brake. Flanking these on either side were two gauge frames with separate shut off cocks, while further outboard still were the combined steam valves and clack boxes of two live steam injectors. Above the right hand one could be found the blower valve and high on the spectacle plate near roof level, the solitary steam pressure gauge. Protruding from the plate below this were both the whistle and steam shut off valve for the 'sight feed' cylinder lubricator mounted on the upper left cab side sheet.

Strangely enough, a modern LMS pattern sliding fire-hole door was fitted to No. 58167 instead of the two piece Midland style and on either side 'umbrella' handles sprouted from the floor, the left being for the single front damper, the other controlling cylinder drain cocks, in both cases they were open when in the up position. The reversing lever was positioned between cylinder drain cock handle and cab side, while attached to the rear edge of the latter was the injector water control support bracket. A similar arrangement served the injector on the left cab side.

Although boasting steam sanding gear, this photograph of No. 58281 amply illustrates its inadequate cab and also the 3250 gallon tender without coal bulkhead. At the leading end, above the hand brake handle can be seen the 'trunk' type locker referred to in the text. However, with such an open footplate, fire irons could be wielded freely without fear of obstructions during disposal.

When driving the engine, a certain amount of extra care was needed until one became familiar with its slower response time to controls which, over the years, would appear to have developed considerable free play. Opening its regulator was not met by the accustomed snappy reaction; on the contrary, because the slide valves felt disinclined to become properly seated until a certain steam chest pressure was reached, much of the initial steam entering therein blew past the valves and exited from the chimney doing little more than making a plaintive sigh. However, once things had settled, she would roll quite smoothly into motion giving more of a soft woof than the sharp bark of the larger 3Fs. Even when working hard the exhaust was noticably softer and the blast less vicious with 2Fs, which probably further aided the impression that they were much weaker engines.

Steam brakes were not available until 1878 and up to that period the only retardation, apart from reversing the locomotive, came from the tender hand brake. To modern minds familiar with ergonomically placed, quick acting brake valves capable of instant full application, both the positioning and action of No. 58167s primitive device was somewhat illogical. The brake valve consisted of a brass hand wheel located below the regulator spindle and not only was it out of convenient reach when looking out of the cab, its action was exceedingly slow.

The valve operated like a tap, taking several anti-clockwise turns to fully open which consequently incurred some considerably delay until pressure built up in the brake cylinders. The only rational explanation of such an arrangement seems to be that when steam brakes were first fitted the increase in brake power thus provided was so great the authorities were concerned that its sudden use may have a damaging effect on the train. By slowing both the action and release by a tap type valve would reduce this possibility while at the same time allowing the driver to adjust braking effect within very fine limits. Of course it did not work out this way as progress has showed, because drivers can obtain a much higher degree of control from a brake which operates and releases almost instantly. However, some improvement was effected by lashing a spanner to the brass hand wheel, this not only extended the reach, but also enabled the valve to be spun more quickly.

Being confined to light trip work involving a maximum train of around twenty wagons it was rarely necessary to extend these old locomotives to their limit and I doubt whether I ever exceeded 30mph with one. However at this speed they rode quite steadily, aided in no small measure by a very low centre of gravity and, in keeping with the bypass effect of all slide valve engines, coasted freely.

With a grate area of only 17.5sq.ft., firing the 2F was not very demanding and provided a 'thick back, thin front' fire profile could be maintained the boiler steamed satisfactorily on the low grade fuel supplied to goods locomotives. The 2Fs tiny dimensions did not allow much thermal reserve and the little and often principle, including the injection of water into its boiler, had to be pursued. Due to the limited size of its foot-plate a short handled shovel was the most convenient to use, powerful swings being unnecessary to deliver coal to the front of a firebox less than six feet in length. This lack of size though was much appreciated when it came to disposal and shed men lightheartedly referred to them as 'dustpan and brush' jobs. Rocking grate types apart, they were the easiest of all the classes we dealt with on shed. The whole grate was within reach of a short clinker shovel which could be wielded with abandon in the wide open spaces betwixt cab and tender. Moreover the trips allocated to them were of relatively short duration so not much coal was consumed. This equated with little ash, clinker and char, and since ashpan and smokebox dimensions matched those of the firebox an easy time was had by all.

It may be thought a little unfair to include these few elderly and diminutive locomotives in this assessment but the principal reason for so doing is to contrast the very considerable difference made by upgrading the same basic engine to Class 3F. Substituting a G7 boiler, a practical cab and some updated fittings, brought about a metamorphosis which broadened the engine's utility beyond expectation and certainly far more than diagrams and figures would suggest.

Perhaps it is best to leave the 2Fs by saying that in times gone by they served the railway well but during the fifties they were of very limited use. Furthermore with their lack of comfort and conveniences they were without appeal to crews who regarded them with a jaundiced eye and felt that at the very best they were only a fair weather machine to be endured if nothing else was available.

3Fs WERE something of an enigma because 'on paper' they do not appear to be anything extraordinary and yet from their introduction in 1916 until eventually fading into oblivion in 1964 they enjoyed a most remarkable popularity matched by few other Midland locomotives. Nor was this popularity confined just to enginemen, for with few instances of trains being delayed by lack of steam or mechanical failures, the operating people had no qualms over rostering them for any duty within their power class.

Of course the Midland Railway had produced a round top (H) boilered Class 3 as far back as 1903 but they apparently left something to be desired and so, stimulated by the success of Belpaire type boilers fitted to passenger engines they commenced an extended re-boilering programme. As mentioned in the previous section, this became rather complex in as much that some Class 2s were rebuilt with Belaire G6 boilers and others upgraded to Class 3s with Belpaire G7 boilers, while Class 3s received both G7s and G6s, the latter then becoming Class 2s.

However, it was not just the larger Belpaire boiler that made such a difference, the inclusion of an improved cab with some up to date fittings also played an important part.

The change brought about by these modifications was, in practical terms, quite amazing, producing a performance far beyond that which the 15% increase in tractive effort would indicate. Furthermore, vastly improved amenities provided a level of comfort and convenience on a par with current express locomotives and this also added to their general appeal. Therefore, although these Class 3s shared the same basic chassis as their Class 2 comtemporaries the new G7 boilers pressed at 175 psi endowed them with the power and reserve capacity to make them an incomparably superior engine.

Having established the 3F design, subsequent re-builds varied little from the original concept and even then this was only in minor details such as the fitting of pop safety valves although, as with Class 2s, they retained their former wheel differences – ie 4ft. 10in. or 5ft. 3in. The 3Fs larger, higher pitched boiler together with the enlarged cab gave it a more purposeful look and although the linear dimensions were similar, it seemed much more of a locomotive than the 2F.

Perhaps some of this impression was psychological, but they did not appear anything like as feeble and old fashioned as their smaller stablemates; on the contrary,

in a subtle way they conveyed a feeling of their true worth: elderly but still pugnacious little work-horses. So let us now consider these improvements which endeared them so much to their crews.

The saturated G7 boiler with 28% greater heating surface and 20% more grate area than the G6 was a prodigious producer of steam and could readily supply almost anything that was demanded for lengthy periods. With its extended roof and more practical lay out, including two generous locker-cum-seats, the cab provided a far worthier and acceptable habitat for the crew.

In addition to these two major advantages, which on their own would have won much favour, the cab contained such essentials as a standard LMS vacuum controlled steam brake with accompanying ejectors, steam sanding, a slaking pipe and in some instances, carriage warming equipment together with appropriate gauges. In other words they were equipped to the standard of current modern locomotives and the engines did not, therefore, feel disadvantaged.

Below the running plate, both classes were very similar, even the steam sanding which delivered to the front and rear of the centre coupled wheels was the same as fitted to many 2Fs. The footplate however, presented an entirely different picture, with a boiler back plate of sufficient height to prevent average sized crewmen from seeing over its top. In fact it was necessary to provide a 'driver's platform' which came complete with anti-glare shield, in order to elevate them some four inches so as to be able to comfortably look out through the upper spectacle glasses. These upper glasses pivoted horizontally and provided useful additional ventilation in hot conditions; the lower glasses were fixed. Forward vision in general terms was really very good and both signals and track ahead of the buffer beam could be easily sighted. Large steel lockers running the full cab length were located on either side and the tops being of sensible height, faced with wood and having a hinged centre section, provided very ample seating. With the aid of a little additional planking these could be adapted to form surprisingly comfortable couches should the opportunity arise during the interminable periods of waiting frequently found on night duties. Moreover, they were equally effective whether used head towards the spectacle plate or vice versa, the latter being preferred in hot weather. The left locker was usually the repository for tools while oil bottles and feeder were kept in the other, although this to some extent was dependent upon the

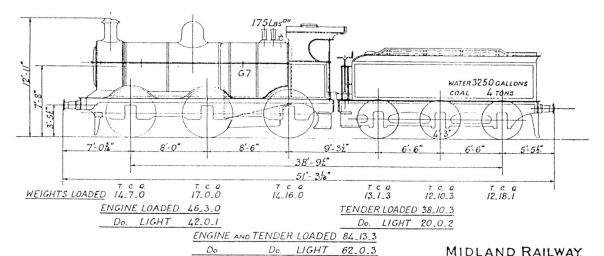

№ 3 CLASS COODS
BETⁿ Nᵒˢ 3130 & 3834
WITH G7 CLASS BOILERS

MIDLAND RAILWAY.

LOCOMOTIVE DRAWING OFFICE

DERBY

CYLRˢ	DRG.WHEELS	TRACTIVE POWER
18" x 26"	5'-3" DIAM.	18720 Lbs - 8·35 Tons
18½" x 26"	5'-3" "	19775 " - 8·82 "

type of tender to which the engine was coupled. Deeley tenders with coal bulkheads had a large central locker for personal effects flanked by two smaller lockers and these were preferred for tools and oil when so fitted.

The boiler face was arranged rather differently to the Class 2F although the regulator, injector steam valves and gauge frames shared the same general disposition. However, the blower was now placed centrally below the regulator with the steam sanding control adjacent, while the small ejector valve occupied the blower's former position. A lever which worked with a fore and aft movement operated the large ejector through external rodding. Both ejectors were mounted behind the smokebox on the handrail-cum-train pipe running along the right hand side of the boiler and these proved effective and reliable.

A standard LMS vacuum controlled steam brake, bracketed from the edge of the boiler back plate, fell readily to hand and could be used while leaning out of the cab. This allowed delicate control and was much appreciated when moving on to a turntable or closing up to stock.

The reversing lever and quadrant were located alongside the driver's seat but they did not prevent him from sitting down even when the lever was notched up.

Quadrants came in two forms, one giving a large number of equally spaced notches and the other which only had two between full and mid gear. The latter, more common version, corresponded to cut-offs of approximately 75%, 55% and 35%. Likewise firedoors could be either Midland double flap type or LMS sliding doors, the former being well suited to the short steeply sloped grate. These Derby designed doors consisted of two flaps or plates, one of which covered about two thirds of the firehole area and was hinged at the bottom and secured when in position by a latch and chain. The upper third was closed by an adjustable flap hinged from the top which possessed the useful advantage of reducing upward glare while allowing variable quantities of secondary air to enter the firebox.

Centrally mounted high on the spectacle plate could be seen both pressure and vacuum gauges while below these were the whistle and steam shut off valve for the sight feed lubricator fitted to the cab side sheet. Damper and cylinder drain cock handles were of the same type as found on 2Fs and similarly located.

As previously indicated, various types of tenders could be attached, but typically these would be Deeley 3250 or 3500 gallon with 4 ton coal capacity featuring a front coal bulkhead. They were quite pleasant tenders giving the 3F a useful duration while at the same time allowing reasonable rearward vision. However, having no rear footsteps or coal space doors required firemen to climb over the coal when watering or shovelling fuel forward.

Drivers found preparation somewhat easier since the 3Fs higher pitched boilers allowed a little more space when oiling motion parts from the running plate. In other respects it was very similar to and just as dirty as with the smaller locomotive.

Preparation as far as firemen were concerned was exactly the same as with 2Fs except that cleaning down was achieved more quickly and efficiently by the use of a slaking pipe. They would also have noticed how rapidly the boiler responded once fire had been levelled over the grate and the blower opened.

The 3Fs usually reacted to movement of their regulators just as quickly as any modern engine and felt very different from the 'soggy' 2Fs, although it would be fair to say that the former were maintained to rather higher standards.

As with all locomotives fitted with LMS vacuum controlled steam brakes, it was desirable to first open the small ejector so as to obtain automatic release of the brake following an application even when moving as light engine. Their regulators were said to have a 'strong first valve' and when opened to half way across its quadrant the engine would be delivering about 75% of its potential power at moderate speeds. In fact it was rarely necessary to use the main or second valve in normal working and, in keeping with most slide valve locomotives, they seemed happier running on long cut-offs with a partially open regulator. Despite having a strong first valve, control was still quite sensitive and this, coupled with adequate brakes and a quick acting lever reverser, made them ideal shunting engines when a longer duration than normal was desired.

Shunting required rapid initial acceleration and 3Fs certainly moved off in quite a lively manner, the raucous exhaust beat contributing considerably to the overall impression of eagerness. Perhaps this aspect was the most noticeable difference between 2Fs and 3Fs from the performance point of view; 3Fs tended to feel like frisky young puppies always straining at the leash.

After leaving the Shed Link at Saltley, novice firemen entered a rather unique link known as The Bank Pilots. Six 3Fs were rostered to provide rear end assistance to westbound trains over the four miles from Saltley Junction to Kings Heath and a better way for firemen to begin learning their trade would be hard to find. Continually banking trains over gradients varying from 1:62 to 1:315 covered many aspects of engine and railway

management, including the ability to maintain steam during that four mile climb when the engine could be working near to full capacity. Any link would seem like heaven after working on shed, but the Bank Pilot's appeal was more than just a release. We all learn more quickly by constant repetition and the Pilots certainly provided that; but we also feel more secure in a familiar environment which with only four miles to learn soon became so. Having the same engine all week helped in this direction and many crews treated their 3Fs as pets, spending much time in making them visually presentable as well as ensuring they were maintained to the highest practical standard. Possibly this early intimate acquaintance with 3Fs initiated the life long liking Midland men had for them, a sort of 'first love' which is never forgotten.

Being such good training, perhaps it would be interesting to take the reader on a trip up the bank behind a typical westbound mixed freight of some forty wagons hauled by a ubiquitous Class 4F.

On passing the pilot sidings, a whistle from the train engine indicates that a banker is required and hearing this some hasty activity takes place. The fireman would open both damper and blower in order to brighten the fire while at the same time filling any holes which may have appeared in the firebed while standing. It was not necessary to build a thick fire at this stage because goods trains often waited for anything up to an hour at Duddeston Road Junction which could be regarded as the commencement of the bank. Also, 3Fs responded so rapidly and steamed so well that considerable liberties could be taken as to how and when the fire was prepared. This is what made them so suitable for banking work, for few engines could match their ability to be ready for a flat out attack on the bank within a few minutes of having stood idle for a lengthy period with a 'cold' fire. Occasionally 4Fs were substituted at times of shortage but they were not welcomed by their crew; firemen found they were slow to warm and did not steam as freely, while drivers did not appreciate trying to relax on the tiny piece of wood placed over the reversing screw which was optimistically referred to as a seat.

By the time the train's brakevan had cleared the pilot siding's points, the banker's hand brake would have been released ready for the ground signal to come off. Then, with the small ejector open, reverser in full forward gear and regulator giving just a breath of steam, the 3F would trundle quietly off to take up position behind the moving train.

At this stage it was only necessary to keep buffered up to the brakevan since any vigorous pushing would not be appreciated by the train engine's driver should he need

Despite sharing the same main frames as 2Fs, the higher pitched G7 boiler and larger cab gave 3Fs a much more purposeful appearance. Nor was this confined to looks alone, for with 28% greater heating surface, 20% more grate area and a boiler now pressed at 175 psi their performance was remarkably enhanced.

to halt at a signal. In the meantime some larger lumps of coal would have been placed in the back corners of the firebox and under the firedoors but leaving the front of the grate with only a very thin layer of fire. After coming to a stand at Duddeston Road there was no way of telling when the signals would clear so the preferred technique was to keep a good depth of well burned through fire at the back and allow a hole to form in the firebed towards the front. With the damper open one notch, sufficient air entered to keep the fire bright but because of the hole, steam pressure remained stable at about 160 psi while boiler water level was maintained at three quarters of a glass. So that they did not have to keep constant vigilance, drivers would compress the buffers on the last few wagons, then, if the train moved the resultant effect would be immediately felt. It was usual policy to hold trains until they could have a clear run at

the bank because, just beyond Duddeston Road, the incline commenced at 1:105 and after a few hundred yards the steepest section of 1:62 was encountered near Brickyard Crossing. Only over the easier first stretch could sufficient momentum be gained to carry the train over the more difficult parts without the possibility of sticking.

As soon as the train was under way, the fireman would fully open the damper and immediately fill any holes in the firebed by the simple expedient of pushing live fire from under the firedoors with his shovel and then firing a small quantity of coal around the box. Even if the distant signal for Landor Street Junction was off the driver would not open up too vigorously because the distant for Brickyard Crossing could not be sighted for another two hundred yards or so and there was always the remote possibility that it may be on. However, once this was seen to be clear the regulator would be opened to full first valve and the fireman could then apply himself in earnest.

The 3Fs draughting was excellent and within a few minutes the fire took on an intense white furnace glare readily consuming even the most indifferent of fuels. If Midland twin flap doors were fitted the preferred method was to fire over the bottom plate, not only did this reduce the quantity of cold air entering the firebox, it also kept the fireman's legs cooler. Over the 1:62 secton speed often slowed to under 10mph but then as the gradient eased to 1:85 approaching Bordesley Junction the pace gradually quickened again.

Here the Banker on first valve and in full gear would probably be pushing about eighteen wagons with the 4F towing the remaining twenty two. There were of course times when the train engine was below par in which case the situation would be reversed and then the banker could be fully extended with its regulator wide open.

Firing on the little and often principle generally maintained boiler pressure between 170-175 psi, while leaving one injector working, ensured a constant water level as the Banker pounded steadily over the 1:85 stretch past Bordesley Junction. Approaching Camp Hill the incline flattens considerably to 1:280 and providing the train engine is not short of steam they would no longer require a Pilot since there is only a short 1:108 stretch through Moseley Tunnel before gaining level ground beyond Kings Heath.

However, the majority of 4Fs seemed to be somewhat winded by the climb and usually whistled for the Pilot to continue assisting through to Kings Heath. We will assume that such is the case and having received their request the signalman will indicate this to the Pilot driver by displaying a green flag in daylight or a green light at night. Despite a steady increase in speed at this stage, the banking engine will have been eased down until the green signal is seen, then with cut-off shortened to 35% it will be opened up once more until the final few hundred yards before reaching Kings Heath. At 30 mph the ride is stable and free from knocks although the exhaust which has now taken on a syncopated beat is as noisy and exhilirating as ever. Firing at this pace proved no problem but over the last half mile the fire is allowed to run down and by dispensing with the injector, steam pressure can be maintained by mortgaging boiler water level. This action is of course necessary to prevent wasteful blowing off on arrival at Kings Heath. Once through Moseley Tunnel the regulator is gradually eased over the final 1:353 stretch until the train draws gently away, when it is finally shut altogether. Then with the reverser returned to full gear the engine is allowed to coast the last hundred yards before a firm brake application brings it to a halt in Kings Heath Station platform. Being down hill all the way, the return journey enabled one to experience a 3Fs remarkably quiet, free running ability when coasting. Vertical

slide valves are held on their seats by steam pressure and therefore with the regulator closed they permit a by pass action which equalises pressure on either side of the pistons. In other words, the pistons do not act as pumps absorbing energy, thereby retarding the locomotive.

With a clear road and the driver in a hurry, speeds of over 45 mph were attained with a smoothness and silence bettered by no other engine, but travelling tender first they were eye watering experiences not improved by being peppered with small pieces of coal.

Since half of a Pilots running was by necessity in reverse and much waiting unavoidable, storm sheets were often rigged during inclement weather. With these in place, heat from the unlagged boiler face was contained and the cab could become very cosy indeed. On the other hand, they did obstruct vision as well as entry into the tender and so were taken down as soon as conditions improved. Whilst on the subject of unlagged boiler back plates, it must be conceded that these old engines were warmer than their modern counterparts when facing into the wind even though they possessed less lateral protection. This unlagged area also provided an excellent cooking surface so that potatoes, onions and even meat pies would be done to a turn after spending an hour or two wedged between boiler back plate and injector clack box.

The 3Fs attributes and behaviour were just as appealing on more extended road jobs as they were on the short sharp effort demanded from the Bank Pilots. Whilst it must be admitted that 3Fs had been relegated to what can only be described as 'third division' freight work by the fifties, these still included a number of through runs which took them to such places as Worcester, Gloucester and Evesham in the West and Derby, Nottingham and Leicester in the North East. Ordinary mixed freight trains did not carry much priority and although theoretically the journey time for a forty to fifty mile run should have taken little more than two hours, it frequently occupied eight or ten due to severe congestion.

Most goods lines operated under the permissive block system which enabled several trains to occupy one section at the same time; this however, led to continual 'stop-go' movements as the queue progressed towards the final destination. The quick response and good steaming properties of the 3F was most useful in coping with this detrimental method of working which caused fires to become clinkered and tubes to become fouled. Unfortunately crews often only became aware of such deterioration when called upon to sprint over a few miles of main line in between these goods line havens, and generally speaking 3Fs under these conditions were less likely to be winded than the larger superheated 4Fs. When they were allowed to stretch their legs on longer sections of main line though, certain shortcomings were exposed particularly when climbing long gradients with a full load.

Slide valve engines suffered from excessive friction losses which became proportionally worse as steam chest pressure increased and so they were usually run with the smallest practical regulator opening. This action, of course, could demand a correspondingly long cut-off to compensate unless an exceptionally light load was being hauled; and long cut-offs did not allow expansive working to take place.

The shortest cut-off available on 'two-notch' quadrants was about 35% but at this setting with a full load over even a modest gradient, would require second valve giving maximum steam chest pressure and consequent loss of efficiency.

Full gear and a partially open regulator would considerably reduce friction losses but by not taking advantage of steam's expansive properties, more would be used and speed restricted by back pressure. Therefore, over these prolonged stretches of adverse gradients, the most usual compromise would be 55% and full first valve. The competent driver constantly juggled with these settings though to suit ever-changing conditions, but whatever he tried he could not make it as efficient or free running as the superheated piston valved 4F.

Occasionally, due to chronic shortage of motive power or some sudden failure, a 3F could be called upon to work a fitted freight train. Because these were booked at a faster pace, they had to be run at shorter cut-offs, friction losses notwithstanding, and both coal and water consumption increased dramatically. However, what they lost on the ups they certainly gained on the downs for they would coast for miles with no noticeable diminution of speed.

Only on one instance was I able to experience working a passenger train with a 3F but it did give an insight into their less well known capabilities.

Because there is far less resistance with coaches for a given weight, the inexperienced are invariably surprised how quickly they can be accelerated when compared with a freight train. It was certainly so in my case and after an initial burst in full gear the regulator was snapped shut, the cut-off quickly reduced to 35% and then the regulator re-opened to full first-valve. This change took place at around 25 mph and from then onwards the five coach special continued to gain speed over level track in quite an enterprising manner. Up to about 50 mph, the ride with steam on was fairly good

but then it developed a harsher feel with distinct intermittent lateral kicks. Towards 60 mph, the ride became far more lively and with the engine and tender moving both laterally and vertically in different directions, the act of firing was somewhat taxing. Nor did the powerful draught of hot air, filled with ash sucked from the pan blowing up between footboards and boiler back plate, make things anymore pleasant. However, the engine steamed well, injectors proved trouble free and as always it coasted beautifully; but one felt bound to admit that passenger work was not their forte.

The Class 3Fs were really at their most useful on local trip work hauling relatively light loads, over shorter distances at modest speeds; though they could still substitute for 4Fs on short haul through freights and, particularly in areas of high congestion, give a creditable performance.

By way of an experiment, in 1923 three Class 3s were rebuilt with Class 4F G7S superheated boilers and other 4F features such as mechanical lubricators for cylinders and axleboxes. It was probably a cheaper alternative to building more 4Fs, but slide valves are very difficult to lubricate in the presence of superheated steam and no doubt the lesson was re-learned on this occasion for within five years they had all reverted to saturated status.

Back on shed, disposal was straightforward since the front of the grate could just be reached with a short clinker shovel and their low tenders did not hamper movement. Even when full, their ashpans and smoke-boxes contained only a fraction of that found in, for example, a Black 5 and this aspect only added further to their universal appeal.

Perhaps the foregoing has helped to explain why such an elderly design remained popular for so many years despite the march of progress. Undoubtedly rebuilding encapsulated the qualities required at the time and it was not until after World War Two that a serious effort was made to bring about replacements. In the event, these Ivatt Class 2s were far too versatile for such lowly duties and the old 3Fs were allowed to gradually dwindle away to extinction in 1964. It is sad that no example was saved for preservation but then that applies to a great number of interesting classes.

Chapter 5
0-6-0 Class 4F Freight

Goods Engine Introduced 1911. Total built 772.

THE 4F IS generally regarded as the Midland Railways ultimate expression of their Standard 0-6-0 Goods engine.

Over the years this design has been much maligned by a variety of authors postulating numerous deficiencies, which in many instances were very well founded. The 4Fs enjoyed a long working life, some fifty five years in fact and with the benefit of hindsight, we can all become very wise in the light of latest developments appearing to our peers as fonts of engineering critique. These criticisms were further compounded by construction continuing virtually unchanged, except for minor details, over the extraordinary long period of thirty years. However, I doubt, in all fairness, whether too many derogatory comments would have been published during their early years and to gain a balanced appreciation we should really review the situation as it existed in 1910.

The movement of mineral traffic over Midland lines was on an awesome scale and yet many routes were subject to severe weight and width restrictions. The most powerful goods engines available at that time were Class 3 0-6-0s equipped with round topped 'H' boilers which in time, proved to be not entirely successful.

The well maintained Midland Class 2 and Class 3 0-6-0s coped quite well, singly on lighter trains and double headed on heavier ones with management convinced that it was less expensive to operate this way rather than upgrading hundreds of miles of track to accommodate larger locomotives which would not be so economical on anything other than the heaviest duties. At the same time they were not adverse to improving the breed and a more powerful, efficient 0-6-0 was a compromise which received much favour. Within this background it was not unexpected that the newly appointed CME, Henry Fowler, applied himself to developing such a machine and, in view of his personal interest in superheating, that this engine would be superheated.

Thus in 1911, two prototypes of entirely new design emerged from Derby which although visually the same, differed slightly in detail. No. 3835 was built with 160 psi boiler pressure, Schmidt type superheater and 20in. x 26in. cylinders while No. 3836 carried 175 psi pressure, Swindon double-pass superheater and 19in. x 26in. cylinders. This gave them very nearly identical tractive efforts, No. 3835 having the theoretical advantage of an extra 289 lbs.

Although these new engines shared the same 8ft. + 8ft. 6in. wheelbase as their predecessors, they appeared, with their high pitched boilers, large smokeboxes, extended cab and squat boiler fittings much more massive machines. Nor was this raising of the boiler centre line a mere styling whim; it became necessary in order to accommodate inside admission piston valves above the inclined cylinders and so as to ensure adequate lubrication in superheated conditions, a mechanical lubricator was fitted. On both engines the short-travel, short-lap valves were operated by robust well designed Stephenson link motion through rocking shafts, which in the course of time, proved accurate and reliable.

Despite continuing pressures to provide more efficient power a comprehensive series of trials were conducted, including the working of heavy coal trains between Toton and Brent. Now it must be remembered that superheating and piston valves were still somewhat new to Derby and quite logically they wished to be certain that these developments would be taking them along the correct path. These trials were primarily to compare coal and water consumption against two saturated 0-6-0 Class 3s in additoin to identifying any advantages or otherwise number 3835 may have over its stablemate. Should it be felt that it was a little unfair comparing what we now call 4Fs against 3Fs, it is worth remembering that these two new engines were also classed as 3s when they first appeared and that 3836s tractive effort was a mere 1050 lbs more than the 'H' boilered machines.

Not surprisingly the superheated locomotives showed better results and 3835 proved to be the superior engine; however being in no great hurry to make decisions they were put into general service for protracted observation.

Exactly when construction may have commenced had not World War One intervened is a matter of conjecture but it was not until May 1917 that the first production batch entered service. By then boiler pressure of 175 psi, and cylinders 20in. x 26in. had been adopted as standard together with the Derby/Schmidt twenty one element superheater. From then onwards manufacture proceeded steadily so that by the end of the Midland aegis, 192 examples had been put into traffic plus a further five constructed for use on the Somerset and Dorset Joint Railway.

As part of the LMS Midlandisation policy, 4Fs were

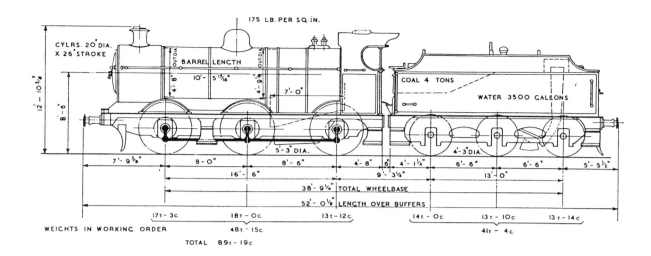

one of the ex-MR locomotives selected for perpetuating as a standard design and with only minor modification manufacture was continued, warts and all, until 1941. Some of the adjustments were cosmetic, while others had a more practical value. Mechanical axlebox lubricators which gave a more positive feed appeared in 1919 but the distinctive piston tail rods, together with the Fowler/Anderson cylinder by-pass valves were removed under Stanier's regime. By way of compensation they acquired air relief valves, pop safety valves and a number of locomotives were fitted with Davis and Metcalfe Class H exhaust injectors. The original tall Midland chimneys were later replaced by a variety of Fowler and Stanier styles in both tall and short form, the latter, together with lower domes, increasing route availability. In 1925 the change was made from right hand to left hand drive with No. 4207 – which seemed more logical since most platforms and signals lay on that side and the LMS added LH drive as standard practice for all new engines.

With the operating people requesting nothing larger, construction proceeded apace peaking during the period 1926-28 and even Stanier, who had in mind more modern alternatives, acquiesced to further demands and allowed 45 more to be built between 1937 and 1941.

My acquaintance with 4Fs on BR was during the period 1950-59 and it is this stage of their life that I propose to describe.

I suppose in 1950 we regarded them as intermediate engines both in size and age. Piston valves and super-heating put them in the 20th Century but they lacked

the panache and performance of truly modern designs. Needless to say this view became modified and placed them even lower 'down market' as the really excellent range of BR Standard locomotives with their outstandingly high level of comfort and convenience came into service later in the decade. However, despite the competition, there was an awful lot of them around and it is true to say that I probably spent more hours on 4Fs during my years with BR than any other locomotive.

Although following the traditional Midland 0-6-0 concept, 4Fs as previously stated, looked and indeed were, more modern than their saturated forebears. Their larger cylinders supplied by more efficient piston valves delivered over 16% greater tractive effort than 3Fs and to take advantage of this, additional sandboxes located below the running plate, delivered sand to the front of the leading wheels. Much appreciated were the footsteps, mounted between front and centre axles, these gave ready access to the foot framing and saved many precious minutes when servicing the engines on shed. The larger smokebox did not allow for a very generous front framing although this was stepped up in the centre which proved useful to smaller crewmen reaching for the top lamp bracket.

This unique raised centre feature housed the tail rod covers but when these were removed they were replaced by small blanking plates. Air relief valves or 'snifters' were bolted to the main plate frame ahead of the leading splashers. When coasting these gave 4Fs a very distinctive but quite unmistakable sound as they tried to overcome the vacuum created in their cylinders. Earlier versions tended to shake themselves to pieces

Although sharing the same 8ft 0ins + 8ft 6ins wheelbase and a dimensionally similar boiler with 3Fs, the superheated 4Fs were pitched even higher in order to accommodate piston valves placed above their cylinders. Squat boiler fittings, larger smokebox and extended cab gave them a much more massive and modern appearance.

and a number of modifications were necessary; even then many older drivers felt they left much to be desired and did not compare with the former by-pass valves.

Between the leading and centre splashers on the firemen's side, two mechanical lubricators were mounted in tandem on a substantial bracket bolted to the top of the main frame. One supplied the valves and cylinders while the other looked after the axleboxes. These lubricators which could be manually primed were not only more efficient than the 3Fs systems but demanded far less attention from enginemen, the one proviso being that each was topped up with its specified grade of oil.

Some locomotives were fitted with an exhaust steam injector the presence of which was denoted by a lagged steam pipe on the fireman's side which curved downwards from the base of the smokebox to pass along the underside of the running plate. This connected with a spherical grease separator mounted ahead of the trailing coupled wheels before leading to the actual injector located behind the cab steps. These H type injectors proved reasonably effective and reliable, but if incorrectly set could waste a considerable amount of water through the overflow. The cab and its layout was in many ways similar to that of a 3F but although the boiler and firebox shared the same dimensions, their higher pitched position made the 4F seem much larger.

In such a big class built over a thirty year period there were a few detailed variations and so for the sake of simplicity I will select an LMS left hand drive version coupled to a standard Fowler 3,500 gallon straight sided tender.

Disposition of controls, pipework and gauges were virtually the same as on a 3F except that there was no sight feed lubricator on the fireman's side, although he still enjoyed the benefit of a full length tool locker cum seat. The driver's side, though, was altogether different, for over a diminutive oil compartment the reversing screw was bolted allowing no room for a proper seat. As if by way of an afterthought, a small piece of wood, divided to expose the reverser sector scale was mounted flush with the top of the screw cover. Needless to say it was of insufficient area to provide comfort for the usually ample posteriors of drivers who not unnaturally felt somewhat hard done by. Hence the derogatory remark 'perched there for hours like a monkey on a stick'. When rostered a 4F on turns which involved a good proportion of waiting, it was quite amazing how generous drivers suddenly became and invited their fireman to 'gain some driving practice' knowing full well they would never refuse.

Unless a giant, it was quite impossible to look out through the cab's top spectacle glasses, the driver was therefore provided with a high 'L' shaped platform which surrounded the base of the reverser assembly and cleverly prevented access to the oil locker in so doing.

Attached to the inboard side of this platform was a substantial steel anti-glare shield which effectively blocked both heat and glare from open firedoors. The LMS 4Fs were always equipped with a V shaped regulator handle which was convenient to use whether perched on the seat or standing behind the reverser. They were also normally fitted with sliding firedoors, although some ex-Midland engines still retained their original Derby twin flap type. Unlike 3Fs, most were provided with carriage warming apparatus, the gauge of which was attached in the usual position on the fireman's side of the cab.

As a class, the 4Fs possessed as wide a variety of tenders as any, but with LMS built locomotives the Fowler 3,500 gallon flush sided version was by far the most common; its four ton coal capacity proved adequate for most duties and, being equipped with a water scoop, enabled the engine to complete non-stop runs of reasonable duration. As always, the water scoop control was located on the driver's side and both the scoop and handbrake handles, mounted on vertical columns, operated in a horizontal plane.

Although they functioned effectively, their handles could intrude on the rather limited footplate area unless correctly parked. Placed centrally in front of the coal bulkhead was a suitably sized locker for personal effects, flanked on either side by small ones used for tools and oil bottles. When not in use, headlamps could be stowed on brackets provided for the purpose in recesses between tender side sheet and locker side.

A tank water gauge also occupied the driver's side

recess but unfortunately its scale was not very visible at night. Rear tender steps were provided making access to the tank top far more convenient than with 3Fs and once there, the fireman felt secure in the footwell when watering. With no coal doors it was necessary for firemen to clamber over the high bulkhead which sported the usual pegs for securing fire-iron handles, their business end being supported by a U-shaped bracket attached to the tender arch brace.

Drivers found oiling a 4F marginally preferable to the older 0-6-0s in as much that there was far more room under its higher pitched boiler and with piston valves placed over the cylinders instead of in between them, it was not so cramped underneath either. On the other hand, two additional sandboxes and an extra stretch to reach smokebox dogs could involve firemen in a little more effort although to some extent this was offset by having the convenience of front footsteps.

The Class 4Fs felt much larger engines than 3Fs and driving them was a completely different experience. Perhaps mounted high on the driver's platform with its elevated view gave an increased sense of being in command or possibly having a screw reverser and twin handled regulator had something to do with it, but 4Fs unquestionably gave the impression of being a superior engine.

With all locomotives equipped with LMS vacuum controlled steam brakes it was routine to open the small ejector before moving off even when light engine. Response to the regulator was much snappier than its slide valve contemporaries and the following initial surge of acceleration by comparison, quite surprising. Moreover, if conditions permitted, this acceleration would continue quickly with very little fuss or noise up to 45 mph or so, which was about as fast as light engines were normally expected to travel. Because of their sharper blast, 3Fs sounded stronger and faster than was actually the case, whereas with the softly spoken 4Fs exactly the opposite applied.

Although designed as freight locomotives, their obvious liveliness must have been quickly noticed because throughout their lives they were used on all manner of duties as a sort of stand-in mixed traffic locomotive. Not that it stopped when proper more up to date mixed traffic engines in their power class became available because with so many to call upon, a 4F always seemed to be waiting in the wings ready for action. They could therefore, be found working local or branch line passengers, excursions, parcels traffic and empty stock quite late in their careers; but crews, to be truthful, would have preferred something more suitable.

Their haulage capacity was never in doubt and if the

route was interspersed with numerous station stops or short sharp gradients which kept speeds relatively low they managed to cope, but because of their limited steaming ability, long adverse inclines or prolonged fast running could leave them somewhat winded.

Short travel, short lap valves mated with small wheels is not the ideal formula for passenger work, but even so, driving technique did not prove too demanding; 4F regulators were endowed with quite a strong first valve so that it was rarely necessary or desirable to open it fully in normal working and, on level track, six bogies could readily be taken off the mark at a brisk pace. Almost immediatley, progressive notching up would commence to give possibly 50% cut-off at 30 mph and 35% at 50 mph. Additionally, the 4Fs reversing screws were just about the lightest and most pleasant to use I have encountered – being beautifully balanced, only a few quick twirls were necessary to take it from full forward to full back gear. In common with short travel valves, reducing cut-off to less than 30% restricted exhaust port openings which then adversely affected the engine's free running capability. Most drivers would adjust the cut-off around this figure until it seemed at its best and then use the regulator to make whatever alterations were needed to suit conditions.

Approaching 60 mph the ride became very lively indeed, with the high pitched boiler seeming to add a rolling motion to at times quite vicious lateral oscillations and harsh vertical movements. Vibration caused a constant stream of ash to fall through the open damper door which was then picked up in the slip-stream and carried back under the cab. Unfortunately, a large gap existed between boiler back plate and foot-boards and through this a veritable gale of ash laden air blew around the poor fireman as he tended his duties. Being constantly engulfed in this blizzard of ash made life very miserable and not a little dangerous, since eyes were being perpetually filled with irritating particles which was not at all conducive to good vision. If the opportunity arose, pieces of sacking would be stuffed into the gap and if kept well watered, some benefit could be obtained; but this ingress of ash into the cab always remained a problem.

However, the main portion of 4F duties were conducted at much slower speeds when both conditions and ride were more comfortable, since even fully fitted freights, at least when headed by 4Fs, rarely exceeded 50 mph. At the other end of the scale, they would plod reliably uphill and down dale with a full load of mineral wagons still pulling strongly on first valve with cut-offs in the 45%-65% range. Perhaps they are best remembered for their work with middle distance through

goods trains which they handled competently enough on the early stages of their journey; but as indicated in the previous section, performance deteriorated when they became bogged down on congested lines.

One of the major criticisms levelled at 4Fs is their reluctance to steam adequately even in the hands of experienced firemen, so it will be interesting to examine some of the possible causes.

Coming from 3Fs with their excellent G7 boilers it was natural that firemen initially used the same techniques with the dimensionally identical 4Fs G7S. However, although the same size, the G7S had twenty one large diameter superheater flues which reduced the heating surface area from 1388.25 to 1167.25 sq.ft. – 19% less. Admittedly the superheater elements gave another 252.75 sq.ft. but these did not boil water in the acceptance sense, only adding energy to that already produced and to function efficiently they needed to be maintained at a higher temperature. When this condition was achieved, less steam by weight together with superheated steam's increased flowing properties and more efficient distribution through piston valves compensated for the lower production rate and gave 4Fs improved economy.

Regretably, heavy line congestion prevented this ideal state of uninterrupted running on all but the most important trains and many duties could hope for nothing better than what amounted to a series of cold starts between refuges offered by lay-bys and goods lines. There is an old saying that the hottest fire burns less coal and my own experience proved this to be so. Small quantities of well broken coal fired frequently on an intensely hot firebed promotes instant ignition and liberation of hydrocarbons which if provided with sufficient secondary air, break down to their constituent elements and burn immediately liberating more heat. As the fire temperature increases so does that of the brick arch which then adds considerably to the speed of combustion apart from becoming a reservoir of stored heat. All this takes time though and it will be seen how important is a progressive build up, followed by consistent running, to obtain optimum efficiency. Because 4Fs with superheated steam and piston valves could produce the same amount of work from a lower weight of steam, exhaust pressures and therefore draught produced was lower. In addition there was something not quite right with 4Fs draughting which left it deficient particularly when being worked lightly. I had this proved when firing one of the preserved examples some years ago and could not understand why it steamed so much better than any 4F I had encountered on BR. Apparently their fireman had experienced problems in this respect so their engineers had installed the modified chimney bell from an 8F and it worked so successfully that on the first run I could not stop it blowing off. It was a sobering thought to realise that such a simple modification might have saved firemen a lot of frustration over so many years and made 4Fs the equal of 3Fs in terms of steaming. Be that as it may, we had to make the best of them and adapt accordingly, for a higher level of skill was certainly demanded. Perhaps concentration would be a better term because provided one applied all the basic principles with care and consistency, adequate steaming could be anticipated; but the least lapse would soon be seen on the pressure gauge. I found that, in general, rather thinner fire beds than would be carried with a 3F were preferable since the lighter draught was better able to keep them bright. The same profile would be used and firing over the bottom flap of Midland doors or the combustion plate found with sliding doors helped to maintained furnace temperature.

The most arduous regular run I enjoyed with a 4F at Saltley was a lodging turn to Sheffield which ran at night from Lawley Street to Queens Road via the Erewash Valley. This express freight ran with at least four vacuum fitted wagons next to the engine to provide additional braking on trains which averaged over forty vehicles. For the first three hours or so we usually managed quite well but then the condition of the fire deteriorated and the final five mile 1:100 drag up to Bradway Tunnel often became a struggle.

This seemed to show that with the indifferent fuel then in use, 4Fs were limited to about three hours continual running before clinker and ash upset the conditions upon which their steaming was so finely balanced. With a grate area of only 21 sq.ft., they were not therefore excessively demanding in physical terms, but to achieve good results, skill and dedication was required for they certainly did not flatter the mediocre.

As with 3Fs, a short firing shovel was preferred on the fairly restricted footplate since, with its tendency to shake forward, the majority of coal was delivered to the rear half of the grate. At normal speeds, firing proved no problems but on passenger work as previously indicated, wild cavorting taxed balancing skills to the limit while perpetual swirling ash made conditions very uncomfortable.

When standing 'right way to the weather' their unlagged boiler faces kept crews very cosy indeed in winter and even if the wind was blowing in the opposite direction their higher tenders, particularly when equipped with side doors, offered rather more protection than was found with 3Fs.

Disposal of 4Fs required the same general method as used with the saturated 0-6-0s, although more care had to be taken when manoeuvring fire-irons because of additional obstructions and also when clearing its smokebox on the restricted front framing. The final major criticism was that of its axleboxes and unfortunately this deficiency had ramifications which affected other locomotives. Their rather inadequate bearing surfaces led to wear rates which called for more frequent attention than was desirable.

Whilst within reasonable bounds on 4Fs, because of their limited weight and power loading, it became unacceptably high when the same axlebox design was incorporated into other engines such as 7F 0-8-0s and Garratts and contributed much towards shortening their service lives. Under Stanier's guidance however, Derby eventually learned their lesson and the LMS produced some really excellent axleboxes, good enough in fact to be perpetuated in the BR Standard designs.

The 4Fs managed to soldier on though, and extra mileage was extracted as wear progressed through rostering them to slower duties which then enabled drivers to help further by using longer than normal cut-offs.

Their basically robust construction had its Achilles heel but even so they earned a lot of revenue over a very long period and possibly missed true greatness by only a short head. The 7Fs front end, some adjustments to the draughting and improved axleboxes would probably have done the trick, but by the time this was appreciated, the design had been around too long and the class too numerous for major rebuilding to be considered. In spite of that, 4Fs were never fully replaced by modern designs and continued to work right up until 1966 on BR while happily, four examples may still be seen drawing the crowds on preserved lines – which is not at all bad for an engine introduced in 1911.

Passenger Tank Engine (Fowler Parallel Boiler).   Introduced 1927. Total 125.

FROM the inception of the LMS in 1923 the need for a powerful medium size tank locomotive with wide route availability had been expressed. George Hughes, the new Company's CME had considered his large 4-6-4 Baltic Tank as a possible contender, but its weight and size precluded acceptance in those areas of the LMS where the loading gauge was not so generous. Whilst this need still remained, other more urgent projects demanded attention and it was not until August 1926 that the Derby Drawing Office was able to commence laying out a design in earnest.

The intention was to use as many standard parts as possible based around the traditional Derby 8ft. 0in. + 8ft. 6in. coupled wheel spacings plus a G8 AS (Class 3 4-4-0) boiler. However, their only experience of a large outside cylindered locomotive was the 2-8-0 constructed for the S & D in 1914 and the incorporation of its cylinders and motion was initially envisaged. As with all other Midland locomotives built at that period, it had short-travel short-lap valves; but even Derby by now was (at least in some parts of the drawing office) becoming aware of the advantages of long-travel long-lap valves already in use on some other designs.

Horwich, meanwhile, had been keeping abreast of the latest developments in this respect and had modified Hughes' 4-6-0 accordingly, although details of this does not seem to have reached the Derby Drawing Office. All was not lost though because apparently in 1918 the ARLE (Association of Railway Locomotive Engineers) in anticipation of the need for a possible range of Standard locomotives for general use after the war had prepared a number of designs. Amongst these was a 2-6-0 and Derby, having been assigned the task of designing its cylinders, was provided with drawings and tables to show the merits of long lap. Fortunately these were unearthed at what turned out to be a most propitious moment for it was proposed that the 2-6-4T's cylinders should be based on the ARLE drawings and surprisingly this was agreed. I say surprisingly because Derby was still stricken with muddled thinking exacerbated by outside interference from a forceful Motive Power Department and therefore lacked positive direction. Sadly this dichotomy continued and the LMS, having for the first time produced such successful, or at least potentially successful modern designs as the 2-6-0 Crab, 4-6-0 Royal Scot and 2-6-4T then spoiled the Garratts and their next new efforts, the 2P 4-4-0 and 3P 2-6-2T by reverting to short-travel valves and inadequate axleboxes.

Also fortuitous in the 2-6-4T saga was the late decision to fit narrow ring piston valves, based on an LNER pattern, rather than the usual Schmidt single wide ring type. These narrow ring valves it may be noted, dramatically improved long term performance on Royal Scots by overcoming serious problems of internal steam leakage.

The final ingredient to ensure long lasting success for the 2-6-4Ts was the inclusion of generously sized axleboxes which were mechanically lubricated. With tanks, cab and bunker derived from the Derby 0-6-4T, this amalgam of components became an instant success when turned out in 1927, and indeed paved the way for the equally successful Stanier, Fairburn and BR Standard 2-6-4Ts.

For their time they were a handsome looking engine, possessing an air of purposeful power rather than grace in their well balanced appearance. Apart from adequate axleboxes, there was also a certain touch of Horwich influence, forward of the centre coupled wheels, although because of the use of a higher boiler pressure and some relaxation of loading gauge restrictions it was no longer necessary to employ the large steeply inclined cylinder layout of the Crabs. The resulting lower running plate while still allowing accessability to robust Walschaerts motion permitted sufficient tank depth to give an ample 2,000 gallon water capacity.

Mechanical lubricators for axleboxes and cylinders were mounted one either side of the smokebox on the running plate and were very accessible as indeed were the sandboxes which supplied efficient steam sanding gear delivering to the forward side of both leading and centre coupled wheels and the rear side of the latter when running in reverse. Although the cab with its T shaped cut-outs was rather traditional, the style blended well with the rest of the design and in fact proved more practical than it looked. Originally both pony truck and bogies were fitted with brakes but since Stanier did not approve of such things they were removed later. Water pick gear was fitted between the rear coupled wheels and the bogie and could be used when the engine was running in either direction.

Prior to producing his own taper boiler 2-6-4T, Stanier made some modifications to the final batches of Fowler engines and 2395-2424 were turned out with side window cab and improved bogies. These cabs certainly altered the overall look of the engine, giving it a more modern appearance in keeping with the early thirties apart from added convenience for their crews.

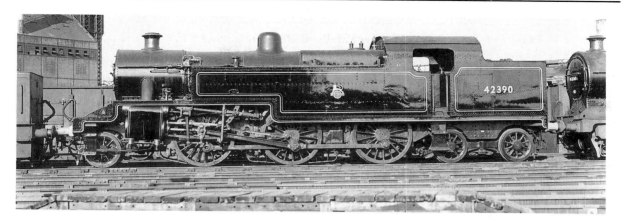

Entry to the cab was via conventional steps and hinged doors and compared with most tender locomotives of that period, it seemed somewhat cluttered and a trifle claustrophobic. This cramped feeling was not helped by the fact that whilst there was a flat area immediately in front of the firehole, raised blocks on either side formed platforms extending to the cab side sheets.

These were necessary to bring average sized crew members up to a comfortable height in relation to the cab cut outs when seated, but it did cause the fireman to adopt a modified stance when at work with the shovel.

The boiler face layout followed traditional Derby practice and having no steam manifold, separate pipes supplied steam to the auxiliary fittings. Two live steam injectors with combined steam valve and clack were mounted outboard of the regulator quadrant with a blower valve situated centrally below it. Water regulators for the injectors were located in the usual place against the cab sides adjacent to the seats, the right one supplying feed to the slaking pipe.

Over on the left was a conventional Midland style reverser with spring loaded locking handle and above to the right could be found the brass handwheel of the small ejector together with the steel handle (which worked in a fore and aft movement) of the larger ejector. The standard LMS vacuum controlled steam brake handle was within comfortable reach of the driver's right hand when seated; however, both sander and whistle handles definitely were not. Instrumentation consisted of the basic boiler and CWA gauges on the fireman's side and vacuum gauge on the driver's, while two water level gauge glasses provided with combined shut off cocks, completed the array.

A deep shelf ran transversely across the rear of the cab just below cut-out level but part of its ample area was occupied by the scoop's water dome. Useful locker

Looking somewhat dated in the fifties, 42390 still has an air of purpose if not grace and could certainly hold her own in terms of on the road performance. Indeed, so successful was the original concept that it formed the basis for the equally superb Stanier, Fairburn and BR Standard 2-6-4T designs.

space was provided above this, inboard from the rear spectacle glasses which were protected by substantial grills. Handles for both handbrake and scoop operating in a horizontal plane were located on either side in front of the shelf and although fairly easy to use, were somewhat intrusive unless correctly 'parked'. The shovelling plate was at a convenient height and set above this were low hinged doors giving a rather tortuous access to the coal space.

Preparation as far as the driver was concerned caused no particular problems for with outside cylinders, access to the motion was relatively easy. Admittedly there were a fair number of trimmings and pin joints to be attended to, but no more than any other locomotive of the period, and it was only when post war designs appeared with increased use of grease lubrication that these additional labours were noticed.

Nor were there any major difficulties for firemen either, since with sandboxes quite accessible, his most onerous preparation task was rendered relatively straightforward. If the initial journey was to be bunker first then it was desirable to trim and restack coal on the driver's side so that unobstructed vision through his rear spectacle glass was obtained. A vertical handrail attached to the bunker rear plate above the left buffer plus two staggered steps enabled this climb to be made without any feeling of insecurity. The complement of fire irons was housed on the right side tank top and secured by means of a peg in front of the fireman's spectacle plus a U shaped bracket located near the forward end of the firebox.

As with all tank locomotives, extra care had to be taken when wielding fire irons within the confines imposed by a fully enclosed cab and this naturally slowed such tasks as spreading live fire over the grate during preparation. Six circumferential dogs locked the smokebox door in position and usually these required to be tightened, but since most pre-Stanier engines used this system, firemen regarded such things as normal.

Filling the 2,000 gallon side tanks also proved a simple operation for not only did the tank top provide a reasonably safe platform, the water column arm needed a much smaller movement to position it. Because a substantial bracing plate ran below the filler orifice, care had to be taken when inserting the column's leather hose for should this become kinked, an unintentioned bath could result. It was also very necessary to ensure that the filler lid was screwed down tightly after watering; heavy braking on approaching a station platform causes water to surge forward in the tank and erupt spectacularly from the filler if not properly secured. This brought forth a not unexpected adverse response from waiting clientele to say nothing of that made by the driver.

When I enjoyed my first road job with one of these tank engines in 1954, they had already been in service some 27 years, yet to me they performed as well as any locomotive I had been on. The impression they must have left with crews in 1927 would I imagine, have been nothing short of startling and the fact that they were an immediate success comes as no surprise.

As with all locomotives fitted with the LMS standard vacuum controlled steam brake it was desirable to open the small ejector even when running light engine in order to achieve automatic release after a brake application.

The brakes themselves were quite powerful and well able to lock the wheels at low speed or if the rail was in anything other than perfect condition. For this reason, some drivers made use of the sanding gear on approaching stations at which a stop was scheduled if they thought track conditions warranted it. This was particularly applicable to branch line working where infrequent services allowed 'slime' to form on the rail head especially when a light drizzle was falling. Heavy rain, contrary to popular belief, affected adhesion very little since it washed the rail clean of slime and grease.

Usually, drivers first became acquainted with a new type of locomotive at a Motive Power Depot and therefore had the opportunity to get the feel of it while running light engine to a nearby carriage siding or station. On opening the regulator, one was immediately conscious of a powerful surge of acceleration quite remarkable for its smoothness and lack of noise, for gone was the lurch of suddenly moving forty to fifty tons of tender and the grinding motion of a fall plate beneath one's feet.

An advantageous power to weight ratio is one of the attractions of tank engines and this shows at its best when working middle distance stopping passenger trains. However, unlike a tender engine, depletion of water and fuel supply directly affects its adhesive factor, an effect which requires slight modifications to driving technique as it progresses. The total engine weight may decrease by eight tons or so during the course of a trip and whilst this may improve acceleration, the reduced adhesion could increase any tendency to slip or wheels to lock under braking.

Usually these stopping trains were truly local, operating within a fifty mile radius of their start point and consisting of between four and six bogies (125-190 tons). With this modest load in tow, acceleration on level track was still very impressive and in normal conditions only the regulators first valve would be used. Progressive reductions in cut-off maintained optimum efficiency as speed increased and in a very short space of time, they were cantering along in the sixties with consummate ease. Perhaps their remarkably quiet, stable ride, free from fuss and trauma was the most notable aspect of these excellent engines. Certainly they produced a very crisp healthy bark when getting under way or when pushed on banks, but at normal running speeds with the cut-off at around 15-20%, only a soft sibilant purr emanated from the chimney.

The coupled wheel size of 5ft. 9in. diameter seemed to suit the engine's characteristics and the type of work upon which it was principally employed. This sound choice was of course a compromise to provide good acceleration and climbing potential combined with the ability to run at 80 mph or so without its wheels achieving undesirably high rotational speeds.

Most of my involvement with 2-6-4Ts was compressed into the period 1954-5, but I was fortunate in as much that the majority of runs coverd two interesting stretches of line, namely Birmingham to Evesham via the single line Redditch branch and Birmingham to Leicester. The former was a superb mix of steepish inclines and short fast stretches interspersed with frequent station stops. Here the major emphasis was on acceleration and climbing prowess since there were few opportunities to achieve really high speeds.

It certainly tested these aspects of locomotive performance in addition to their steaming ability and was ideal for making comparisons between locomotive types. The Birmingham-Leicester section again offered an interesting mix, but being a main line, it was generally run at a faster pace. Even so, it had a number of gradients, the most notable being the summit between Arley and Stockingford approached by an unrelenting six mile drag from the West and a similar five mile climb from the East, the former having a maximum stretch of 1:109. On the whole, though, it gave much more scope for high speed running and therefore the opportunity to compare this important attribute with other types currently in use.

Some of the duties allotted to the 2-6-4Ts over this stretch really fell into the semi-fast category and the non stop run between Hinckley and Leicester frequently gave them the chance to show their paces particularly on the falling gradients to Elmsthorpe. At exceptionally busy periods loadings could be increased to as much as eight coaches (approx. 250 tons) and, being obliged to keep point-to-point timings within the original fairly tight schedules, much vigorous working was called for well prior to the final twelve mile dash into Leicester. No matter how hard these Fowler 2-6-4 tank engines were thrashed, they never seemed to be short of steam, indeed they revelled in this type of work and were as eager at the end of a hard climb as at the beginning. Normally the injectors worked reliably and when used in unison were well able to maintain the boiler level against even the heaviest demands.

Assisted by the 1:320 gradient, departure from Hinckley was always brisk and continued rapid acceleration ensured by a further two miles of 1:162. With a well opened regulator and 20-25% cut off indicated, they often achieved speeds of around 80 mph when passing through Elmsthorpe. With only a normal wrist watch available it was of course impossible to be too precise when recording seconds between ¼ mile posts, but frequently, as near as I could judge, barely eleven seconds elapsed which represents 82 mph, which figure would seem to be in accord with reliable reports more accurately recorded in many other areas since their introduction in 1927.

At these high speeds the ride was truly superb and in quite a different class to any tender locomotive I had experienced at that time. Being quiet and stable they showed no sign of stress and gave the impression of always running well within their limit. Nor did this impression change when working bunker first, although because of altered aerodynamics, powerful draughts entered the cab via the cut outs and below the bunker doors making it an eye-watering experience for the crew.

Forward vision was not particularly good when seated but this could be considerably improved by standing on the raised side platforms when, from this elevated position, it was possible to see over the boiler through the upper spectacle glasses. Reverse running on the other hand, with only a few feet of bunker and no steam to obstruct the view, made the signals easier to sight especially when some of the coal supply had been used.

Firing the Fowler 2-6-4T was a mixture of pros and cons. With a 25 sq.ft. grate area nearly 8ft. 0in. long it would have been easier to fire with a long shovel but, because of the constrictions imposed by its cab layout, to use one would be at the risk of barked knuckles. Most firemen therefore opted for a short version even though this meant adopting a more shuffling stance and the need for a heftier swing – which could then be executed with a greater degree of confidence. Unfortunately the short shovel would not reach very far into the bunker and therefore the coal doors had to be opened earlier thus creating another undesirable obstruction. Once aware of these problems I tended to carry both types of shovel whenever possible using the long one only to disturb blockages which frequently occurred in the tortuous passage between bunker and shovelling plate and to draw coal forward.

However, perhaps the most endearing quality of the 2-6-4Ts was their remarkable stability at all speeds, a stability of course enhanced by the absence of a separate tender and mobile fall plate. With a continuous solid platform from which to work, the fireman no longer had to perform acrobatic feats in order to retain his balance during the act of firing and this alone did much to reduce fatigue.

The sloping grate was typically Midland and responded well to the time honoured practice of a thick bed at the back tapering progressively to just sufficient body at the front to prevent holes being drawn in it. The actual thickness was as always, dictated by the amount of work to be done and its duration.

Draughting was first class and there never seemed to be any problem in maintaining a bright fire even when lightly worked, providing of course no clinker obstructed the free flow of air through the firebars. One damper was provided at each end of the ashpan and most firemen tended to open the leading one relative to the direction of travel. By so doing, admission of primary air was assisted by the locomotives movement when the ashpan then acted as a scoop. Its capacity was quite generous and more than adequate for the relatively short distance duties allocated to these tank engines.

Apart from having a large grate area, the firebox was also fairly deep enabling a good depth of fire to be carried and because of this a lot of energy could be stored for times of abnormal demand. Since passenger quality coal was normally supplied, fires could be rapidly built up prior to bursts of heavy working without detriment to steaming and then, with a little judicial mortgaging, short periods of exceptional effort could be indulged in without 'winding' the locomotive.

Tank engines always tend to be rather hot in warm weather, especially for the fireman performing hard physical work in front of a white hot furnace. Having a rather inadequate cab roof ventilator, the Fowler 2-6-4s were worse than most, although opening the upper spectacle glasses which pivoted on their horizontal axes helped particularly when running chimney first. Reverse travel was somewhat less torrid since, apart from additional draughts entering the cab as previously described, boiler heat tended to be carried away from the crew. In winter the opposite applied and it was the driver who suffered more from cold, although by comparison with contemporary tender locomotives, they were undoubtedly more comfortable and offered a much higher degree of protection from the elements.

On later engines built in 1934 prior to the side window version, the rear cab cutaway was reduced in order to improve protection and exclude some of the draughts when running bunker first, but in all honesty I cannot recall noticing much difference.

When it came to disposal, 2-6-4Ts were just about at the bottom of the ratings list and to shed crews they were not a welcome sight. With their limited capacity, the side tanks invariably required filling, not that this was particularly difficult nor indeed was coaling, but it involved additional work nevertheless. When static, conditions in the cab were always hot, intolerably so in summer, but they had to be endured. However, most frustration was caused by the confinement of the full cab enclosure and the limitations which its layout of fittings and fixtures imposed. Only a short clinker shovel could be manoeuvred effectively within that restricted space and even then it often became annoyingly hooked over some unseen handle or latch just as a full load was being withdrawn through the firehole. The red hot ash and clinker then either dropped back on to the grate from whence it came or spilled over the oil soaked footboards with interesting effects. Footplate conflagrations were therefore more common on 2-6-4Ts than any other locomotive as their charred floorboards testified.

Unfortunately a short clinker shovel would reach but two thirds of the grate's length and because a long one could not be accommodated a rather individual technique was usually employed. Assuming the engine was to remain in steam, live fire would be pushed forward to form a ridge half way along the grate. Using a bent dart,

any clinker in the back corners and under the firehole was broken up and likewise pushed against the ridge which then acted as a 'backstop'; thence clinker and ash were removed by means of the short shovel. Once this had been completed, sufficient live fire to ensure the combustion of fresh coal was then brought back under the firehole.

With care, a longer clinker shovel or rake could be inserted so as to reach the front of the firebox and any clinker here pulled back over the ridge and paddled out as before. One benefit of keeping only a thin fire at the front was that very little clinker tended to form in this area, especially with good quality coal, so it was often merely a case of raking over the grate which then caused loose ash to fall into the ashpan below. Although not unduly difficult, the whole process was rendered slow and tedious by not being able to wield fire irons within the confines of a very hot cab. Fortunately, because of the better grade fuels used on generally short duration runs, fires were rarely in a bad state which compensated in some measure for the additional discomfort involved. For the same reason neither smokebox nor ashpan entailed exceptional effort although the latter naturally had to be cleared from the pit below the engine.

From the foregoing it will be seen that these Fowler 2-6-4 Tank engines were an instant and remarkable success proving, along with Crabs and Royal Scots, the advantages of long travel long lap valves coupled with high degree superheating set on a well shod chassis. The fact that these lessons took a little longer to be learned at Derby does not detract from the excellence of their design and although I did not work on them until many years after their introduction, they appeared fully able to compete with more modern developments of this type.

Obviously improvements were made over the years and later versions of 2-6-4Ts were tailored to changing conditions but I shall discuss how the Fowler compared with Stanier and Fairburn versions in the next section.

Class 4P LMS Passenger Tank Engine (Stanier Taper Boiler) Introduced 1935 Total 206

Although Stanier became CME of the LMS in 1932, another batch of Fowler 2-6-4Ts had been authorised in the 1933 building programme. He did however, have some modifications made to a number of these including the fitting of side window cabs and improved bogies; but for the final five he introduced his own version. General layout and dimensions were basically similar to

The elegant Stanier 2-6-4T certainly looked thoroughly modern and to some eyes its taper boiler and high, angled bunker added a touch of extra grace. Apart from appearance, the twin side window cab offered better all round vision and was rather less draughty than the Fowler version particularly when running in reverse.

the Fowler engine but it was equipped with a taper boiler and provided with a three-cylinder layout which it was believed would give smoother and better acceleration.

Early examples were fitted with low degree superheat domeless boilers but as was the case with his Jubilee (3A) and Black 5 (3B) boilers they were not initially suited to LMS conditions and required subsequent development. With an urgent need for additional modern motive power on the Southend line, a further 32 locomotives of this type were constructed specifically for the purpose. When tested against the Fowler engine they showed no significant improvement in performance even though possessing a 1,475lb tractive effort advantage. Having caried out this experimental exercise Stanier quickly realised that there was nothing to be gained by the additional cost, complication and weight of a three-cylinder design and for the following year, production reverted to his own version of the original simpler layout.

Although the initial batch of eight engines possessed domeless low degree superheat boilers, dimensionally identical to those of the three-cylinder 2-6-4Ts,

subsequent examples had the improved type with separate dome, top feed, larger grate area and 21 element superheater. In this form they proved to be excellent engines and since overall dimensions were identical to those of the Fowler, direct comparison was inevitably invited.

Aesthetically they presented a delightfully balanced appearance of modern efficiency and in keeping with the rest of Stanier's designs, practical features blended harmoniously with near perfect lineaments. The taper boiler added a certain grace to the impression of raw power enhanced in no small way by external steam pipes to its cylinders, side windows and high inset bunker.

It will be seen from their diagrams that there were many similarities between the two designs. They both shared a common wheelbase, axle spacings, wheel sizes, overall length and width in addition to fuel and water capacity and the same boiler pressure. The principal differences with a potential to affect performance lay in the cylinders (which had ⅝in. greater bore) and the taper boiler. This boiler not only possessed a grate 1.7 sq.ft. larger in area but also the tubes gave an additional 140 sq.ft. of heating surface; surprisingly though, even with a twenty one element superheater, it still lagged behind the parallel boiler figure by 21 sq.ft. or approximately 8%.

At 85% boiler pressure its tractive effort at 24,670 lbs. was some 1,545 lbs. greater than the Fowler engine although to some extent this was offset by an extra 1½ tons weight.

Most of the other differences were those of details and fittings and related more to convenience rather than performance. Commencing at the front, the deeply dished smokebox door was secured by a central dart which was far easier to use than circumferential dogs and remained air-tight for longer periods. Because of its longer boiler there was less room on the front framing but even so, quite adequate when cleaning char from the smokebox, while the small step beneath was much appreciated by firemen reaching to attend lamps on the top bracket. Sanding and lubricating systems were very similar and their boxes therefore disposed in approximately the same places. The cab and bunker design not only presented a much more modern appearance, they also offered the crew a higher level of comfort and convenience. The coal bunker, arranged to be as self trimming as possible, was of the inset type and its high top was angled in towards the rear end so as to give even better vision when running in that direction.

The cab interior seemed lighter and more spacious than the Fowler version due in part to double side windows, the rear one of which could be moved forward to open. Large rear spectacle glasses, unobstructed by coal, allowed further light to enter and if so desired, illumination could be also enhanced by opening the sensibly sized roof ventilator. Use of a main steam manifold above the firebox gave rise to the tidier pipe work and general layout established on Stanier locomotives and which is described in detail under the section dealing with Black 5s. There was also rather more space at the rear of the cab and the fact that both hand brake and water scoop handles operated in a vertical plane made them somewhat less intrusive, although the benefit of this was noticeable more when disposing than firing.

Preparation of the Stanier version was virtually the same as far as the driver was concerned and perhaps a little easier for the fireman in as much that there were no smokebox door dogs to tighten nor coal to remove from before the bunker spectacles. However, it was always good policy to check and trim the coal in the interests of safety and climbing up to the bunker top likewise proved fairly easy. Steps on the bunker back plate were positioned differently, there being an additional one in the centre plus foot blocks on either side of the inset and a hand rail ran horizontally across the full width, but on the whole, the arrangement proved quite convenient.

Driving the Stanier tank was remarkably like driving the Fowler; it possessed the same quiet and rapid acceleration which if pursued quickly achieved normal running speed. To arrive at this, much the same regulator and cut off positions would be used and even when in

full flight the superb stable ride was very similar.

In fact the main differences lay in the area of vision and protection from the elements especially when seated.

The large front spectacles permitted a rather better view around and over the taper boiler which itself was less obstructive when trying to sight awkward signals. Rearward vision was excellent and undoubtedly superior to the parallel boiler engines. Equally large spectacles allowed an unobstructed wide angle view past the inset bunker so that there was rarely any need for the driver to peer round the cab side during normal running. However, as with all flat spectacle glass they picked up annoying reflections at night when the firedoors were open.

The sliding side windows were also much appreciated, since they offered the best of both worlds. When shut they protected the driver from side winds or lashing rain while at the same time permitting ample lateral vision. Open, they provided extra ventilation and allowed the driver to lean well out which was the usual stance when closing-up to stock.

With some 6½% more tractive effort theoretically available, they should have had the edge over the Fowler engines but on normal loads little difference could be detected. Both types were equally tolerant of being worked on a partially opened regulator with a longer cut-off or expansively with a wide open regulator. Because there was rarely any need to fully extend these powerful tanks on day to day scheduled trains, most drivers found the first valve of the regulator quite adequate.

On the Leicester runs I tried as before to determine maximum speeds at Elmsthorpe but my rudimentary methods produced exactly the same timings which merely confirmed that the Stanier engines were also capable of travelling in excess of 80 mph. Again the ride was superb but it did not perhaps feel quite as taut as the Fowler and its cab and fittings certainly rattled a lot more. On the other hand it was undoubtedly less draughty, particularly when running at speed in reverse when improved vision past the inset bunker was also much appreciated.

Although the Stanier firebox was 6in. longer, most firemen still preferred to use a short shovel for exactly the same reasons as with the Fowlers. In all the usual places, obstructions again threatened knuckles so that as before I only carried a long handled version to help clear blockages and draw coal forward. Despite its purported self trimming features the passage from bunker to shovelling plate became clogged by large lumps of coal just as easily as with the former design. Similar folding doors allowed access to the coal space but when open they did intrude and I preferred to keep them closed whilst firing.

Its sloping grate responded best to the 'thick back, thin front' profile and because of its slightly more generous area, coupled with what seemed a softer blast, they could generally be fired a touch lighter. Not that the blast was at all woolly in any way; on the contrary, it was clean and well defined, but it possessed a rounder more mellow tone which sounded less explosive. With only the leading damper open, maintaining a bright fire posed no particular problems irrespective of how the engine was being worked, merely a case of varying the firebed depth. Nor did they tend to throw sparks as much as the Fowlers, this unfortunately was always a problem when accelerating hard or climbing banks and could lead to trails of lineside conflagrations after a dry spell. However, their ability to produce steam was never in doubt and the injectors were quite capable of keeping pace with even the heaviest demands made upon the boiler.

Firemen appreciated their sliding side window for much the same reasons as the driver and the large roof ventilator certainly helped to keep temperatures more tolerable, indeed one could say that the Staniers were rather cooler in summer and more cosy in winter.

Working in a vertical plane, the water scoop handle seemed rather easier to operate and to me, involved a more natural action. It could be used when running in either direction but as with the Fowler, the indication when to withdraw the scoop had to be relayed by the driver, since the water gauge was located atop the tank in front of his spectacle glass.

Disposal presented just about the same difficulties, although with an extra few inches of depth and better disposition of handles, fire irons did not get entangled quite so often. Also with the cab ventilator open, conditions were not quite so torrid even though the same fire cleaning method was normally adopted.

To make a choice between the two designs was not easy, rather a case of swings and roundabouts and most enginemen if given the opportunity would I suspect, unhesitatingly select the most recently shopped locomotive irrespective of type. The Fowler probably gave a tauter, quieter ride and seemed to steam a little more freely particularly with poorer quality fuel. The Stanier offered a less cluttered more comfortable cab, albeit at the expenses of some additional rattles, and improved vision especially to the rear.

As far as performance on the road was concerned, there was in all honesty no detectable difference in terms of pulling power, acceleration, speed and economy of fuel and water. Both were excellent machines more than able to master the duties assigned to them and because of the confidence this engendered they always remained extremely popular with their crews.

LMS Class 4 Passenger Tank (Fairburn Taper Boiler). Introduced 1945. Total 277.

We now come to the final LMS variant of 2-6-4T, known as the 'Fairburn' which, because of its similarity to the Stanier, I am including in this chapter. The type arose because construction of a further batch of Stanier 2-6-4Ts, programmed to be built in 1940, was deferred until after the war, by which time conditions had changed considerably. With the need for ever greater route availability and ease of servicing very much in mind, the opportunity was taken to modify Staniers' powerful tank engine in line with such ideology. This was achieved by shortening the coupled wheelbase by 1ft. 2in. which then permitted the engine to be used on 5-chain curves instead of the 6-chain curve limit of the original version.

Further weight reduction was gained by the absence of plating ahead of the cylinders and the use of lightweight open type steps. Despite retaining the same water and fuel capacities, the total weight in working order was then 85.25 tons compared to the Stanier's 87.85.

Being over 2½ tons lighter should have given them a slight advantage in acceleration and although this was difficult to detect in service, they have been reported attaining speeds into the mid eighties. Certainly these engines were every bit as fleet of foot as the other two and everything that has been said about the Stanier equally applies. Only in the ride could a subtle difference be sometimes noticed, it being perhaps a little more harsh at higher speeds on certain sections.

Much appreciated by firemen was the provision of additional vertical handrails running up the back of the inset bunker and steps now fitted to both sides. Drivers too, were happy to find increased use of grease lubrication, but by far the most endearing features were the fitting of self cleaning smokeboxes, rocking grates and hopper ashpans. If every any locomotive needed these wonderful labour saving devices it was the 2-6-4T for the reasons already described. Also of course, the self cleaning smokebox acted as a very effective spark arrester, since only cool particles could be ejected from the chimney and with this additional bonus, drivers felt less restrained on heavy gradients in dry weather.

To some traditionalists open steps and the absence of plating detracted from the Fairburn's appearance, but changed conditions demanded emphasis on ease of maintenance and the absence of plating certainly speeded up routine piston and valve inspections. However, most appreciated as far as loco crews were concerned was the fitting of rocker grates, hopper ashpans and self cleaning smokeboxes, because if any design ever needed these wonderful aids, it was the 2-6-4T. In this photograph of 42096 the spigot which opens the hopper ashpan can be seen adjacent to the lower end of the trailing couple wheel's brake hanger.

With its lighter weight and ability to negotiate tighter curves in addition to rapid servicing capability on or off shed, this latest addition to the family of 2-6-4Ts was more versatile than ever. They so suited prevailing conditions that construction continued until 1951 with many being supplied for use on other BR regions, the final batch indeed being built at Brighton.

If a choice had to be made between the trio then it would always come out in favour of the Fairburn if for no other reason than its rapid disposal facilities and improvements in crew conveniences.

On the road there was little detectable difference as far as engine performance was concerned, although as with all locomotives fitted with rocking grates, steaming efficiency could be maintained for a longer period. This feature was apparently subsequently taken into account since Fairburns seemed to be used all over the country on a wide variety of duties.

Tailpiece

When the BR Standard 2-6-4Ts came to be produced, they were based on the Fairburn version wheelbase, but in order to conform with the universal L1 loading gauge a reduction in cylinder diameter from 19⅝in. to 18in. was necessary. By increasing cylinder stroke to 28in. and boiler pressure to 225 psi, together with a 1in. decrease in diameter of the coupled wheels, not only was the objective achieved but also the engines' tractive effort enhanced – by a further 845lbs to 25,515lbs.

With the curved outer tank side, BR style cabs and raised footplating in front of the cylinders they were to my mind the best looking of all the 2-6-4 tanks. Furthermore, if experience on other BR types is anything to go on, their ergonomic excellence and profusion of practical improvements would have made them the most comfortable and convenient to work with as well.

I regret to say, though, that I never had the opportunity to even get near one whilst with BR let alone clock their speed through Elmsthorpe but from all accounts they were every bit as sprightly as the others and well able to live up to the term 'ultimate expression'.

From the above it is obvious that the development of 2-6-4 tank engines on the LMS/BR was from start to finish one of outstanding success. Admittedly they only ran on mundane, unglamorous duties which received little publicity, but they were masters of their work and highly popular with crews. What more can you really ask from an engine?

Chapter 7

4-4-0 Class 4P Compound Type
EXPRESS PASSENGER ENGINES

Midland Introduced 1902. Total 45. LMS Introduced 1924. Total 195.

The history of compounding as applied to steam loco-motives is as intriguing as it is complex and possibly more has been written discussing its merits or otherwise than any other aspect of locomotive design. Although experiments were conducted as early as 1850 it was not until 1876 that the first successful design went into regular service in France. Indeed it was mainly on the continent and in America, driven by various economic reasons, that compounding was pioneered and finally reached its most efficient form in Chapelon's remark-able 4-8-4 242A1.* The story of compounding in Britain is rather convoluted and as a system it seemed to draw more acrimonious controversy around it than just about any other major engineering development particularly within two of the constituent companies of the LMS. Nor did it cease after the grouping in 1923 took place; on the contrary this acrimony became more intense during the mid-twenties due to the persuance of policies involving compound locomotives that were not always appropriate. Although the involvement of Midland Compounds will always be associated with this period of political turmoil, much good eventually came from it. A number of volumes describe the fascinating develop-ment of the Midland Compound and for those so inter-ested I would suggest they read the books of O.S. Nock and D.F. Tee. It will then be seen that the Midland compound's development was inextricably linked with other major advances such as superheating and a more scientific understanding of valve gear design to say nothing of a better appreciation of compounding principles.

Compounding is the use of the same charge of steam by allowing it to expand in more than one cylinder of an engine before exhaust. By the end of the last century it was very much in vogue and although continental designers had achieved considerable success, it had not made much headway in Britain.

F.W. Webb's great compound experiment on the LNWR went through all manner of vicissitudes and with some classes, came near to success, but the under-standing of certain basic principles seemed to be lacking and Crewe Works reverted to simple expansion engines

once more. Sadly, however, memories of Webb's efforts and the frustrations they created lingered with LNW locomen long after the grouping and were to have certain reprocussions in due course.

In the meantime a much greater degree of success was being enjoyed on the North Eastern with two cylinder compounds based on the Von-Borries type; but then, in 1898, W.M. Smith who was chief draughtsman under Worsdell produced a much more logical design. This was a re-build of one of the two cylinder compound 4-4-0 express passenger engines but now it had one high pressure inside cylinder and two low pressure outside cylinders, all driving the leading coupled axle. The performance of this locomotive aroused the interest of Midland Railway CME S.W. Johnson who was on ex-tremely good terms with Worsdell and was at the time contemplating the introduction of more powerful 4-4-0s to cope with demands for increased loadings.

In 1902, without any previous experience of com-pound locomotives, Derby constructed the first two of what was to become the best known and undoubtedly the most successful engines of this type in the country. Being fast and economical they quickly proved superior to their Midland contempories and a further three examples were built the following year albeit with simplified valve gear.

R.M. Deeley succeeded Johnson in 1904, whereupon he set about preparing his own version of the Smith system and when it emerged from Derby a year later the appearance was radically change. The locomotive was essentially in the form it retained for the next half century or so, except for such later modifications as an enlarged smokebox (when converted to superheating) and changed boiler fittings.

Important mechanical changes had also taken place. The already generous firebox of the Johnson engines was now extended to give a grate area no less than 28.4 sq.ft. (the largest for any 4-4-0 in this country) and boiler pressure increased from 195 psi to 220 psi. Deeley also simplified the driver's controls by intro-ducing an ingenious pattern of regulator the working of which has already been described in Part I.

Having provided continued satisfaction in service, the original batch of ten Deeley compounds was followed by a further twenty in 1906 although these, together with ten more built in 1908-9 had modified frames and

---

* For a definitive study of the whole international scene see 'Compound Locomotives' by J.T. van Riemsdijk – Pendragon Books – 1994.

smokeboxes. The next step was to apply superheating since this had considerably improved performance on Deeley's 999 class 4-4-0 'simple' engines. Initially only one locomotive, No. 1040, was converted, but having conducted coal consumption tests with this and another compound using saturated steam, the superheated engine showed savings in coal and water of 26% and 22% repectively. Unfortunately the outbreak of hostilities slowed matters so that only four more were converted before the war ended. Even then progress was far from rapid so that at the time of the grouping in 1923, 21 Compounds still remained with saturated boilers and it was not until 1928 that the superheating programme was completed.

Naturally, grouping so many companies together, some of whom had been fierce rivals, inevitably resulted in trials, tribulations and not a little antipathy which rumbled on for some years. The situation was not helped by a rather intransigent Board of Directors and Senior Management drawn mainly from the former Midland Railway who seemed rather insensitive when it came to the imposition of their ideas, one of these being perpetuation of the well tried Midland philosophy of frequent light loadings hauled by small engines. Their champion was the 4-4-0 Compound (which was actually quite big for a 'small' engine!) and, focussed around this locomotive, a series of trials were conducted over the next two years or so. Meanwhile boiler pressures had been reduced and then brought up again to stabilise at 200 psi in addition to valve settings being re-adjusted.

These trials brought the Compounds into direct competition with probably a greater variety of locomotives than any other class before or since. Furthermore, the outcome was, for their advocates, a happy one since they not only quite easily saw off most of their adversaries in terms of economy and spritely running, but also displayed unexpected haulage power on inclines. Not that this latter discovery was particularly welcomed in certain quarters because it did not accord with preconceived notions and operating policy.

Hardly had the first trials ceased when the initial batch of Standard Compounds emerged from Derby. Whilst their general appearance was almost identical to the original superheater rebuilds they differed by having both high and low pressure cylinders ¾in. larger and coupled wheels reduced to 6ft. 9in. These were quickly followed by a further variation, modified to conform to the more restricted Scottish loading gauge by having shorter chimneys and Ross pop safety valves.

Additional trials that year brought about a reversion to the original cylinder dimensions for engines built from 1925 onwards and also a change was made from right hand to left hand drive, which then became standard for all subsequent LMS locomotives. Midland men were naturally happy to receive more examples of a well tried and popular class as the influx of compounds spread all over the system. Scottish drivers also accepted them readily and soon acquired the necessary techniques to produce good results but with the LNWR crews it was a different story. Still mindful of the problems experienced with Webb's designs, compounds represented trouble so understandably drivers viewed these new 'foreign' engines with suspicion. Also having their favourites displaced when they were performing more than satisfactorily was, as far as they were concerned, provocative and even insulting to their abilities. Furthermore the methods needed to extract optimum performance from a Compound were rather different to those traditionally employed on the LNWR. Hence the stories of wild variations in time keeping, disappointing fuel consumption and drivers running the whole trip on 'simple engine'.

In due course things settled down and Compounds ranged the length and breadth of the system on even the most prestigious trains. Admittedly they were often piloted but they coped well and they coped economically until the Royal Scots with their vastly superior performance arrived in 1927, a year incidentally in which the bulk of Compound production ceased. Derby completed the final batch of five locomotives in 1932; but by then William Stanier had become CME and was about to change the motive power scene on the LMS for ever.

As more of his excellent 4-6-0s became available, many Compounds were displaced from their main line duties and this gradual relegation to the second division continued until the outbreak of the 1939-45 war when, during the early years, they experienced a short revival. Priority given to increased freight traffic made heavy demands on available 4-6-0MTs which were more capable in this respect but when production of Black 5s and later, 2-6-4Ts recommenced their fate was sealed and the first withdrawals were made in 1948.

This continued steadily throughout the 1950s, but even so, the remainder were still able to perform usefully on more humble duties. Towards the end of the decade their decline was accelerated by the introduction of Diesel multiple units and so the last example was taken out of service in 1961, nearly sixty years after their introduction. Not a bad record for a first attempt at compounding. Had the efficiency obtained from modern well designed long travel long lap valve gear coupled to high degree superheating been applied to the compound principle who knows what might have resulted? As it was, we left it to the French to develop the idea to the full.

My experience with Compounds was, of course, during their final decade with most activity confined to 1955 while working in one of the passenger links at Saltley. At this time they were being used principally on secondary passenger duties, parcels traffic, specials and the occasional pilot.

Compounds were at their best worked by regular drivers on long distance non-stop expresses, when their potential for economical operating showed to advantage; nevertheless, some of the middle distance stopping passenger trains allowed them to stretch their legs on a regular basis and the operating people still seemed happy to use them. However, by then they were com-

STANDARD COMPOUND CYLINDER ARRANGEMENT

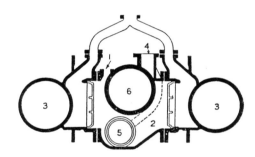

I AUXILIARY STEAM PIPE
2 LOW PRESSURE RECEIVER
3 LOW PRESSURE CYLINDER
4 MAIN STEAM PIPE
5 H.P. PISTON VALVE
6 H.P. CYLINDER
7 NON RETURN VALVES
8 L.P. SLIDE VALVES
9 AIR VALVES

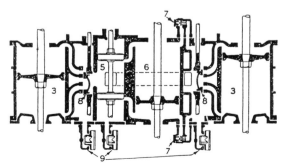

FIG. 37

PLAN IMAGINING ALL THE CYLINDERS DRAWN IN ONE PLANE

peting not only with the latest LMS examples of 2-6-0, 4-6-0 and 2-6-4T, but also with completely new BR designs specifically built with versatility, low maintenance and rapid servicing in mind. It was little wonder then that most enginemen regarded them as one would an old race horse – with respect and gratitude for past services, but also with the underlying feeling that it would now be kinder to put them out to grass.

For simplicity I propose to describe only a typical LMS built left hand drive Compound as it would have been found running in 1955 equipped with a Fowler tender.

Viewed from a distance through the eyes of a keen young fireman a Compound seemed to me rather archaic and, being a 4-4-0, definitely inferior to more modern six- and eight-coupled types. Yet it displayed a certain dignity blended with an indefinable air of grace, even when standing all dishevelled on an ash pit; and one could not help feeling that little pang of sorrow one experiences on seeing a celebrity who has fallen on hard times.

There is a tendency to pre-judge the size of 4-4-0s and bracket them all within the small locomotive category, but at close range the Compound's true dimensions became surprisingly apparent. With a boiler barrel one inch longer than that of a Stanier Class 8F, a grate area virtually the same as a Black 5 and in working order weighing five tons more than an Ivatt Class 4MT 2-6-0 there was nothing dwarfish about them. Compounds certainly looked what they were supposed to be, express passenger engines and one can only admire the modern appearance with which Deeley managed to endow his design in 1905. Indeed certain features he embodied were to become Midland and LMS practice and were perpetuated until production of Class 4Fs ceased in 1941.

The Compound's cylinder design and layout was entirely unique on the LMS and its plan and cross-section are illustrated in Fig. 37.

It will be seen that a single high pressure cylinder, 21in. diameter by 26in. stroke is placed between the frames and two low pressure cylinders 21in. diameter by 26in. stroke are mounted outside. Steam is distributed to the HP cylinder by an 8in. diameter outside admission piston valve and to each LP cylinder by a slide valve, a separate set of Stephenson's link motion being used for each cylinder.

All cranks drive on to the leading coupled axle, the two LP crank pins being set 90° apart with the right hand crank leading and the HP crank is set to bisect the obtuse angle between them placing it 135% from each (see Fig. 38).

Both in action and in use the Deeley regulator was extremely simple and unless some defect existed in the operating gear which might cause the starting valve and main valve to stick together, it was not possible to have the main and starting ports open simultaneously. Should this occur, though, it would be detected by the registration of excessive pressure on the LP receiver gauge. It was of course necessary for enginemen to have some understanding of what took place when the regulator was opened and this was explained quite lucidly in basic training.

"At starting, saturated steam is fed via the auxiliary steam pipe to the LP receiver and operates, in conjunction with their slide valves, the two LP cylinders as a simple engine. At the same time a small supply of live steam fed by way of the balancing port in the regulator valve, passes through the main steam pipe and superheater to the HP piston valve, which distributes it to the correct side of the HP piston. Balancing pressure is then obtained on the opposite or exhaust side of the HP cylinder past the open exhaust port. However, in certain positions one or both steam ports of the HP cylinder might be covered by a lap of the HP piston valve and in the former case excess pressure could build up on the exhaust side of the HP piston due to LP receiver steam passing back via the port which was open to exhaust so producing a negative turning effort at the HP crank pin. To guard against such a contingency a non-return valve is fitted to each end of the HP cylinder. The non-return valves are simple mushroom type steam valves each of which is placed in a port running respectively from the front and back of the HP cylinder to the LP receiver. The non-return valves are arranged to lift only towards the HP cylinder which means that they cannot operate and allow steam to pass if pressure in the LP receiver exceeds that in either or both ends of the HP cylinder at any time. Obviously the non-return valves can only function at starting or possibly on occasions when working 'simple engine'. With the regulator over to full compound position the steam pressure in the HP cylinder must at all times exceed that in the LP receiver into which it is exhausting, consequently both non-return valves will then be held firmly down upon their seats".

Compounds enjoyed a long and relatively trouble free life due in no small part to the benefits bestowed by the action of compounding itself. There are several areas in a steam locomotive where wear is of major significance and which directly affects the scheduled period

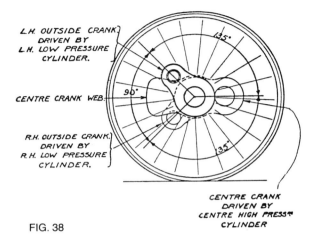

CRANK POSITIONS OF
3-CYLINDER COMPOUND ENGINE

L.H. OUTSIDE CRANK DRIVEN BY L.H. LOW PRESSURE CYLINDER.

CENTRE CRANK WEB.

R.H. OUTSIDE CRANK DRIVEN BY R.H. LOW PRESSURE CYLINDER.

CENTRE CRANK DRIVEN BY CENTRE HIGH PRESS™ CYLINDER

FIG. 38

between light and heavy repairs and eventually the total life expectancy. In a number of these areas compounds showed a distinct advantage which probably not only extended their life, but also enabled them to maintain a higher level of condition for longer intervals.

At the time when Compounds were at their peak, steam leakage past piston valves accelerated rapidly as mileage between overhauls increased, causing not only a fall off in performance but an unacceptable rise in coal and water consumption. Even the Royal Scots were afflicted with this problem when first introduced in 1927 and was only cured later when multiple narrow piston rings were fitted.

With compounds, any leakage on the HP piston valve only tended to contribute to the power output on the LP side and therefore did not affect overall performance to the degree it would with a simple engine. Periodic attention to valves and pistons was consequently dictated rather more by wear on the pistons which, in the case of the LP ones, was less because of the lower pressure involved. For the same reason glands and packings also were less affected.

Another major cause which restricted mileage between repairs was wear on little end and big end bearings since after a certain point had been reached, not only was it damaging to the journal, the knock produced made conditions extremely unpleasant on the

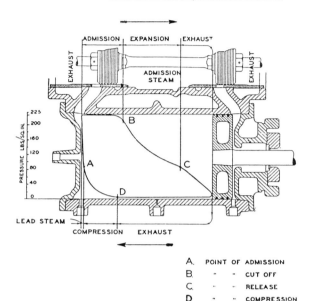

DIAGRAM SHOWING THE DISTRIBUTION OF STEAM ON ONE SIDE OF THE PISTON FOR A DOUBLE STROKE.

A.   POINT OF ADMISSION
B.   "   "   CUT OFF
C.   "   "   RELEASE
D.   "   "   COMPRESSION

FIG. 39

footplate. The longer cut-offs employed by compounds promoted a much smoother more even turning movement resulting in a less destructive action on the bearings and because of this, even when they were worn, it was far less noticeable. On many occasions with high mileage simple engines I have found it necessary to work them at long cut-offs on a partially opened regulator in order to ameliorate excessive knocking.

With a simple engine, work is obtained from expanding steam in a cylinder against a piston and then exhausting it. To obtain maximum economy at a given power output it was generally desirable to use the shortest practical cut-off which then allowed for maximum expansion before release to exhaust (see Fig. 39).

Pressure against the piston is therefore highest at the beginning of the stroke and then reduces steadily after cut-off until release point when it falls rapidly as exhaust takes place. The action resembles that of a short sharp blow which becomes more vicious as cut-off is reduced and speed increases and it must be remembered that exactly the same thing happens on the return stroke.

Long cut-offs on the other hand give rise to what is in effect a prolonged steady push; but for a given power output the commencement pressure would be considerably lower and pressure fluctuations within the cylinder far less. With a simple engine, loss of economy would result from not making full use of the expansive properties of steam and speed restricted due to a late release causing back pressure.

Because steam was allowed to expand through two separate cylinders in sequence over an extended period, full use could be made of steam's expansive properties while at the same time obtaining all the aforementioned benefits. Modern simple engines were often worked at around 15% cut-off, but this would equate to 40% on a Compound and at 30% (about the least at which locomotives with short travel valves could be effectively operated), would be equivalent to 73%.

On the Standard Compound both HP and LP valves were controlled by a single common reversing screw for simplicity but the LP cut-off was set rather less than the HP so that for example, at 73% cut-off on the HP the LP would be giving 64%.

Yet another factor contributing to the Compound's longevity was the better balance achieved by its three cylinder layout which virtually eliminated the wracking stresses associated particularly with designs using two outside cylinders. These stresses frequently led to rapid wear in axleboxes and fatigue cracks appearing in frames. Whilst this problem also beset some three cylinder simple locomotives, it was mainly those with divided drives whereas the Compound's drive was concentrated on one axle.

It will be seen then, that because Compounds demanded less from their bearings and tended not to shake themselves to pieces, they retained their quality of ride far longer, indeed I cannot recall ever having worked on a really rough one.

The G9AS Belpaire superheated boiler looked elegant and, aided in no small measure by its very generous grate area, was a very effective producer of steam. 6ft. 9in. driving wheels indicated the traditional long stride of a true express locomotive and above these, imposing splashers, the rear of which blended gracefully with the cab side sheet. By modern standards the cab was rather basic but in 1905 it must have represented a wonderful advance over the elementary shelters provided on Johnson's engines.

Mechanical lubricators for both cylinders and axleboxes were mounted on the running plate above the bogie's rear wheel and forward of each splasher were sandbox fillers flush with it. Steam operated sanding apparatus delivered only to the leading side of both coupled wheels, it being thought unnecessary to provide this facility for reverse running. Between the coupled wheels could be seen the Compound's somewhat unusual steam brakes. These were horizontally mounted cylinders with a brake block at each end which when operated, thrust against the inside of both wheels while at the same time through a simple system of cranks and rods, drew other blocks on to their opposite sides. Due to their relatively small size, exposed position and distance from the brake valve, they suffered far more from condensation than a single large cylinder located beneath the footplate. As a result the first application from cold took a long time to take effect and even when hot, retardation was not very reassuring, fortunately the tender brakes were up to normal standards and probably provided more of the initial braking effort.

Other than the braking system, an extremely neat and tide appearance was presented below its running plate by the absence of valves and valve gear, while its round cylinder casings with long tail rods always remained a distinctive feature. In keeping with the British tradition at that time of hiding as many parts as possible, this tidiness extended to above the running plate as well, with only the vacuum brake ejectors at handrail level on the driver's side being a minor aberration on an otherwise unblemished boiler.

A variety of Deeley and Fowler tenders were fitted to Compounds and as was the usual LMS practice, these became changed from time to time so that engines did not always retain the tenders they started with. However, for simplicity I will describe the Fowler tender as supplied to the last batch built.

Both engine and tender steps possessed pleasing symmetrical curves which in addition to their aesthetic appeal also proved safe and practical in use and were far easier to mount when ladened with equipment then the single ladder type steps found on some more modern locomotives.

On first acquaintance, the interior of the cab seemed rather cluttered and was not over generous either in depth or width, the latter dimension not being helped by two large box structures projecting in from the cab sides. The reversing screw cum drivers 'seat' surmounting the left, while the fireman's, fitted with a hinged wooden lid, served as both seat and tool locker. Neither were practical as seats while running nor was it possible to adopt a comfortable stance around them; however, the fireman was able to enjoy a somewhat more relaxed posture when activities ceased. A substantial wooden platform complete with metal anti-glare shield surrounded the drivers box and further encroached on the limited footboard area.

This elevated him so that if of average height, he could see over the boiler through the cab top glass which, being hinged, enabled a useful stream of cooling air to enter when required. Vision through this and the lower glass was somewhat restricted and produced reflections at night so that drivers were obliged to spend a lot of time peering round the cab cutaway.

The reversing screw handle was rather small, did not provide much leverage, required twenty four stiff turns from full forward to full reverse and was locked in place by a separate handle which moved in a fore and aft direction. High on the cab side above the reverser was mounted a gauge which registered pressure in the LP receiver, while to the front the curved copper train vacuum pipe climbed upwards partially obstructing the lower glass. This then coiled itself behind a lagged steam pipe from the small ejector valve to connect with a standard LMS vacuum controlled steam brake located against the boiler face. Tucked under the train pipe and operating fore and aft parallel to the firebox, was the flat metal handle which opened the large ejector. Inboard from the brake valve and mounted on the boiler face was the combined steam valve and clack of the live steam injector and almost above this the small ejector control valve.

A total of five pipes from the injector and brake combined to descend in a cluster to the floor and between these and the reversing screw could be seen the umbrella handle which operated the cylinder drain cocks. In pride of place on the boiler face was a twin handled regulator and below this adjacent to each other, were the blower and steam sanding valves. Boiler water level was registered in two gauge glasses complete with brass protectors located equidistant from the centre line, these had separate shut off cocks and consequently were not as convenient to shut down in the event of a broken glass as more modern types with combined handles.

To the right, either an exhaust steam or another live steam injector valve matched the position of the live steam one and outboard from this, the control and reducing valve of the carriage warming apparatus the pressure of which was shown on a gauge attached to the cab side. Another umbrella type handle protruding from the floor adjacent to the leading end of the fireman's locker operated a single damper in the front of the ashpan while the water regulator for the exhaust injector was positioned some distance behind. The live steam injector's water regulator was inconveniently mounted low down to the rear of the reversing screw although the injector overflow could be observed when setting it. Only the exhaust injector supplied water to the slaking pipe, the control valve of which protruded from the forward end of the fireman's locker. Standard LMS hollow sliding doors were simple and efficient to use and shrouding these from above, the drip tray which was much appreciated as a repository for tea cans.

Finally a steam pressure and vacuum gauge mounted on the spectacle plate between the upper glasses completed the fairly basic instrumentation.

The Fowler tender with its nominal 5½ ton coal and 3,500 gallon water capacity provided the Compound with a useful duration quite adequate for the duties to which it was normally assigned. Most useful were the folding doors which gave safe and easy access to the coal space and avoided the hazardous practice of climbing over the tender front in order to bring coal forward on a long run. Small lockers either side of the coal doors provided stowage for personal effects and located in the recess between the driver's locker and the tender side sheet was a vertical tank gauge which, although visible in daylight, tended to be shaded from firelight at night. Atop vertical columns were the hand brake and water scoop handles which rotated in a horizontal plane and whilst they could be intrusive unless correctly 'parked' they were generally free running in use. The scoop handle located on the driver's side was restrained from accidental movement by the usual ring and safety chain. The flat shovelling plate suited firemen of average stature and conveniently situated on either side of this were the shut off cocks for the injector's water supply. Two vertical 'pegs' at the leading end and a 'U' shaped bracket fitted to the coal space brace provided a useful and secure location for the fire-irons when a certain amount of coal had been consumed, but if fully coaled they were normally carried on the back of the tender. Being of modest height, one step attached on either side of the tender back plate sufficed for the climb to the top for watering purposes, but once there, the fireman felt quite secure in the foot well since raised plating around the periphery provided a useful leverage point when pulling round a heavy water column arm. With three separate sets of Stephenson's motion inside the frames, preparation for the driver was a tedious and dirty task particularly when conducted at night. The rest of the engine, though, posed no serious problems – in fact it's exposd brake gear was very accessible. Likewise the fireman found preparation straightforward with only four sandboxes to deal with, although it was important to ensure that these were well filled.

Moving a Compound light engine was an operation which had to be approached with more care than usual, especially when manoeuvring in confined spaces such as running on or off a roundhouse turntable. As previously mentioned, the rather feeble brakes were slow acting and with twenty four turns to a fairly stiff reversing screw, rapid changes in direction were not feasible. It was therefore a wise driver who applied the brakes for a minute or two before a move was contemplated so that the cylinders would be thoroughly warm and free from condensation. The other problem was that on initially opening the regulator, steam was supplied to the low pressure cylinders via a very large LP receiver which often needed to be completely filled before the engine would start. Even with the regulator shut, such was the receiver's volume that once movement had commenced it would continue to do so for a number of revolutions and those 6ft. 9in. wheels had a big stride. Should slipping take place, and this was not an unusual event, the driving wheels then possessed more inertia than the brakes could overcome resulting in some very anxious moments for the driver.

When low on steam, following disposal, this problem was far more acute and few would argue that Compounds were possibly responsible for more unofficial exits in shed walls than any other class of comparable numbers. However, once these points had been assimilated, they could be accurately positioned provided a light and sensitive hand was used. Attached to a vacuum braked train, any deficiencies in the engine brake passed unnoticed and it was only the method of driving which was different at which stage, it is worth reiterating certain characteristics of the Compound design which was pertinent to its performance and therefore driving methods.

Its regulator was unique in as much that on opening to the half way position across its quadrant the locomotive operated exactly as a simple engine with saturated steam being supplied, albeit at slightly reduced boiler pressure, direct to the outside LP cylinders. With the outside cranks set at 90° to each other, maximum tractive effort was available for easy starting just as in a simple engine. When a specific speed had been attained and this was dependent on load, gradient &c., then the regulator would be pushed right across the quadrant, opening the main valve so that steam then flowed through the superheater to its HP cylinder. At the same time, saturated steam to the LP receiver was cut off and replaced by steam exhausted from the HP cylinder so that the engine was now working in compound mode.

Full gear on a Compound which was twelve turns of the reversing screw from mid gear, worked out at 87% for the HP cylinder and 81% for the LP cylinders, rather more generous than most simple engines which averaged about 75-78%.

The majority of drivers tended to calculate cut off by

The true size of a Compound may be appreciated rather better when placed against another familiar locomotive. 41188 is seen reliving her former 'glory days' piloting a Black 5, the boiler and grate dimensions of which are only slightly larger.

so many turns of the screw (sometimes referred to as notches, a term derived from lever reversers) from full gear. This was a far more convenient method than trying to see what was indicated on a scale which in any case would be quite invisible during hours of darkness. Drivers therefore used the colloquialism: "I pulled her up six turns or I had her on the sixth notch" which, in the case of a Compound, would be 67% HP cylinder and 55% on the LP cylinder, equivalent to about 27½% for a simple engine.

The major deficiency of short-travel short-lap valves is that if cut off is reduced to less than about 30%, port openings become too constricted to allow the free passage of steam at speed and this is especially applicable to the exhaust port which can create excessive back pressure. With these locomotives there is a particular gear position where it runs most freely and having found this the driver adjusts for speed and power requirements by altering the regulator opening.

So too with Compounds, since they also suffered the handicap of short-travel short-lap valves and, like many other engines, worked through their long lives restricted by this design limitation. On the other hand, they developed a surprising amount of power between 30 and 50 mph which is the usual speed range when slogging hard up gradients with heavy loads. This is one reason why they showed up so well during the many trials conducted during the twenties over the rigorous Settle to Carlisle section.

As previously mentioned, my principle involvement with Compounds was during 1955 by which time quite a number had been withdrawn and the remainder had been relegated to mainly secondary duties. Often though, they were rostered for these duties on a regular basis which offered the opportunity of comparing

individual engines of the same class and also against different designs performing similar tasks over a familiar line. One of these familiar lines was the quite taxing stretch between Birmingham and Leicester which, with its mixture of inclines and fast downhill runs stretched most locomotives when hauling a well laden semi-fast passenger.

With their usual load of six to eight coaches, Compounds on these trains initially accelerated steadily on the level with the cut-off being reduced a turn or so at a time as speed increased. Four exhaust beats per revolution of the 6ft. 9in. wheels was deceptive though and tended to give the impression of more leisurely acceleration than was actually the case.

At around 30 mph in normal circumstances, drivers usually changed to compounding and with the screw set at two or three turns up from full gear the engine took on a different feel. The rather ponderous exhaust note softened and it seemed as if a restraining hand had been lifted. Now with the HP cylinder producing around 50% of the total power and steam flowing much more freely through slide valves relieved of several tons pressure, the ensuing smoothness and increased vitality was quite a revelation.

Acceleration into the fifties was surprisingly brisk and effortless by which time the reverser would have been wound back to five or six turns. Provided conditions permitted, speed would increase rather more slowly but just as effortlessly until it seemed to settle in the low seventies at which point the front end deficiencies once more began to take affect. Fortunately on the Leicester turn we enjoyed the benefit of the 1:160 descent from Hinckley which enabled the effect on a Compound's free running at speed to be noted when the regulator opening was reduced. With cut-off still at around six turns (67% HP, 55% LP) it became just that little bit quicker and gained a few more mph on passing through Elmsthorpe. With my rough and ready method of checking speed with a normal wrist watch and quarter mile posts, the best figure came out at a close on 80 mph, but this was the exception rather than the rule. Over this same section they were therefore a few mph slower than the 2-6-4Ts with comparable loads and despite their small wheels, the latter never seemed at their limit, so much for modern valve events.

In view of the foregoing description of the Compound's characteristics it will be appreciated that they were not at their best on runs entailing station stops at frequent intervals and found it hard to compete with modern small wheeled simples. However, on longer journeys with a good measure of banks they performed remarkably well for a design introduced so many years ago. At any speed their ride was really quite good and I cannot recall ever having had one with knocking bearings. When well extended it became lively with intermittent, lateral movements accentuating a natural rolling gait, but there was never anything vicious about it on well laid tracks.

To those familiar with firing ex-Midland locomotives, the Compound posed no problems either, except that it required a fairly powerful swing with a long handle shovel to reach the front of its 9ft. 0in. firebox. Although the grate was about the same length as that of a Black 5, it sloped more steeply and was therefore easier to fire since there was more tendency for coal to roll forward. Fortunately, despite intrusions of the fireman's locker and driver's platform, there was just room to fire from either side although it was more convenient to work from the right. It responded best to using the traditional 'thick back, thin front' shape and it paid to keep a good depth of fire if the run involved frequent station stops and/or a good proportion of banks to climb. When on long stretches of compound running, the depth of fire could be rather less, but draughting throughout its working range was very effective and there was no difficulty in keeping the fire bright providing one adhered to the little and often principle.

The injectors were adequate although occasionally suffered from sticking clack valves which fortunately could be conveniently dealt with from the footplate but operation of the live steam one could only be achieved by disturbing the driver from his stance.

When in motion it was possible for the fireman to snatch a few minutes rest on the ample locker lid, although to look ahead while seated required the upper body to be twisted in an uncomfortable posture. A fully lagged boiler face together with a shallow cab kept temperatures to bearable levels in summer although during inclement conditions it offered scant protection from the sides and rear. Even at high speeds, though, such draughts that entered the cab were those to which Midland men were accustomed and, reduced by folding tender doors, largely passed unnoticed.

Disposal could be a long and onerous process with a Compound if the engine had been out in service for a lengthy period. Fortunately, during the fifties regular schedules were mostly of short duration, so that only specials and mail train workings resulted in engines with really rough fires.

Since only two sets of bars were used in the grate their proportions were such as to dissuade removal and therefore most crews opted to paddle the fire out in the usual manner. Typical procedure was very similar to that required by 2-6-4Ts and is described in detail in that chapter. It was rather less taxing with a Compound on two counts: first of all there was far more room for the wielding of fire-irons and secondly, it was by no means as hot. The ashpan had to be tackled from a pit beneath the locomotive and with three sets of obstructive motion dripping oil, it could be a trifle more adventurous than with some other engines. The smokebox door, fastened by six peripheral dogs, had to be opened with care since the front plating was not over generous; however, cleaning out the char was no worse than any other locomotive of comparable size.

It was difficult not to compare Compounds with the very latest designs when they were both in daily use but this is obviously unfair on the engine which preceded its successors by nearly half a century. It should be compared with its contempories and fortunately this was done on a grand scale during the formative years of the LMS with surprisingly successful results – so successful in fact that 240 were eventually built, running premier trains all over the LMS system for a number of years. Then progress in the form of long-travel long-lap valves with high degree superheat overtook them and compounding as a system seemed to fade from designer's minds in this country. Perhaps it was because of commercial pressures that Compounds were not brought up to date with modern valve gear, perhaps the other mechanical benefits were not fully understood or just disregarded, but whatever the reasons, Compounds came very near to true greatness and compounding as a system in this country could well have trod the same path as it did in France.

Chapter 8
H.G. Ivatt 2-6-0 Class 2MT

Mixed Traffic Locomotive. Introduced 1946. Total 128.

To anyone familiar with Ivatts background and interests, the layout and features of his Class 2 2-6-0 and 2-6-2T locomotives were just about what would have been expected from him. Commencing as an apprentice at Crewe Works in 1904, he gained a wide range of experience in a variety of appointments at such notable centres as Stoke, Derby and Glasgow. He was not so much an academic as a practical engineer with a deep instinctive perception of things mechanical who possessed the desire and ability to improve on established practice. This flair also extended to wider aspects of working methods such as the repair procedures of locomotives. At Derby for example, when Works Superintendent, he was largely responsible for cutting the time engines spent in Works for overhaul by over half. Over the years Ivatt contributed numerous technical improvements including not only innovative original design, but also improved methods of construction which, in additoin to saving time and labour, resulted in a more consistent and better product.

However, it was the harsh operating and maintenance conditions imposed by World War Two that showed up certain mechanical deficiencies and in 1944 under the new LMS CME, C.E. Fairburn, attention was focussed in this direction. Because it was correctly assumed that the problems caused by shortages of certain materials and skilled labour in all departments would prevail for some considerable time, measures should be put in hand to make locomotives more rugged and extend their shopping mileages. Although Ivatt was deeply involved from the outset, these measures were intensified when he succeeded Fairburn following the latter's untimely death in October 1945. Two parallel paths were pursued: firstly the attention to and refinement of detail and secondly, the testing of more fundamental developments such as roller bearings and poppet valve gear.

Taking the former path, perhaps the most significant contribution to mechanical longevity was the introduction of manganese steel liners on coupled axlebox faces and flanges and on axlebox guides and hornblocks. This modification on Black 5s nearly doubled the mileage between periodical repairs apart from adding to the comfort of crews in the meantime. With regard to more radical departures from conventional practice, Black 5s were also used as guinea pigs for comparing the benefits of roller bearing axleboxes and Caprotti poppet valve gear, not so much with a view to increasing performance but again rather to facilitate ease of maintenance and lower servicing costs.

It will be seen therefore that Ivatt was not reluctant in introducing new ideas and methods which would enable engines to spend less time under repair and also to achieve a faster turn round at depots between duties. It is not surprising, then, that Ivatt's new locomotive designs were slanted towards these aims of simplicity, accessibility and ease of servicing, whilst still incorporating all that was latest in steam engineering practice.

For many years there had been a growing need to replace ageing 0-6-0 locomotives (some dating from the 1870s) in the Class 2-4 power categories which had been 'retired' at a steady rate under Stanier's regime. During the war, the Derby Design office diagrammed a number of possible contenders, some of which were a touch bizarre to say the least, although others were merely developments of ideas proposed as long ago as 1932 when it was suggested that the Standard Fowler Class 4's boiler could be replaced by a tapered version. This idea was later taken a step further with scaled down varients for power classes 3 and 2 since the motive power people were still asking for Victorian 0-6-0s as straight replacements. Fortunately, Ivatt was able to influence matters sufficiently to establish that the new engines must be straightforward but completely modern 2-6-0s and 2-6-2 Tanks.

Production design of the Class 2 'Twins' proceeded through 1945 and the first examples were completed after Ivatt had been appointed CME in 1946. Thus materialised the first thoroughly up to date small engines specifically designed for secondary duties to appear on any British railway for many years. Moreover, with a coupled wheel base of only 13ft. 9in. and maximum axle weight of just over thirteen and a half tons, they showed an advantage in both these areas over the engines they replaced and were truly capable of going anywhere.

The general appearance of the Class 2 was neat and functional and although concessions had been made to ensure ease of maintenance and operation, it still followed traditional British lineaments. It did however, remind me in some respects of the American Baldwin Moguls imported by the Midland Railway nearly fifty years earlier. That it soon proved a success and was popular with footplate crews is hardly surprising when the improvements offered over their Victorian forebears are considered.

Although overall dimensions were comparatively modest, they were equipped with a full size cab with

An effective tender cab provided a high level of protection when running tender first and did not inconvenience the fireman during disposal since, as with all Ivatt designs, these engines were equipped with rocker grates. The long box-like structure alongside the firebox contained the fire irons which could then be withdrawn and used without the need to swing them outside the cab. The flat tender decking provided a safe platform for firemen when watering or trimming coal, a feature much appreciated in icy conditions.

side windows, the rear one sliding forward to open in the usual manner. In addition to this new standard of comfort, a tender cab was provided which not only gave excellent protection from the elements when running tender first but also much welcomed shelter if standing 'wrong road' to the wind on an exposed lay-by.

Access to the cab was via open steps attached to the tender and then through spring loaded folding doors leading on to the footplate where a conventional fall plate covered the gap between the two units. Cab layout with regard to controls and gauges closely followed current LMS practice at that time and was rather similar to a Black 5s which is described in detail in that chapter. Although perhaps out of context, it is nevertheless interesting to recall that when BR 'adopted' these Class 2s for their 78000 Standard series, one of the most obvious differences was changing the cab interior to the established BR pattern. This of course included a regulator handle operating fore and aft with its attendant rodding running alongside the boiler. However, prior to the emergence of these 78000s, 38 Class 2s were built at Darlington 1952/3 which, in the circumstances, may be regarded as a tribute to their effectiveness on lightweight duties.

Matching open steps located just behind the front buffer beam allowed easy access to quite generous footplating in front of the smokebox. This gave a secure feeling when opening the smokebox door for inspection or cleaning purposes. However, the need for the firemen to do so normally only occurred during disposal prior to a washout since, like all Ivatt engines, they were equipped with self cleaning smokeboxes.

The small diameter boiler likewise allowed for plenty of lateral room when working atop the relatively low running plate so that filling sandboxes was rendered somewhat easier than on some locomotives. The fact that there were only two either side also contributed in this respect and the rear ones, standing proud on the framing, were particularly accessible. These delivered sand to the rear of the centre coupled wheels when running in reverse, while the front sandboxes fitted between the frames and, filled by the usual tube extension, provided sand ahead of the leading coupled wheels.

Mechanical lubricators, one for axle boxes and one for cylinders, were mounted on each running plate just forward of the motion bracket. The latter supplying atomised oil to the steam chest and droplet oil to the cylinder and valve spindle and piston rod glands.

An unusual feature in the form of a box section tunnel was also fitted on the fireman's side running plate adjacent to the firebox. Extending from spectacle plate to dome, this housed the complement of fire-irons, it being considered safer stowage here since there would be no need to swing them outside the cab when put to use. These engines were, of course, equipped with rocking grates and hopper ashpans which not only made disposal a much simpler task but also reduced the need to use fire-irons when on the road to negligible proportions. As described earlier, regular use of the rocking grate facility in its limited stroke position tended to prevent the formation of clinker and also enabled excess ash to fall into the hopper below. Properly used this allowed clean fires to be maintained over greatly extended periods thus enhancing overall performance to a considerable degree.

Another not so apparent benefit of rocking grates was that there was far less chance of fire cleaning being scamped at disposal thereby reducing the possibility of engines leaving the shed with clinker in the grates on commencing a duty. It has been suggested that many firemen did not make full use of a rocking grate's limited stroke action when running due to fear that the firebox sections might jam when partially open. Personally I never encountered this problem on any locomotive so equipped no matter what quality of fuel being used. However, I suspect that it could happen on occasions.

Two live steam injectors mounted one on either side below the cab supplied feed water via the latest Ivatt clack valve arrangement located atop the front ring of the boiler well ahead of the dome. These proved quite reliable and able, when used in unison, to supply even the heaviest demands made upon the boiler.

The flat sided six wheeled tender had an inset bunker which added to the box like effect presented by straight horizontal and vertical lines and was reminiscent of those provided for Riddles' austerity 2-8-0s. However, the base of the 3,000 gallon capacity tank was at the same level as the bottom of the cab side sheets and blended quite well into the overall design. Four tons of coal provided adequate bunkerage for the duties intended and matched the water capacity, which could be supplemented on the road by use of the standard water scoop apparatus.

Access to the tank top was via a rear mounted ladder which proved easy to use and since this tank top was not particularly high and provided a flat deck upon which to walk, one felt safe and secure when watering at a column or trimming coal. The tender cab did not look at all out of place nor did it obstruct normal operations on the footplate due to the incorporation of such modern features as the rocking grate facility; giving almost tank engine-like enclosure, the cab appeared and was indeed spacious for a locomotive of this size – and proved to be incomparably, better in every respect to those of the engines it replaced.

Being 'full width', vision around and over the relatively small taper boiler was exceptionally good but at night the flat spectacle glasses produced undesirable reflections. Rearward vision too was excellent when travelling in reverse, signals and track being easily read over the low tank top and past the inset bunker without having to resort to leaning out of the cab. Only when setting back against stock was it necessary to do so.

Compared to the old 0-6-0s, the cab offered far greater protection from the elements particularly from the sides and rear. However, as with most things, there were pros and cons and with regard to crew comfort it really depended on which side of the footplate you were working and what was being done that influenced your view. In keeping with modern practice, the boiler back plate was effectively lagged, a feature much appreciated in summer by both members but it did not radiate much heat in cold weather when in motion. This was of little consequence to the fireman who apart from benefitting from regular physical exercise, performed much of that exercise in front of a white hot furnace. On the other hand, the driver was more or less static, often with his head thrust into an icy slipstream and sheltered from any furnace radiation by the anti glare shield; he therefore suffered in consequence. When static, things were rather more even and the only way either could keep reasonably warm was by constant visits to the open firedoors.

Both driver and fireman were provided with wood faced tip-up seats attached to the cab side sheets which, when not in use, gave unobstructed access to the side windows. These were quite satisfactory when at work and as far as the driver was concerned, a distinct improvement on the small 'board' placed over the reversing screw on 2P 4-4-0s and 4F 0-6-0s. When it came to relaxing though, they in no way compared to the large tool box lids provided for the firemen on these engines; but then perhaps he deserved the luxury of being able to lay down more than his driver.

Controls were laid out as per current LMS practice at that time with a centrally mounted regulator operating in the conventional manner. Immediatley in front of the driver was the reversing screw above which were mounted the large and small ejector valves, while a standard LMS vacuum controlled steam brake valve was located within easy reach of his right hand.

A main steam manifold fitted above the boiler inside the cab supplied all auxiliary equipment except for the blower. Pipe runs to these followed the usual pattern and all could be isolated by a central shut off plug on the manifold. Gauges were the normal boiler pressure and carriage warming apparatus pressure on the fireman's side while the driver only had the vacuum gauge before him. Two standard LMS water gauges with combined shut off cocks indicated boiler water level and were illuminated at night by a standard rape oil fuelled gauge lamp. Access to the 17.5 sq.ft. sloping grate was via hollow sliding firedoors below which was located a small flip up combustion plate.

Preparation of these little 2MTs posed few problems for the driver, designed as they were with visibility and accessibility in mind. Likewise the fireman had a relatively easy time since the low running plate and only four very accessible sandboxes entailed the minimum of climbing. Nor did scaling the short ladder to the tank decking present much of an obstacle for watering and coal trimming purposes.

Driving was quite a delight, particularly when compared to the Victorian engines they replaced. Small engines do not necessarily have light controls, but those of the 2MTs required no great effort and were quite sensitive in operation. Even when heading a Passenger train at its load limit, no special techniques were needed getting under way and providing cut offs were not reduced too early, then acceleration was extremely lively. Admittedly their small 5ft. 0in. diameter coupled wheels assisted in this respect but the excellent valve and cylinder porting proved very capable of handling high volumes of steam enabling longish cut offs to be used even at relatively high speeds. However, under suitable conditions they were very happy running at around 20% with a wide open regulator when they could romp along in the seventies without showing any sign of distress. At this pace, the ride could be described as lively, but was in no way uncomfortable for either member of the crew and compared very favourably to that of say a 4F at some 15 mph less.

In 1950 a Class 2 was sent to the Swindon test plant with a view to tuning up Ivatt's original draughting design. The LMS chimney proportions were changed from 1ft. 1½in. diameter at the choke and 1ft. 5in. at the top, to 1ft. 0in. and 1ft. 2in. respectively, together with some slight adjustments in vertical height. According to E.S. Cox these modifications raised the maximum evaporation from 9,850lb, of water per hour to 14,000lb using Blidworth grade two coal. Apparently during road trials in this form the little engine was able to lift a 455 ton, 15 coach train up nearly five miles of 1 in 300 between Little Somerford and Badminton at a minimum speed of 40mph. Here, at a steam rate of 13,378lbs per hour it was using coal at 2,501lbs per hour, a consumption figure few experienced firemen would find difficult to maintain even over lengthy periods. On this occasion it was exerting 625 drawbar hp at 42% cut off, coal per dbhp hour being 3.6lbs, steam temperature 585° and boiler efficiency 55%.

Performance of such quality rather belies the 2MT power classification given to these fine little locomotives, nor was this just an isolated instance. The author's description of a particularly inspired run from Birmingham New Street to Derby in 'Saltley Firing Days', thoroughly endorses the attributes of these engines and their suitability for use on stopping passenger trains.

Little physical effort was needed to fire the comparatively short sloping grate which in keeping with this design responded best to a well filled back reducing to just sufficient thickness at the front to prevent holes forming in the firebed. Indeed when working hard it was only necessary to deliver coal just over the raised combustion plate when the combined action of blast and vibration would feed the forward half. However, certain elementary precautions had to be borne in mind, particularly when building up the fire before starting a run. Because of the small grate area it was all too easy to over fill or 'charge' the firebox with unburned coal in a short space of time. With best quality cobbles this action would not prove irredeemable providing sufficient time was available for the coal to burn through before any serious work was required. However, if the fuel was of poor quality and contained a high percentage of slack, a clogged and therefore dead fire would often result. Then, despite desperate use of the fire-irons, a considerable period would elapse before it became thoroughly burned through and capable of supplying steam in quantity.

When drivers became aware that all was not well in the steam generating department they not unnaturally tended to work the engine as lightly as possible, but this only exacerbated the problem which usually resulted in the train limping along in an uncertain manner with inevitable loss of time. From experiences gained when booked with a particularly heavy-handed driver, I found that the cure for a clogged fire was in fact just the opposite — a right good 'thrashing' usually rectified matters!

Admittedly the pressure gauge needle initially adopted a downward swing and the boiler had to be mortgaged more than somewhat, but then the fierce blast took effect drawing sufficient volume of air through the firebed for proper combustion to take place. Indeed these little 2MTs responded better than most to what might be considered brutal working, in fact the harsher they were treated the more they seemed to like it. Certainly I can never recall being short of steam on any duty with the aforesaid driver. There was also another factor with these 2MTs which possibly effected the method of working.

Ex-Midland drivers were, on the whole, used to working light trains in former days and if loadings were even slightly over the limit they resorted to double heading. As a consequence, drivers treated their charges rather gently since excessive exhaust noise was considered uncouth and not in keeping with a refined upbringing. However, when opened up these 2MTs produced a sound like the crack of a Bofors gun which was entirely out of all proportion to their size. Therefore as with Caprotti 5s, there was a tendency to reduce the cut off too quickly and then run them at a shorter percentage than was strictly desirable for optimum results. Most ex-LNWR drivers, on the other hand, felt that they were honour bound to take anything that happened to be attached to their drawbar and had no inhibitions whatsoever in this direction. On the contrary, many seemed to take a great delight in making as much racket as possible, even though it gave their firemen a little more exercise – and with these eager little locomotives they had the ideal vehicle in which to indulge such whims.

Despite the tender cab enclosure, firemen found they had plenty of room in which to prosecute their activities. In keeping with old Midland Railway and LMS traditions, both firehole and shovelling plate were at the same sensible height above the footboards which for a person of average stature required only the minimum of bending thus reducing back fatigue. Although designed to be fired from the right hand side there was sufficient space to stand beside the driver if the fireman felt so inclined, although with such a short grate there was no need to deliver a hefty swing in order to place coal at the front end. Even those not yet adept at firing 'left handed' had few problems with these locomotives. Either a short or long handled shovel could be used but the latter were generally preferred since with its greater reach a more solid stance could be adopted and there were no footplate obstructions to inhibit movements.

As with Stanier tenders, both handbrake and water scoop handles were vertically mounted on the tender front plate; they were unobtrusive, smooth in operation and the latter was held in place by the usual ring and safety chain. Folding doors, which when opened could be secured by a simple latch, gave easy access to the self-trimming coal space.

As previously mentioned, fire-irons were stowed in a compartment formed along the running plate in front of the fireman. This sensible arrangement allowed them to be withdrawn in the correct alignment for use and therefore avoided the need to swing them round beyond the sides of the cab which was the case when stored on the tender. Short grates naturally required only short fire-irons, particularly when that grate was of the rocking

variety, and therefore such an arrangement could be readily adopted on these engines.

Disposal of these 2MTs was an extremely easy and speedy operation requiring little effort or skill. The method of fire cleaning with a rocking grate has been described earlier and so far as the fireman was concerned this part of the disposal sequence took but a few minutes.

Coaling of the small inset bunker required rather more care than with full width tenders if spillage was to be avoided, but the platform provided by the flat topped tank allowed 'hand' stacking to be accomplished in safety if extra capacity was required for a special duty. As with preparation, the driver's final examination was simplified by the visibility and accessibility of the more important components and was as much appreciated by them as rocking grates were by firemen.

It will be deduced from the foregoing therefore, that not only did the 2MT offer new and wider possibilities to the operating department, they were also very acceptable to their crews whether out on the road in traffic, or being serviced on the shed.

One could be unkind and say that almost any locomotive would be an improvement on the machines they replaced and to some extent this may be true. However, locomen are traditionally conservative by inclination and new engines have to earn their respect. That these little Ivatt Moguls did so on pure merit in a short space of time is ample testimony to the excellence of their design, a design which BR considered worthy of replicating, except in minor detail, for inclusion in their range of Standard locomotives.

The reasons for this general acceptance are not hard to find. Their appearance despite some innovations, was modern but conventional enough not to offend those nurtured on traditional ideas. They were lively performers having excellent powers of acceleration, pulled well on banks and yet ran freely at speed while at the same time giving a tolerable ride. Their spacious cabs offered almost tank engine-like protection from the elements and allowed first class vision both fore and aft. Firemen too were well catered for since, if operated correctly, they steamed freely without excessive physical effort. And when it came to disposal, that onerous task was rendered almost pleasant since they were perhaps the simplest of all LMS locomotives to service.

With so many attributes they could not fail to be a success and it gives much relief to note that a number of these fine little locomotives have been saved from the scrap yards and are now running in regular service on preserved lines.

Introduced 1947. Total 162.

FOR many years a replacement for the ubiquitous Fowler 4F 0-6-0 had been contemplated and E.S. Cox lists in his Locomotive Panorama Vol. 1 no less than eight diagrams of suggested designs prepared between 1932 and 1944. These ranged from a straightforward taper boiler replacement through various modified versions of 2-6-4 tanks to an 0-6-0 with bar frames, wide firebox, Allen valve gear and a stove pipe chimney.

However, as outlined in the chapter dealing with the 2MT 2-6-0s, Ivatt was able to bring his sound engineering judgment and influence to bear and by 1945 the proposed Class 4 2-6-0 looked rather like a larger version of the Class 2 as built. Then, as Cox succinctly puts it "Coleman's wild men set about it again", so that when it eventualy appeared in 1947 the style displayed a strong transatlantic influence which left the more staid eyes of British traditionalists somewhat aghast. Perhaps the high running plate and even the indecent exposure of pipes and rodding might have been tolerated but certainly not the large excrescence atop its smokebox which served at the chimney. This huge double chimney not only seemed completely out of proportion to the rest of the locomotive but it was of a singularly unattractive shape. Its excessive dimensions were occasioned by the fact that it catered for a double exhaust in which the exit tips were splayed outwards at an angle instead of the normal vertical arrangement. It might have given some purists a certain degree of satisfaction to learn that when these engines were put into service their draughting was found to be far from satisfactory, indeed they soon gained an unenviable reputation for poor steaming.

These same purists may then have given a sigh of relief when Derby investigated the problem and in due course produced a much more handsome single chimney

system which also achieved the desired result. Replacement of the offending double chimneys fitted to the original fifty engines was put in hand and new manufacture from 43050 onwards possessed the single version which without doubt transformed their appearance to a remarkable degree. Not that development stopped there, because in 1951 an example was sent to the Swindon Test Plant so that Sam Ell could bring his particular talents to bear. By merely reducing the chimney choke from 1ft. 2¼in. to 1ft. ¾in. and altering the taper slightly, a very considerable improvement was achieved. In fact it raised the maximum continuous steaming rate by no less than 89% and now at last properly draughted, the excellent boiler was able to reach its full potential.

Aesthetic appeal, or rather lack of it apart, the Class 4 design did possess a certain air of functional efficiency and many of its innovations and features were perpetuated in the BR range of locomotives which followed. In this respect there is some justification in regarding it as the blueprint for the final expression of steam on British Railways. As with the 2MT it too was adopted with only minor changes to become a BR Standard design while during the interim some 82 examples were built at Doncaster and Darlington for use on their own regions.

It must be borne in mind that from the outset these locomotives were designed with ease of maintenance and operation as a high priority and still being in a period of general austerity, less thought was given to the niceties of appearance. At first sight, possibly the most notable departure from previous LMS practice was the very high running plate attached to the boiler flanks rather than the framing which, together with the wheels, was left completely exposed and therefore

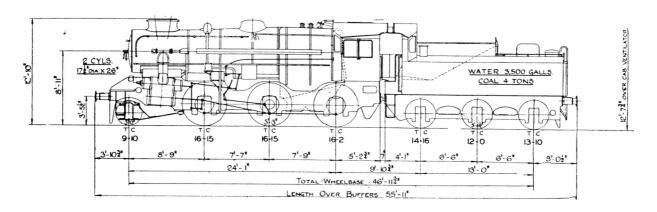

extremely accessible. The generously sized twin side window cab with its angled weather boards looked streamlined and thoroughly modern.

A regulator handle working in a fore and aft plane delivered its action via external rodding running from the front of the cab alongside the boiler to a point just below the dome. Another departure from former practice was that of mounting the main steam manifold over the firebox outside the cab and running the steam supply pipes externally to the injectors which were both mounted below the cab on the fireman's side. Feed water from these entered the boiler via top clack valves located in the current Ivatt position well forward of the dome. Mechanical lubricators for cylinders and axleboxes were attached one either side to extensions of the motion brackets and their tops were flush with the running plate. Unlike the 2MT, a reversion was made to the usual steam sanding disposition where sand was delivered to the front of the leading and centre coupled wheels and the rear of the latter.

At 3,500 gallons the tender tank had rather greater capacity than its smaller stablemate but in most other respect the tender was very similar in concept. It likewise possessed an inset bunker carrying the same four tons of coal and had a neat tender cab albeit with angled spectacle plates which matched those of the cab. The tank was also angled inwards towards the top, a feature which may look pleasing but was definitely not appreciated by firemen since working up there was rendered more precarious. However the tender did allow excellent rearward vision of signals and when setting back onto stock.

As with the 2MTs, open frame steps attached to the tender led to the footplate which was enclosed by folding doors and here, departures from previous LMS practice were very noticeable. Perhaps the most obvious was that two regulator handles, situated one either side of the cab and attached to a common transverse rod, were provided so that operation could be accomplished from whichever position the driver chose. Originally, the Standard LMS vacuum controlled steam brake was similarly interlinked, but this feature was removed at an early stage although the second regulator handle remained.

The reason for these innovations was never entirely clear because although the ability to drive from either side was theoretically sound, most drivers seldom took advantage of it and a hefty metal bar making sudden, unexpected movements in the dark could be hazardous to the fireman as I can painfully testify.

Having the main steam manifold placed outside the cab allowed for a neat and uncluttered boiler face which

added to the air of spaciousness. Whilst the driver's controls were conventionally arranged, the fireman was treated to a new experience by having the two injector steam valves and water regulator handles within easy reach while still seated. These injectors possessed a very high flow rate in relation to boiler capacity and even with only one in use, one could literally observe the water level rising up the gauge glasses.

Also new were the damper controls consisting of a brass handwheel through the centre of which ran a threaded rod connected to the damper levers. These could be very finely adjusted and once set would not move no matter how much vibration they were subjected to. As an added bonus, these damper wheels which projected from the floor, doubled up as very comfortable foot rests for firemen. Like the 2MT, fire-irons were housed in a convenient tunnel running at footplate level alongside the firebox on the fireman's side, this of course had the same advantages as already discussed in the previous chapter.

Mounted at a convenient height were LMS hollow sliding firedoors and below these, the rocking grate spigots and catches could be found. The portable lever for operating both grate and hopper ashpan was retained by efficient clips attached to the cab side beneath the fireman's seat. This and the driver's was of the current wood-faced tilt-up type, being tolerably comfortable and allowing good access to the side windows. At the leading edge of the sliding side window was fitted an effective windshield which proved a great boon when viewing ahead, particularly in inclement weather; it could also be folded flat along the cabside when not in use.

Instrumentation consisted of two water level gauge glasses with combined shut off cocks, boiler and carriage warming apparatus pressure gauges on the fireman's side with the usual vacuum gauge ahead of the driver. A large sliding ventilator in the cab roof helped to keep temperatures bearable despite the almost total enclosure although of course it let rain in just as effectively as it let heat out. The tender layout was similar to that of the smaller Mogul except that the spectacle plates were angled which helped to prevent unwanted reflections at night.

When the Ivatt 4MT first appeared in double chimney form its draughting was less than satisfactory and since bad news always spreads rapidly, it did not take long for its reputation of inadequate steaming to become widely known. At the time I joined BR in February 1950, some of these double chimney examples were still to be seen and were viewed with askance except by disposal crews. Human nature being what it is, even those with single chimney modifications were regarded with suspicion and because of this expectation of trouble, problems on the road did arise.

I have already mentioned what could go wrong with 2MTs when the firebox was over charged with poor quality coal and the same applied to the Class 4s. Working the engine lightly only exacerbated the situation and because of the injector's remarkable flow rate they could only be used in short bursts.

It was all too easy forget momentarily that one injector was on, whilst engaged in some other essential activity – and realisation only dawned on finding how much water had been delivered to the boiler during the short space of time involved. This of course caused an equally rapid reduction in boiler pressure which, because of the poor combustion conditions prevailing, was proving difficult to maintain. Unfortunately no amount of thrashing with the double chimney version would produce sufficient draught to rectify this type of firing error, although the modified type responded quite well if only drivers could bring themselves to do so.

It took some time though for crews to become familiar with their traits and to realise that the single chimneys had effected a considerable improvement and then it was a case of gaining sufficient confidence to properly exploit the full potential of their new charges.

For the driver, preparation was a relatively clean and straightforward task since everything had been designed with accessibility in mind. There was of course no inside motion to become entangled with, most items that required inspection were in full view and there was a wide use made of grease lubrication to pin joints in the motion, suspension and brake system.

Preparation was fairly typical for this size of engine as far as the fireman was concerned. The high running plate involved somewhat more climbing when filling sandboxes and checking the mechanical lubricators, but this was barely noticed. Admittedly there were two extra spectacle glasses to clean, but the feature I was not entirely happy about was the sloping sides of the tank top. A ladder offset to left (platform) side at the back of the tender was simple enough to climb but once up there one encountered a problem. In order to grasp a water column chain which was provided to enable the column arm to be swung into position, it was usual to stand at the extreme edge of the tender. Due to its upward slope that edge was at least a foot inboard so that the fireman had to lean well forward in order to obtain it. Leaning over that sloping edge with the ground some fifteen feet below ones eye level definitely instilled a feeling of insecurity, even in daylight. In foul weather on a dark night when the tank top could be encrusted with

snow or ice, the task was made doubly hazardous and worst of all were the columns which merely had a hose attached to the top. These heavy leather 'bags' required to dragged up hand over hand until in position, a difficult enough procedure even when standing in the relative safety of the tank wells found on former designs.

This potential danger must have been realised because when BR versions of inset bunker tenders were brought out they had large footblocks mounted on their rear flanks and whilst not the perfect answer, they did help.

Although initially, the Ivatt Class 4 was berated because of its boiler's inability to produce sufficient steam, even the most critical driver had to concede that they were an exceedingly lively locomotive. The driver's first acquaintance was usually with a light engine and the response to opening the fore and aft regulator which had a very free action was almost alarming.

They set off with an alacrity hitherto not previously encountered, even better than the 2-6-4Ts, which were no slouches by any means. No doubt its good power to weight ratio, small 5ft. 3in. couple wheels, excellent cylinder design, adequate adhesion and light controls all contributed to the overall impression of a machine eager to get to grips with the job in hand. Fortunately the braking system with twin blocks on the coupled wheels was well up to standard and could easily lock the wheels if injudiciously used. Forward vision over and around the taper boiler from the full width cab was good and the angled spectacle glasses which considerably reduced reflections at night were much appreciated.

As with the smaller mogul, running tender first was rendered much more tolerable by the rear cab enclosure, since it not only kept the elements at bay but also allowed observation of signals from a seated position past the inset bunker. However in cold weather, drivers did complain of draughts when running in either direction. Having entered the cab, these draughts attacked him from directions he had not previously experienced and were therefore immediately noticeable. The more active fireman was not so badly affected although even he was aware of the gale which blew in from the partially empty bunker when travelling in reverse at speed.

Most of my experience with these 4MTs was on stopping passenger trains, particularly on that delightfully exciting stretch of mainly single line from Barnt Green to Ashchurch via Redditch. Short fast sections of undulating track, liberally interspersed with quite severe gradients, provided a good testing ground where comparisons of engine performance could be assessed. Loaded with up to six bogies (approximately 200 tons gross) on quite a tight schedule was the type of duty on which these engines excelled. The superb Fowler 2-6-4Ts had been working these branch line stopping trains for many years with consummate ease, but their numbers were limited and with the need to meet increased traffic demands, the new moguls were the preferred choice. On purely passenger work over this line there was little to choose overall between the 4MTs and the big tank engines, merely a case of swings and roundabouts. With an extra 1400lbs of tractive effort and smaller coupled wheels, the 2-6-0 had the edge in pure acceleration and climbing ability. On the other hand the tank engine seemed far less fussy at higher speeds and no matter how brutally driven it could not be winded. As would be expected the 2-6-4 gave a better ride and generally provided a higher level of comfort although they could be intolerably hot in summer and were more awkward to fire. Where the mogul won hands down was in respect of its greater endurance, ease of servicing giving a quick turn-round and an ability to handle even loose-coupled freight trains with equal competence. These attributes gave the operating department far wider scope when arranging work diagrams and allowed for much more intensive use of a particular locomotive. This could be extremely useful on branch lines where there were few loco depots, when perhaps an engine would work a late evening passenger train out and then return at night with a freight duty. It must be borne in mind that during the 1950s there was more traffic moving by rail than could be comfortably handled and once it was realised that such a versatile locomotive existed then entirely new schedules were drawn up to suit, or so it seemed.

Once over their initial steaming problems, loco crews' attitudes changed, complaints faded away and cautious acceptance was in many instances replaced by a degree of enthusiasm one would not have thought possible in their early days. Thus, with the comforting assurance that in general, boiler pressure could be maintained at maximum level, drivers were able to concentrate on extracting the desired performance from them. So, taking a stopping passenger train of 170-200 tons gross as a typical example, let us see how they faired on the road.

As previously mentioned the regulator had a rather easy action, but even so, starting proved no problem providing the driver was not ham-handed or impatient. Obviously getting under way on a gradient, or if the rail was very slippery, required a more sensitive touch, but then this was so with all engines. However, should the regulator be opened too suddenly then a violent slip could be readily induced even on a dry rail. Fortunately the 4MTs sanding equipment always seemed to function rather better than most with the result that lack of adhesion rarely gave concern. This initial impression of eagerness persisted as the regulator was progressively opened and was no doubt enhancd by the delightfully sharp, rapid exhaust bark derived from wheels of only 5ft. 3in. diameter. Excellent porting allowed quite long cut-offs to be used until normal running speeds had been attained, this asset contributing much to its robust powers of acceleration.

Unless on a steep rising gradient, a wide open regulator was rarely used and gradual progressive linking up of the reverser was sufficient to maintain optimum efficiency in the cylinders and the desired increase in pace with minimum use of steam. Under suitable conditions on level track they would readily achieve the high sixties which was about the maximum attainable on branch lines where distances between stations was rather short. However, where longer runs permitted, a further 10mph could be added without the engine showing any signs of stress, although the already lively ride then became distinctly so with lateral kicks and oscillations being particularly noticeable. Whilst this ride quality could be considered fairly typical for a modern 2-6-0, I suspect that it was the cavorting footplate rather than any lack of ability on the engine's part that curbed the driver's enthusiasm to push them to higher speeds.

As with most modern LMS designs using long-lap long-travel valve gear, they were fairly tolerant to different driving techniques and would respond well when driven with a partially open regulator related to a longish cut-off. Because of the greater smoothness this method imparted, it was often resorted to when nursing a worn engine and of course with non-fitted freight trains where speeds were normally low. At the upper end though, they were equally happy working expansively with a wide open regulator and at around 15-20% cut-off when they would run very freely indeed.

A fully lagged boiler face complete with adequate anti-glare shield ensured the driver was kept reasonably cool in summer and as frozen as with any other engine sporting these features, in winter. The cab though, as previously mentioned offered almost tank engine-like protection from the elements even if it caused his interest in new draughts to be stimulated more than somewhat.

By and large the 4MT was a pleasant, even exciting machine to drive; in fact, when compared to the dated 0-6-0 they were intended to replace, it was rather like changing from a riding school hack to a thoroughbred eventing horse.

Once its draughting had been modified, firing the mogul posed no particular problems. At 23 sq.ft., the sloping grate had only 2 sq.ft. more area than the Fowler 4F and if you could fire a 4F then you could equally well fire the 4MTs since the techniques required were very similar. As usual with this type of grate, a thick body of fire was carried in the back corners and under the firehole, from where it sloped gradually down to just a few inches depth at the front. In keeping with current LMS practice, a small combustion plate hinged below the firehole contributed to efficiency when maximum output was needed, although sadly not all firemen took advantage of this useful fitting. There was plenty of room in the spacious cab to fire from either side and although the front of the grate could be reached without undue effort a long handled shovel was always preferred.

Providing all the standard rules relating to firing were adhered to, then with average quality fuel, reliable steaming could be maintained for the duration of a run. Regular use of the rocking grate facility in partial stroke mode assisted considerably in achieving this. In relation to work performed both fuel and water consumption proved extremely economical enhancing its already useful endurance. The super efficient injectors had to be treated with respect and only used in short bursts, but once the technique had been acquired it was comforting to know the boiler could be filled so quickly.

With a conventional mobile fall plate betwixt engine and tender, the fireman's sense of balance was tested to the limit when travelling near maximum speed, but the act of firing never became hazardous. Access to the modest coal space via standard folding doors could be accomplished in complete safety and dragging coal forward to the shovelling area did not prove a particularly stenuous activity. Although the water scoop was normally quite light to use the tender water gauge was not particularly visible at night and over filling could easily occur, but this was so with most pre-BR tenders. And as with all locomotives fitted with rocking grates, hopper ashpans and self cleaning smokeboxes, disposal was almost a pleasure and required only a few minutes work.

How well did Ivatt's 4MT fill it's intended role as a replacement for the Fowler 4F? With only 162 example built (and even if the 115 BR 76000 Class are added) they did not, nor could not replace the 772 old stalwarts which went about their mundane business until 1966 by which time a number of the moguls had also been withdrawn.

Once it was appreciated how much improvement had been incorporated during some 36 years of steam locomotive development, the Operating Department realised that these new engines were far too good and versatile to be used just as a straight replacement for 4F activity. It has already been mentioned that traffic density was at a very high level during the late forties and early fifties so that all the 4Fs were fully occupied with the work they had coped with for many years. Some of the duties admittedly were middle distance vacuum fitted express freights and even some passenger work when more suitable motive power was not available, but no one would deny that they were on their limit performing these tasks and it was often a case of just struggling through. With the quality of coal and general maintenance far below pre-war standard this struggling did not favour good economy nor was it comfortable for the crews trying to maintain schedules in such conditions.

So whilst the Ivatt engines did not oust 4Fs from their traditional work except for a few more exacting duties, they did, in many instances, take over from or at least become an alternative to 2P 4-4-0, 4P Compound 4-4-0, 4P 2-6-4Ts and even 2-6-0 Crabs. Needless to say they executed these tasks efficiently and with a high degree of economy while at the same time providing their crews with an unaccustomed level of comfort and convenience. Moreover, full advantage was taken of their reverse running ability and quick servicing facilities so that new, more intensive operating was diagrammed.

Had steam traction continued for another decade or so then perhaps they would have adopted their replacement role as more 4Fs were withdrawn. However, even that possibility is doubtful since with the ongoing demand for heavier and faster services and with track improvements to make this possible, larger, more powerful more versatile designs were already being prepared.

The Ivatt 4MT was therefore an engine of its time, ideally suited to that exciting if austere period of British Railway history. Built to suit changed conditions, it successfully fitted an important niche and with its many innovations pioneered the way for better things to come.

Chapter 10

2-6-0 5P5F (Crab)

Introduced 1926. Total 245.

A NEW design of locomotive usually arose from some specific operating requirement motivated by a need for improved profitability. Reduced working hours and consequent increased material costs following the First World War had created pressures to maximise efficiency and one way of achieving this would be the more intensive use of locomotives. However, it really hinged on an engine's versatility, for the more able it was to operate both passenger and freight trains with equal facility the easier it could be incorporated into wide ranging and even opportunist working diagrams. Mixed Traffic 2-6-0s with coupled wheels between 5ft. 6in. and 5ft. 9in. had already appeared on the other grouped companies and were proving to be extremely useful, but despite inheriting nearly four hundred different classes of locomotives in 1923, the LMS did not have anything suitable for development in this category as a standard locomotive.

George Hughes the CME, was therefore instructed to formulate his proposals and consequently conducted a quick review of what was being progressed in the various pre-grouping Drawing Offices at the time. It appeared that St. Rollox had a design well in hand which fitted the general concept but unfortunately in terms of overall size would not suit the rather restricted Midland loading gauge and, moreover, its axle weights would impose severe limitations on general route availability. Having decided to start afresh it took, according to E.S. Cox, some nine different proposals and twelve months before the necessary compromise between size, power and availability was reached and the final diagram agreed.

Because of Hughes insistence that boiler pressures should not exceed 180 psi, relatively large cylinders 21in. x 26in. were required to achieve the desired power and so that these should meet the necessary loading gauge restrictions, they had to be steeply inclined. This in turn dictated the very high running plate at the front and which, at the time, proved a distinctive if controversial feature of the design.

The cylinders and valve gear were entirely new and followed the very latest American practice, incorporating long-travel (6⅜in.) long-lap (1½in.) 11in. diameter valve pistons with generous porting. Another departure from Horwich tradition was the fitting of flexible, small cross section piston rings instead of the previous stiff thick ones. Also of American origin was the extremely robust Walschaerts valve gear, largely based upon

Pennsylvania Railroad layout and details, which gave very accurate and reliable steam distribution.

The new parallel boiler, designated 9HS was some 3¾in. longer and 8in. greater diameter than the Compound's 9AS and while its firebox shared the same 9ft. 0in. length, it possessed an additional 13 sq.ft. surface area. However, the grate area at 27.5 sq.ft. was slightly less and had a similar arrangement consisting of two sets of large firebars.

The stout plate frame, in time, proved to be very trouble free and although its coupled wheels conformed to the now sacred Midland 8ft. 0in. + 8ft. 6in. spacing, the axle boxes were of extremely substantial construction. With so many new features derived from the latest current developments, success was virtually guaranteed and for the first time the LMS possessed a locomotive equal to just about anything within its power class.

Regrettably Hughes retired before the first example had been completed which allowed his successor Sir Henry Fowler to bring Midland influences to bear and make a number of changes. These included the fitting of Derby injectors with combined steam valve and clack and the Midland vacuum controlled steam brake with its associated boiler mounted ejectors. Such changes were perhaps understandable in the interests of standardisation, but what tends to deny logic was Fowler's insistence on replacing the original L & Y style tender with one of his own standard units some 18in. narrower. This mis-match not only looked incongruous but it was the source of discomfort for countless engine crews for the entire lives of these engines.

Even in 1950 when I first encountered a 'Crab' (as they were soon nicknamed), they still gave the appearance of a modern locomotive, in fact high running plates were just coming back into fashion which rather re-enforced the impression. Viewed from a front angle in particular, the large diameter boiler together with equally large prominent cylinders presented a look of hunky power emphasised in no small measure by fully exposed coupled wheels of modest size. The gracefully curved Belpaire firebox blended neatly with a full width twin side window cab of handsome proportions and style the like of which had never been seen on the Midland before. Indeed it is not hard to imagine that quite a few eyebrows were raised on that region where they were mainly familiar with traditional inside cylinder designs of more moderate dimensions.

From a side view the Fowler tender did not seem too much out of place since the cab bottom aligned with the tank base and their steps were also compatible. In fact few would disagree that the Crab looked at its best from the side with the squat chimney and dome intensifying the impression of powerful utility.

Originally, steam sanding apparatus delivered only to the outside of the leading and trailing coupled wheels, but later this was altered to the more usual layout of supplying sand to the front side of the leading and centre couple wheels and the rear side of the latter when in reverse. Another feature altered later was the front pony truck brake. Stanier did not approve of brakes fitted to bogies or pony trucks and consequently they were removed from all engines so equipped. With being suddenly confronted with so many alien aspects, Midland observers may not have noticed the pop safety valves which were positioned side by side rather than in line, nor the reversing rod angled upwards towards the weight shaft, but whatever else, Crabs undoubtedly presented a unique picture on the LMS and however viewed, their outline was quite unmistakeable.

As with all outside two-cylinder engines, drivers found preparation relatively clean and straightforward although the upper parts of the motion could be a bit of a stretch for men of modest stature. There were, of course, the usual number of trimmings and pin joints calling for attention, but on the whole oiling a Crab was far more preferable to oiling a 4F. Nor were there any major difficulties for the fireman because, although the engine was above average size, everything which concerned him was very accessible.

As a cleaner I found climbing over a Crab quicker and safer than most, the high running plate in particular giving easy access to smokebox and boiler top. Therefore an extra step up the running plate passed unnoticed when filling sandboxes, the tops of which were flush with the ample foot framing, or checking the cylinder and axle box mechanical lubricators nestling behind its first downward curve. Admittedly the large diameter smokebox door required eight dogs to secure it, but this was but a minutes work with a 7/8in. spanner and there was ample room on the front framing to move in safety.

Mounting the cab steps was relatively easy, even when laden with tools or equipment and passage on to the footplate was in no way obstructed by tender side doors which folded neatly behind the uprights. The large full width cab must have been quite an experience to former Midland men in 1926 because, although in my time we were familiar with Stanier's generous designs, it still compared favourably in terms of space. Indeed the impression of airiness was no doubt enhanced by the discrepancy in size between the tender and engine. The fact that the edge of the cab projected some 9in. beyond the tank side sheets was probably the first thing crews noticed since it gave a certain feeling of insecurity until the side doors were closed. As is often the case, this particular aberration had its pros and cons. When travelling tender first or standing wrong way to the wind especially during inclement weather, the only dry spot on the footplate was a small area immediately in front of the firedoors and even if no precipitation was falling it could be a cold and draughty experience. On the other hand when running forwards the tender deflected fewer uncomfortable eddies around the drivers posterior, while the gap certainly improved vision when setting back onto stock.

To Midland eyes, probably the next feature to be noticed were the L & Y style seats which consisted of steel tubes sprouting from the footboards and topped with substantial wood discs. They did not look at all inviting and as one of my drivers succinctly put it "they're like ruddy toadstools"; however, looks were deceiving and the seats proved quite convenient and comfortable. Following the seats, attention was then drawn to the reversing screw which also bore the hallmark of L & Y practice. This was operated by a wheel, which with its spiral spokes, appeared very old fashioned and rather like a Victorian mangle. It was locked in position by a separate spring loaded catch, similar to that of a Compound, but the wheel moved freely and was easy to use, although its sector scale was not very visible especially at night.

Apparently Horwich had planned to incorporate a steam manifold, 'drowned' injectors and top feed and the fully lagged boiler face certainly seemed to have been designed for different fittings to the Midland ones it actually received. The layout therefore was very similar to that described for the Fowler 2-6-4T but being larger, it accommodated the pipe runs and fittings more readily and appeared less cluttered.

While Crabs normally featured sliding firehole doors, some examples ran with the Derby twin flap arrangement in which one plate covering about two thirds of the firehole area was hinged at the bottom and secured when in position by a latch and chain. The upper third was closed by an adjustable flap hinged from the top which possessed the useful advantage of reducing upward glare while allowing variable quantities of secondary air to enter the firebox. Midland crews were of course familiar with these doors but they were probably more suited to shorter, steeply sloping grates and did not possess the infinitely variably quick action of sliding doors.

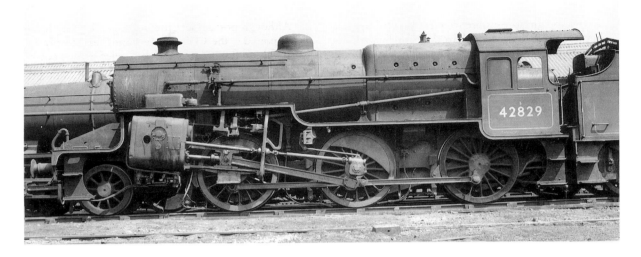

The five Lentz (and later Reidinger modified) poppet valve versions performed reliably over the years, showing slight improvements in economy and lower maintenance costs. Crabs usually looked at their best when viewed from the side when the mis-match with their Fowler tenders was less obvious.

Large flat spectacle glasses allowed reasonable vision directly ahead but it was not possible to see over or around the large diameter parallel boiler and its high running plate obstructed the view immediately in front of the buffer beam. Being flat they also gave rise to unwanted reflections at night, which was another reason why the drivers spent much of their time peering round the cab side. Unfortunately when so doing they did not have the benefit of those excellent windshields which was a feature of Stanier, Ivatt and BR locomotives.

As with all engines equipped with standard LMS vacuum controlled steam brakes it was necessary to open the small ejector in order to obtain automatic brake release even when moving light engine.

The Crab's regulator was rather different from most in as much that the pilot valve porting only permitted a modest steam flow, so that even when the regulator was half way across its quadrant steam chest pressure was lower than normal. In enginemen's terms it was said to have 'a weak first valve' and if any serious work was contemplated the second valve had to be used.

Coupled with its long handle, this attribute endowed extraordinary sensitivity to the regulator, permitting very delicate control when starting. This was of course extremely useful when working long, loose coupled trains or when getting under way with a heavy load in adverse conditions. It was this characteristic which gave

the initial impression that Crabs were rather leisurely performers as far as acceleration was concerned. However, on opening the main valve a dramatic change occurred, its exhaust took on an explosive bark and with a distinct lateral twitch at each piston thrust, it would start to pound along, gaining pace in a most enterprising manner. The nickname of Crab is generally attributed to the rather ungainly cylinder and valve gear layout bearing a passing resemblance to that creature, but I rather suspect that the sideways movement it developed when working hard had something to do with the sobriquet!

With a tractive effort at 85% boiler pressure of 26,580lbs and 5ft. 6in. coupled wheels, Crabs were quite powerful engines, stronger in fact than Black 5s. The choice of wheel size seemed to be about right: small enough to give good acceleration and hauling capacity and large enough in conjunction with its modeern valve events to achieve a reasonable turn of speed.

In keeping with their mixed traffic designation they could and indeed did, particularly in their earlier years, cover a wide range of duties but as further modern specialised types and even more effective mixed traffic locomotives appeared in greater numbers, Crabs became relegated to less glamorous tasks. Whilst in the fifties they could still be seen heading holiday excursions or occasionally standing in for a failed secondary passenger, they had by that time found their true niche. Crabs were undoubtedly ideal for middle distance express freights and whether they be loose coupled, semi, or fully fitted, all were handled with great competence. I grew to appreciate their qualities from both sides of the footplate during the period 1957-8 when booked in Saltley's Sheffield Link.

In this top group we were frequently called upon to relieve through freights and work them forward for distances of around fifty miles. These freights were often perishable traffic loaded to between forty and fifty vehicles travelling as semi-fitted (at least one third of its vehicles fitted with vacuum brakes) or fully fitted trains. In order to keep to rostered paths involving many rather tight point-to-point timings, brisk acceleration and maximum speeds of up to 55mph were necessary. Crabs then, were at their best in these situations for they were certainly spritely starters and could run very comfortably at one mile per minute while at the same time possessed of the reserve boiler capacity to maintain schedules on the steepest of gradients. Moreover, they could achieve all this with commendable economy and without overtaxing their crews. Much of this economy was probably due to being able to maintain time over less rigorous routes using no more than the first valve with cut-offs around 15-25%. Only during acceleration and on adverse inclines was it necessary to 'crack' the main valve unless trains were exceptionally heavy. They responded well to expansive working although even when used on longer cut-offs, economy did not appear to be unduly affected.

Quality of ride was to some extent determined by the position of both the regulator and the reversing screw; admittedly this is the case with all locomotives but it was considerably more so with Crabs. As previously described they developed a pronounced lateral 'kick' under heavy power at low speeds, but as the pace quickened and power eased, this rapidly diminished so that by 50mph when using only first valve, progression was smooth and stable. There were always irregular twitches and wiggles denoting a certain looseness in the axle boxes but at 'fitted' speeds this caused little concern and the crew could remain comfortably seated. It was only on passenger duties calling for an altogether faster pace that the lateral oscillations became more noticeable again. Passing through the sixties the twitches reverted to kicks and sudden random vertical movements accompanied the kicks when approaching the low seventies by which time the ride could only be described as very lively.

This was about the maximum speed I experienced with Crabs and whilst I do not doubt they would have gone faster if pushed, neither drivers nor myself felt the desire to explore their limit. Indeed, it was on passenger workings that one appreciated the all round superiority of Black 5s and I for one am very grateful to Sir William Stanier for deciding that neither Crabs nor his own 2-6-0s were quite what he had in mind for the ideal mixed traffic locomotive.

Although possessing a firebox of similar length to a Compound's, the Crab's grate sloped less steeply and therefore to fire its front end demanded a more powerful swing of the shovel. Fortunately coal tended to burn at much higher rates in the rear half of the box, a bias greatly valued by fatigued firemen since not all engines were so considerate.

Why this should be so was not entirely clear; possibly the large ashpan with its single front damper concentrated air in that area and was assisted by a peculiarity of the exhaust arrangements entraining gases in a unique way. Whatever the reason it compensated for fire not shaking forward as it did with more sloping grates so that on the whole they were about par for their size. Most firemen tended to carry a rather thicker firebed at the front than with the majority of engines which was perhaps another reason why more rapid burning at the rear took place. The profile though, more or less followed normal practice in being level with the bottom of the firehole plus well filled back corners tapering slightly in depth towards the front.

Draughting always seemed excellent since they consumed poor quality fuels, including briquettes and dust, with great gusto and steaming in general was so good that lapses in technique such as overcharging the firebox frequently passed unnoticed.

It therefore came as a considerable surprise to learn that tests at Rugby in 1954 disclosed the Crabs' maximum steam output to be only 16,000lbs per hour. By some minor adjustments to chimney choke size and taper and a $\frac{3}{8}$in. reduction in blastpipe tip diameter, output was boosted to 20,000lbs per hour, although by then it was considered too late to modifiy the whole class in retrospect. The foregoing rather highlights the fact that Class 5s were rarely extended to near their maximum during normal freight workings, whereas Class 4s, particularly the older designs, were frequently at their limit in terms of steam production.

On freight trains of any type, firemen were generally not over stretched. A long handled shovel could be lustily swung from either side of the commodious footplate, despite a substantial anti-glare shield near the driver, and the injectors were able to reliably supply any demand. The Fowler tender, as described elsewhere, having coal access doors was safe and convenient to work from despite the need to stand on and over the usual mobile fall plate, and the discrepancy in width between it and the cab. Only when travelling at higher speeds were the firemen's balancing skills and reflexes taxed to a high degree if firing in earnest.

In 1931 five Crabs were fitted with Lentz rotary cam poppet valves so as to compare performance against the normal Walschaerts gear. Initially they showed a 1% saving in fuel consumption but over a five year period this rose to 5% indicating that poppet valves were less susceptible to steam leakage and could be better maintained. One drawback with the Lentz system was that it would only allow a limited number of cut-off positions, rather like some of the older locomotives' notched quadrants. However, in 1953 the original mechanism was replaced with a new camshaft system devised by the Lentz engineer, Reidinger. Like the Caprotti gear it was infinitely variable but by then insufficient time remained for it to be properly assessed for inclusion in current BR designs.

It was therefore engines equipped with Reidinger gear which we worked during the 1957-8 period mentioned earlier and to be truthful there was little noticeable difference from standard Walschaerts locomotives as far as freight duties were concerned. Possibly they were a little stronger at shorter cut-offs above 40mph but this would have shown up better on passenger work so driving technique was virtually the same. As would be expected, similar firing methods produced similar results and although one liked to believe that slightly improved economy was being obtained it was impossible to tell whether 57lbs of coal instead of the usual 60lbs per mile had been swallowed on the grate during a run.

With regard to disposal, Crabs came fairly low down the popularity list of tender engines and were in fact only about one place up from the dreaded 'Super Ds'. Crabs were principally used on longer runs which in those days of high congestion often resulted in being at work for very many hours without servicing. When they eventually arrived on shed they could have been in the hands of two or three sets of crews during which time most of their coal supply would have been consumed and coal consumed equates with ash and clinker. More often than not then, the grate presented a formidable scene, filled from mouthpiece to brick arch with a red hot slurry and when the fire was rough both ashpan and smokebox were generally likewise. Having only two sets of large firebars dissuaded many men from attempting to extract three or four in order to drop the fire through the ashpan. Most therefore, opted for the long and tedious business of paddling it out through the firehole. Whilst the rear could be dealt with by using a short clinker shovel wielded in a carefree manner, a long version was needed to reach the front half and this could only be manoeuvred slowly. Unfortunately maintaining a deeper bed of fire on the forward section produced more clinker in this area which made the task doubly difficult.

Tackling the capacious ashpan through its single leading damper from beneath the engine was equally daunting especially if the wind was blowing from the wrong direction and it usually involved ten minutes back breaking labour enveloped in clouds of drifting spray and dust. Then came the smokebox where battle was done in heat and fumes to remove a few hundredweight of gritty, sulphurous char which seemed to find its way into every pore and crevice no matter how much care was taken.

However, apart from potential difficulties with disposal, how did the Crabs measure up as Class 5 mixed traffic locomotives?

When introduced in 1926 they filled a need for there was no direct competition and since they incorporated all that was most modern in steam locomotive practice they were bound to succeed. On the freight side, Crabs were able to handle the most prestigious and arduous runs with consummate ease – runs with which 4Fs had struggled over the years hauling lighter loads, burning more coal per mile and providing less comfort for their crews.

Perhaps it is a little unfair to compare them with 4Fs but they were being built concurrently and running the same mix of duties. On the other hand Crabs were equally competent handling cross country or excursion passenger trains where their ability to accelerate rapidly and pull strongly on inclines was more important than prolonged high speed running. For some eight years or so Crabs reigned supreme but then they found themselves completely outclassed by the advent of the Black 5. With its tireless capacity to run at express speeds, the Stanier design became the obvious choice for passenger work and Crabs were gradually ousted from these duties. Having proved that they possessed superior duration and quality of ride, Black 5s were then selected for the super long distance freight hauls such as the Birmingham to Carlisles; but as stated before, this still gave the Crabs plenty of scope to show their mettle with a wide range of fast goods traffic. Here they proved their worth and being of very rugged construction suffered few ills so that they were able to continue performing useful and varied work virtually to the end of the steam era.

Just as the larger Crab demonstrated improved efficiency and economy in use over the 4F, so in time did the even larger 9F eclipse the Crab in these respects, such is progress. However, for over forty years this unglamorous 2-6-0 won the respect of countless enginemen and proved to the LMS that long-travel, long-lap valves with high degree superheat was the correct path to travel.

Chapter 11

Stanier 4-6-0 Class 5 (Black Five)

Mixed Traffic Engines. Introduced 1934. Total 842.

THE circumstances leading to the appointment in 1932 of William Stanier to the post of Chief Mechanical Engineer on the LMS has been extremely well documented. So too have his remarkable efforts in revitalising the LMS stock of locomotives which was at that time woefully in need of modern engines to cope with improving and expanding services. This need extended from the largest type of express passenger through to heavy freight locomotives, and although the greatest initial urgency was for express passenger power, there was a growing requirement for an efficient 'Maid of all Work' with an axle load kept down to about eighteen tons. Apart from the ability to operate just about everywhere over the system, it would have to be capable of a good turn of speed, sufficient endurance for longer runs and be equally competent with both freight and all but the heaviest express passenger duties.

Prior to Stanier's appointment, the 245 Horwich inspired 2-6-0 Crabs were the only modern mixed traffic engines available to the LMS and although a great improvement on earlier types, they did not fulfil what Stanier apparently had in mind. He did 'test the water' with forty taper boiler 2-6-0s of equivalent power to the Crab which were introduced in 1933 but these were fundamentally similar in performance. However, the following year there appeared the 4-6-0 Mixed Traffic locomotive which ultimately became a legend in its own lifetime, the Black 5.

Coming fresh from Swindon, where modern design practices had been long established under Churchward and Collett it was only to be expected that as many as possible of these practices would be incorporated by Stanier. Indeed as E.S. Cox stated in Locomotive Panorama, the Class 5 owed much, in concept if not in precise design, to the highly successful GWR Hall Class 4-6-0.

Sixteen years of evolution and refinement had already gone into the LMS Class 5 engines before I was privileged to work on them in 1950, so naturally I had no personal experience of their earlier shortcomings. Furthermore, by then there were a number of variations, some very apparent such as the fitting of Caprotti valve gear, others less obvious, so perhaps it would be useful to recall some of the major areas of their design and developments.

It is, of course, well known that Stanier's three cylinder 4-6-0 express passenger engines, later to be known as Jubilees preceded the mixed traffic version into service by some five months. Whilst the Black 5s performed adequately from the outset, the Red 5s (actually 5X Jubilees) struggled to maintain steam.

Both the 3A (Jubilee) and 3B (Black 5) boilers were of similar size and they initially shared the well tried Swindon principal of low superheat using only fourteen elements. However, whereas the proportions and draughting arrangements on the two cylinder engine were reasonably satisfactory, they were very much amiss on the three cylinder Jubilee. In 1934 getting these matters correct was as much an art as a science but after a prolonged period of intensive testing involving seventeen variations of the 3A and ten variations of the 3B boiler, success was eventually achieved. The development of these boilers is a complex and fascinating story in itself and quite beyond the scope of this narrative. Suffice to say that they commenced with domeless vertical throatplate fourteen element boilers and ended with sloping throatplate domed boilers with between twenty four and twenty eight superheater elements many of the earlier boilers being modified in the light of later experience. No matter, in fully developed form both boilers proved to be excellent and indeed the 3B boiler provided the basis for the later BR Standard Class 5s.

Although the Swindon principle of low-superheat did not suit LMS operating conditions, many other features Stanier bought with him showed improvement. Perhaps the most notable of these were his coupled axleboxes, the success of which had a very long lasting positive effect on locomotive repairs and availability. With their carefully machined generous bearing surfaces properly lubricated, failures from hot axleboxes dropped to negligible proportions. Equally successful was the new 6ft. 6in. wheelbase side-bolster bogie which followed closely the De Glenn-Churchward pattern. With adequate side control provided by helical springs fore and aft of the bogie centre casting it gave an exellent ride and was reliable enough to be adopted virtually unchanged by BR Standard locomotives.

Laminated spring design and manufacture came in for much attention and a change made to silico-manganese ribbed plates. However, both attachment and weight adjustment methods required continued refinement and the latter never was fully resolved. The cylinder configuration was excellent and the use of direct steam and exhaust passages no doubt contributed much to the first class overall performance these engines demonstrated in service. Inside admission piston valves were ten inches in diameter or 54% of the 18½in. cylinder bore and gave a clearance of 9.5%. Robust Walschaerts Motion provided a maximum travel of 6.47in. with a nominal lead of ¼in. a steam lap of 1½in. and exhaust clearance of ¹/₁₆in., producing a maximum cut-off in forward gear of just over 75%.

Cylinder lubrication was by means of a Silvertown mechanical lubricator mounted on the right hand foot framing and actuated from the expansion link thus giving a constant movement irrespective of cut-off. It supplied atomised feeds to an annular ring round each valve chest liner plus 'droplet' feeds to top and bottom centre of the cylinder barrel and to the piston rod gland and rear valve spindle bushing. The system generally produced good results in respect of wear and would doubtless have been better if all drivers had heeded instructions regarding coasting. They were enjoined to use 45% cut-off with a breath of steam and to help identify this position a letter D was inscribed on the reversing sector plate. Many had difficulty in breaking the habit of a lifetime acquired from handling slide valve equipped engines where full gear was preferable when coasting. As described in the section dealing with valves and pistons, long valve travel at full cut-off aggravated the suction effect, thereby drawing a greater volume of hot gases and char down the blast pipe. I found that at Saltley most drivers coasted with the reverser in the 'drift' (D) position but few, if any, could be persuaded to do so with a breath of steam on.

Originally balance weights were cast solid on coupled wheels which left something to be desired in terms of accuracy and for that matter foundry practice. The Swindon method was to use plates riveted over the spokes and then filled individually with a molten lead/antimony mixture. This proved so effective that the process was used by the LMS and BR until the end of the steam era. As was general at that time, the first batch of Black 5s were built with 66% of the reciprocating masses balanced equally divided between coupled wheels. In 1936/7 this was reduced to 55% and finally in 1938/9 50% was adopted with earlier engines eventually converted in retrospect.

Although the flowing curves of the 3Bs inner and outer wrapper plates which formed part of its Belpaire firebox were a great improvement over the very square Midland variety, their grates did cause some difficulties. Initially only two sets of long firebars were used giving a 55:45 ratio of slope and flat respectively. At 3.2:1 this rather steep slope at the front made firing somewhat awkward since it was not easy to keep a uniform depth

of fire over the hump so formed. Later, in the sloping throatplate boilers, three sets of firebars were fitted, the rear set being level and the others sloping more gently at about 4.3:1. This not only eliminated the firing problem but enabled fires to be cleaned more easily.

Not all things GWR were superior to Midland practice as experience in due course showed and one such feature was the well proven steam sanding equipment used by the latter. Stanier at first fitted Western style mechanically controlled dry gravity sanding, supplemented with a water de-sanding device requested by the Signal Engineer to prevent excess sand interfering with track circuits. It proved difficult to maintain in service. Consequently from 1936 reversion was made to the Midland system.

Nor was the topfeed clackbox and water distribution as first fitted too popular either. Although little trouble arose from sticking clacks, leaking flange joints were always a problem and although modifications and the use of 'Metaflex' joints improved matters, the leakage fault was never completely eradicated. Having entered the boiler, feed water was distributed into shallow zinc trays arranged either side of the main steam pipe. These rapidly filled with sludge allowing raw feed water to discharge directly on to the tubes causing serious deposits to form. The trays were supposed to be cleaned out at regular intervals but being an onerous task it was not always done as prescribed. When H.G. Ivatt became CME in 1946 he had these trays replaced by a simple 'saddle' plate fixed over the tube nest. This allowed feed water to flow over the plate and make its way down the sides of the boiler, carrying any sludge to the bottom.

Main frame plates were not particularly generous, being no more than 1in. thick on the first 225 engines. It was then increased to 1¹/₁₆in. from No. 5225 and then in 1947 1⅛in. was adopted until production ceased in 1951. Many accounts have documented the problem of cracked frames which dogged the Black 5s throughout their lives and the efforts made to correct this malaise. Although improvements were made over the years the problem was never completely overcome and they continued to remain below average in this respect.

On the other hand the Stanier circular smokebox was a great success; sitting on a cast or fabricated saddle, it no longer suffered the problems of leakage which affected D sectioned smokeboxes of the Fowler era. The deep dished door and door ring mated on inclined faces and was conveniently secured by means of a central dart which provided a reliable seal. In keeping with Swindon practice, domeless Black 5s had the regulator valve located in the superheater header but due to subsequent maintenance problems, later construction reverted to dome regulators. These were disposed horizontally (see section under regulators) making them more accessible for servicing and generally speaking they proved effective and reliable.

The above are a few of the principles, practices and innovations Stanier imported from the GWR and whilst many showed considerable advances over current LMS procedures, there were some which were just the opposite, or at least, did not translate well to LMS operating conditions.

However, it is a measure of Stanier's greatness that he did not insist on Western dogma in all things, nor did he place personal ego above the success of a design. If it was not up to standard he would change it or seek an improvement and if the Western article was not as good as the LMS one, then the latter would be retained. His designs therefore were an amalgam of the best practices from both these great institutions placing them at the leading edge of steam engineering in this country. That said, however, in order to give a personal opinion of a locomotive, it is necessary to restrict comment to the period of acquaintanceship and resist any temptation to speculate on aspects of development prior to that time.

By 1951 the last Black 5s had been built which was some nineteen years after their conception and of course these incorporated the results of trials, tribulations and much corrective and innovative development. Although to me they still represented that which was most modern and efficient in motive power, what effect must they have had on the crews when first introduced in 1934? These were, on the Midland Division, men, who on fitted freight workings, had known nothing better than Class 4F 0-6-0s or the occasional Crab, while for passenger duties they still relied mainly on Compounds. Little wonder then that even 'undeveloped' Black 5s made such a favourable impact and soon gained acclaim and universal respect.

Over the years this respect grew as the engines themselves improved, inspiring supreme confidence in crews and operating staff alike so that in time the Black 5 became the standard by which others were judged. So let us look at some of the features that contributed towards this popularity which was in some instances tantamount to almost reverence.

Few will disagree that aesthetically, the Class 5 was a most handsome locomotive no matter from which angle it was viewed. With the running plate just clear of the coupled wheels it curved gracefully down in front of the cylinders and also at the cab so that the bottom levels of these were in perfect alignment with those of the tender. A sleek tapered boiler surmounted by elegantly proportioned chimney and dome did much to enhance

With development continuing over the long construction period of seventeen years and also being used as guinea pigs for innovative engineering experiments, it is doubtful if there was ever two Black 5s exactly the same. However, to many they were the ultimate 4-6-0 mixed traffic engine, equally competent with almost every type of duty.

the appearance of perfect balance and poise which evoked a definite sense of power, speed and efficiency.

It therefore came as something of a shock to the purists when in 1948 they first viewed the original batch of Black 5s fitted with Caprotti rotary cam valve gear, for gone were the balanced curves and alignments. Prominent steam pipes connected to the leading end of equally prominent cylinders and cam boxes, emphasised their inherent ugliness. A short separate running plate extended back some 40in. from the front buffer beam while the main running plate ran at a lower level with no drop at the back to give deeper cab side sheets.

However the cab floor was still the standard height of 5ft. 4in. above rail level but new open footsteps up to it only served to exaggerate the mis-match between tender and cab running angles. Long sand box filler necks, higher pitched boiler and repositioned chimney likewise did nothing for the overall appearance although rather trim individual splashers perhaps managed to redress matters a little. On the premise that 'if it looks right then it is right' the Caprottis would have been condemned by many enginemen before they even climbed on board.

The last two Black 5s built, 44686-7 used a completely revised Caprotti motion, having an outside drive line on each side and twin exhausts. With these, the running plate was carried above the camboxes and joined the cab just below the window line giving a much improved appearance and a hint of things to come. With such a long period of development coupled with their use as 'guinea pigs' for experimental purposes there were very many variations in the Class and although some modifications were adopted in retrospect, one wonders if any two examples were identical in every respect. Even so I cannot recall ever having heard a bad word said about the design as a whole. Admittedly there are always instances of complaints over individual engines near to shopping or carrying a temporary defect but this was so with every class. Hardly surprisingly, therefore, when a crew knew they were booked a Black 5 they were happy and confident that they had the best available tool within that power class no matter what the job entailed.

With a heating surface in excess of 1,500 sq.ft. it fell into the category of engines for which sixty minutes was allowed for preparation. Having two outside cylinders and therefore all the motion readily accessible, drivers had a much cleaner and easier time than when oiling engines with inside cylinders, even if those engines were much smaller. Moreover the increased use of grease points on later types lightened the task still further. This visibility and accessibility also helped considerably when the driver was inspecting for defects during preparation and disposal.

Nor were things too difficult for the fireman either with the possible exception of filling sandboxes. The usual six boxes were carried to provide front sanding to the first and second coupled wheels and back sanding for the second pair only. The forward four boxes were within the frames and had three foot filler tubes mounted in angled plates above the foot framing. It was difficult to see the level of sand in these boxes and there was therefore a tendency to top them up until the sand became visible in the tubes, quite often unnecessary for the trip involved.

I have already described earlier the effort involved in filling sandboxes and of course it had to be carried up to a far greater height than with for example a 4F 0-6-0.

While attending to the sandboxes the fireman also checked oil levels in both mechanical lubricators which were located in tandem on the right side foot framing. Obviously care had to be taken when topping these up that the correct grade of oil was used. Axlebox oil did not perform very satisfactorily in cylinders nor vice versa for that matter.

The Stanier cab was on a completely different scale to former Midland engines both with regard to size and convenience. Being flush sided it was large and offered good protection from the elements, while spring loaded folding side doors helped to eliminate draughts and added to a sense of security. Large flat, hinged spectacle glasses in conjunction with the tapered boiler gave good forward vision in daylight but unfortunately reflected glare at night. Large side windows, one fixed, one sliding, enhanced the impression of light and space. Fitted to the outside of the cab just ahead of the sliding windows were folding glass windshields of ample size which provided very effective protection when peering around the side of the cab when in motion. Robust profiled wooden tip up seats were provided for both driver and fireman and when not in use enabled either crew member to easily lean out of an open window when necessary. On early locomotives the firemans seat was the top of a small tool locker, but on later versions a larger locker located below the spectacle glass replaced this and the firemans seat then became as decribed. They were not however, very comfortable when used for their intended purpose, particularly if the engine was run down and rough-riding.

In keeping with modern practice the boiler face was fully lagged and together with a large sliding cab roof ventilator, temperatures within were more tolerable than some of the older designs in hot weather. On the other hand standing 'wrong way to the weather' on a bitter winter's night could be very cold and uncomfortable. Not that it was much better for the driver when running during these inclement conditions because, apart from the absence of boiler heat, an efficient anti-glare shield mounted to the left of the firedoors effectively blocked any furnace radiation from reaching him. Although in contrast to Derby tradition a main steam manifold was mounted above the boiler, it was inside the cab and consequently all the principal steam supply pipes ran to it across the boiler face. It could however, be isolated from the boiler by a single central valve.

Knowing no better at the time, it was generally felt that the controls were reasonably placed and easy to operate. A conventional reversing screw was mounted in front of the driver and although usually light to use,

In 1950 I considered the Black 5 cab layout to be spacious, modern and efficiently arranged. Five years later, after experience with the BR Standard 5, it seemed just the opposite – such is progress.

the cut-off scale was not very visible at night. Not that this proved a particular disadvantage since drivers tended to gauge cut-off by number of turns given to the screw. While seated he could reach the hand wheel of the large and the wooden handle of the small ejector without difficulty and of course the LMS vacuum controlled steam brake fell readily to hand. Not so the blower placed centrally below the regulator quadrant and the whistle handle beneath the cab roof. The regulator itself had a long unbalanced handle which could at times be very stiff, requiring two hands and a standing position to open fully. They could also be annoyingly slack and tended to close of their own accord which is why most drivers carried a small wood block to wedge against the quadrant stop.

The fireman too needed to move around the cab to perform his duties. The injector steam supply valves were mounted either side of the regulator quadrant, exhaust right, live steam left and while the exhaust

injector water regulator was by his seat, the live steam injector's was adjacent to the driver's. However, the firehole was the same sensible height as the shovelling plate and in conjunction with efficient sliding doors did much to reduce fatigue particularly on long runs. Although designed to be fired from the right there was ample room to fire from either side despite the presence of that large anti-glare shield.

Instrumentation was fairly basic being confined to a boiler pressure and CWA gauge on the right and a vacuum gauge above the driver. The water gauges were quite easy to read and capable of being shut down by means of a single handle, extremely useful in the event of a gauge glass breaking. Illumination of these was by means of the usual standard LMS rape oil fuelled gauge lamps. The ashpan was fitted with both a front and a back damper and on early examples the controls for these were quadrant levers in the right side floor. Later versions reverted to pull up umbrella handles but neither were particularly satisfactory after a certain amount of wear had taken place and often needed to be propped open by wedges or spanners.

The Stanier tender was a vast improvement on previous LMS designs and without doubt complemented the overall excellence of the Black 5 not only in appearance but also from the practical point of view. With a nominal capacity of nine tons of coal and four thousand gallons of water, it gave this already economical locomotive a superior endurance. Being flush sided it was easy to coal and would, with a little judicious stacking, take an extra ton or so without being a danger. This capability was regularly taken advantage of on the super long distance Birmingham to Carlisle fitted freights. Furthermore, unless blocked by large lumps, coal would normally fall on the shovelling plate to at least the half empty stage when access to the interior was readily gained via a large folding door which could be hooked back out of the way.

Water pipes with spaced perforations ran along both upper inside edges of the coal space and could deliver a curtain of spray to damp down dusty fuel when the exhaust injector was on. The control valve for this much appreciated device was located below the fireman's seat adjacent to the slaking pipe control. Handbrake and water scoop handles, operating in a vertical plane flush with the tender front plate were unobtrusive and smoothly efficient, the latter being restrained by the usual ring and safety chain when not in use. A locker on the driver's side provided dry and adequate space for the crew's belongings but it did tend to mask the tank water level gauge from the fire's illumination at night.

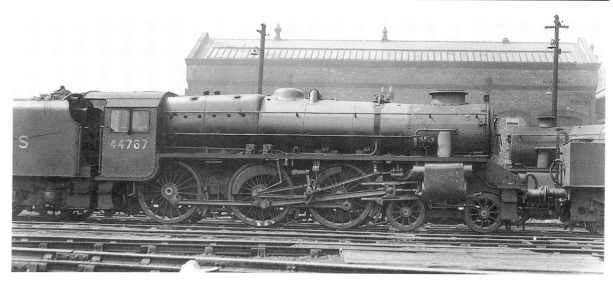

During H.G. Ivatts regime, Black 5s were used to test a variety of ideas and innovations. One such experiment was to explore the advantages or otherwise, of Stephensons motion (which gave variable lead) against that of the standard Walschaerts gear. The results were rather inconclusive and only 44767 was converted, however, happily this one example has been saved for preservation. Not everyone approved the appearance of the double chimney, but loco crews appreciated electric lighting supplied from the steam generator located on the smokebox.

Over on the fireman's side a cavernous tunnel was capable of holding a double complement of fire-irons, although as with all locomotives, care had to be taken when manipulating these while on the move since most were longer than the engine width. Umbrella handles either side of the shovelling plate controlled the water supply to the injectors, it being usual to leave the injector water regulator valves 'set' and just operate these main supply controls.

Although the tender rode well the usual mobile fall plate lay between this and the engine and of course it was necessary for the fireman to stand astride the plate when firing and neither unit moved in unison for more than a few seconds at a time.

Climbing on to the tank for watering purposes was accomplished via the usual side steps and three foot-steps attached to both sides of the tender back plate. The tank filler hole cover, hinged at the leading edge was a distinct improvement over the detachable types of former designs, while generous curved side plating enhanced the feeling of security provided by a substantial well. This was much appreciated when hauling round a heavy column on a wild winter's night.

Compared with some of the older types, the Black 5 really was a delight to drive, not the least attractive feature being the ability to operate most of the major controls while still seated. Admittedly the blower and whistle were out of reach and one usually had to stand up in order to open the regulator fully, but most of the time one could remain 'in situ'.

When moving off it was necessary, as with all locomotives fitted with an LMS Standard vacuum controlled steam brake, to first open the small ejector if one wished

use the automatic release provided by vacuum in the train pipe. The cylinder drain cocks could be closed by pushing forward a small lever attached to the cab side adjacent to the driver's left leg.

The long regulator handle gave plenty of leverage and sufficient sensitivity to render the task of getting a heavy train under way even in bad conditions relatively straightforward. This was of course assisted by an efficient steam sanding system and the adhesive advantage of a 4-6-0 compared to, for example, an uncompensated 'Pacific', provided that spring settings and tyres were in good order.

The Black 5 was a lively engine and unless heavily over-loaded, accelerated well under progressive notching up and often required no more than 'first' valve to maintain freight or passenger schedules.

With the latter, on level track they seemed to settle easily into the 70-80mph bracket which could be achieved either by using a wide open regulator at perhaps 15-20% cut-off or first valve at 25-30%. Obviously this would depend on load, prevailing winds and the actual condition of the locomotive. Although expansive working i.e. fully open regulator, was officially recommended it was not always feasible or desirable to pursue this. Stanier locomotives were smooth, quiet and rode well when new but they soon made the crew aware of deteriorating clearances in motion bearings and axleboxes. Once past the halfway point between shoppings, conditions on the footplate generally became far less pleasant and in the later stages they could be almost intolerable.

Violent hammer blows at every revolution caused everything, including the crew, to shake and rattle while unpredictable lateral and vertical lurches made sitting impossible and effective firing open only to those masters of balance who possessed lightning reflexes.

It was when a Black 5 had reached a certain stage of discomfort that working with the shortest possible cut-off was not desirable since this only exacerbated the effects described above. Using a partially opened regulator and longer cut-off reduced knock considerably and this method was used to give both engine and crew a less traumatic time. Fortunately such was the efficiency of its cylinder design and steam circuits that the Black 5 could still perform very adequately driven in this manner. Indeed it was so tolerant to these differing techniques that it tended to flatter the less skilled, thereby advancing still further its universal appeal. The same could really be said with regard to firing, since the 3B boiler in its final form was an excellent producer of steam and being tolerant to methods used, again flattered the less adept.

Unless prolonged heavy working was anticipated, a remarkably thin fire could be carried, given reasonable fuel. Normally this would be just below the firehole at the back of the grate then sloping to the front where it would be only sufficiently thick as to prevent holes being dragged in it. While like all engines it responded best to the 'little and often' principle, it would still steam adequately even if 'charged' quite heavily providing suitable coal was used. Nor did the fire shape affect output unduly for although most favoured a dished profile, i.e. thicker at the sides, some preferred the haycock style.

Reaching the front of the grate some eight and a half feet from the firehole required a fairly hefty swing of a long handled shovel although this was made rather easier by 'bouncing' the blade off the mouthpiece ring (firehole protection casting). Most firemen quickly acquired this delicate, energy saving art which greatly assisted the accurate placement of coal at the front end. However, it required much practice to become expert when trying to balance on a wildly cavorting footplate with one foot on the engine and the other on the tender.

One problem to be aware of was that of drooping smoke plates (baffles). When wear took place they tended to drop at the leading end and this obstructed the flight of coal from the shovel blade. Instead of travelling as intended to the front of the grate, it fell in the middle causing a ridge, which then prevented proper coverage of the forward section. To cure this defect firemen usually inserted a large bolt, (chair screws were readily available) over the centre of the plate to cock it up although care had to be taken so that the bolt did not move in such a way as to jam the doors when shut.

For an engine to be popular it had to steam freely and this the Black 5 certainly did whether running relatively lightly or being hammered for long periods.

One of the most demanding duties they were called upon to perform was the Birmingham to Carlisle fitted freights. The 226 mile run via Ais Gill was taxing enough in sheer duration, but on the down run most of the really hard work came after some five hours and 140 mile into the journey. By then the fire was past its best and the coal was in the back of the tender, a combination guaranteed to expose any steaming deficiency in a locomotive.

With a heavy train, even in calm conditions, the fourteen miles of mainly 1:100 gradient from Settle to Blea Moor usually required a wide open regulator and cut-offs in the order of 45%. If a full blooded storm was blowing then anything up to 75% was needed just to keep moving. (Ref. my previous book 'Saltley Firing Days').

Admittedly we were normally given the best Black 5s at Saltley for this marathon run, but despite such heavy working over a prolonged period I cannot recall boiler pressure ever varying more than a few psi from the optimum 225. On the contrary, the more they were thrashed the better they seemed to steam. This was one occasion when a much thicker fire needed to be carried on the grate otherwise holes would soon be torn in it causing not only a great loss of combustion efficiency but also an increased risk of setting embankments on fire with blazing cinders carried through the tubes and ejected by the powerful exhaust blast. It was therefore, prudent to gradually build up the thickness of the fire-bed prior to reaching Settle. With the prospect of some forty minutes of unrelenting climb, most firemen aimed to retain approximately the same fire shape but the back would now be level with the top of a small hinged combustion plate which was normally brought into use in these circumstances. Although rising only three or four inches above the bottom of the mouthpiece ring, it provided a flat base to the firehole and by altering the flow pattern of secondary air, seemed to accelerate the combustion of gases over the firebed. Providing lumps were broken down to the prescribed size, normal firing could be continued with the plate in positoin but since it was so simple to flip up or down with the shovel blade some firemen only used it between bouts of firing.

Of course Black 5s suffered with clinkered fires as did all steam locomotives, but because they could be run with relatively thin firebeds and also possessed a good reserve capacity, they seemed to be affected less than most. Although it was possible to complete the Carlisle duty without cleaning the fire, it certainly made a noticeable difference when the rear set of bars was cleared at the Skipton 'train examination' stop. With those later Black 5s fitted with rocking grates it was usually sufficient to merely give the bars a good 'rattle' every half hour or so. Provided the coal was of reasonable quality, the grate could be kept in excellent condition for the duration of the Carlisle run.

The Black 5 therefore did not demand too much in terms of either skill or effort and the average crew could invariably obtain good results on any duty within its power class. It would however, respond exceptionally well when in the hands of dedicated men and produce results far beyond normal expectation.

Apart from seeking to improve shortcomings applicable to a specific locomotive, engineers also continually viewed the wider scene and investigated methods and ideas which might, if adopted, effect the whole range of motive power. For this they required a 'Mr. Average' as a test bed and what better vehicle could be chosen than a good, medium size, general purpose engine like the Black 5. Having been thus selected, Black 5s henceforth almost invariably served the role of LMS guinea pig, which proved not only of benefit to them as a class but also their progeny yet to come.

Much of these engineers' endeavour was aimed at improving the life of components and times between major overhauls particularly during the immediate post war period and perhaps the most obvious and significant of these modifications was the fitting of alternative types of valve gear, one such experiment being the equipping of No. 44767 with Stephensons motion which gave a variable lead. Not having worked on this engine I only mention it in passing, but it was reputed to pull strongly although it never quite ran as sweetly as a Walschaerts locomotive and there was apparently always a hint of axlebox knock.

Of greater interest were the twenty locomotives, Nos. 44738-44757 built with British Caprotti poppet valve gear manufactured by Associated Locomotive Equipment Co. of Worcester. Also, as an additional experiment, the first ten had plain axlebox bearings while the remainder were equipped with Timken roller bearings on all axles and all benefitted from the latest Ivatt treatment to improve ease of servicing.

It was not expected that they would show any marked improvement in performance, but it was hoped that valve and piston mileage between examinations could be extended from 30-36,000 to 40-48,000 miles. After a lengthy settling down period during which much experience was gained, this goal was indeed achieved. Not the least contribution towards this substantial improvement coming from the by-pass feature which greatly reduced any tendency of flue gases being drawn into the cylinders when coasting. Certainly the front end generally kept much cleaner than on a piston valve engine.

There was no mistaking the Caprotti's distinctive appearance which as previously described, was generally thought less pleasing than the Walschaerts version. Complaints were indeed soon made, not however regarding any offended sense of the aesthetic but rather the more practical allegation that they were weak on banks and sluggish on acceleration.

Investigation of the problem resulted in auxiliary exhaust cams being fitted but it also revealed that the cut-off scale plate was grossly optimistic. In fact when 20% was indicated, it was actually 13%, 40 = 26%, 60 = 40% and full gear was only about 70%. These false indications would naturally add to any impression of factual weakness and needless to say the scales were rapidly changed. Later, single 'solid' exhaust cams were installed and their success did much to rectify the situation.

I must assume that all the Caprotti locomotives I worked on had been so fitted, since I could detect little difference either on banks or in initial acceleration between these and Standard engines. In fact, one of the most notable trips I ever had with a Black 5 with regard to sustained power output was with Caprotti No. 44744 on a Birmingham to Bristol parcels. With a very determined driver using full gear and full regulator, it accelerated its train up the bank out of New Street Station in a manner which belied any weakness in this area, despite a 44 ton overload. Gaining time easily on a fairly tight schedule all the way up to Blackwell, it then treated us to some exceptionally high speed running over the falling gradients towards Eckington where it attained the highest speed I have ever experienced with a Black 5. (See 'Saltley Firing Days').

Firing technique was exactly the same as with a Standard locomotive and perhaps it was the luck of the draw with this small batch of engines but I never had a rough one, which gave the perhaps, not entirely accurate impression that they were superior to Walschaerts versions in this respect.

To obtain the best performance, drivers had to

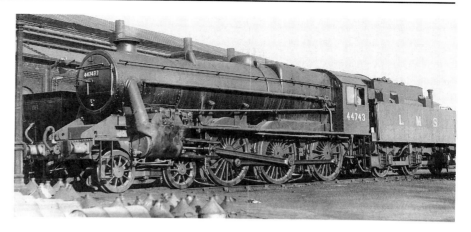

This photograph shows 44743 in single chimney form which to some eyes was less objectionable than the double chimney version. The original batch of 'Caprottis' used a single central shaft driven from the leading axle to operated the cams. However, the last two Black 5s built (44686-7) used a completely revised Caprotti system with twin outside drive lines, and subsequently this pattern was adopted on BR5s. Note the 'weigh' tender used for fuel consumption tests.

modify their methods of working slightly. It must be borne in mind that a driver adjusts the cut-off to suit conditions partially on feel and partially on sound, the latter becoming more predominent at night or in the darkness of tunnels. These combine to give him a sense of what is right to maintain optimum efficiency on a particular section. Because of their valve events, Caprotti's produced a sharper and louder exhaust bark especially at shorter cut-offs than a Standard Black 5, consequently drivers instinctively tended to notch them up much further than usual and this would pass unnoticed if the scale was not visible. Hence one possible reason for the alleged weakness on starting. Without doubt though, they did produce more power on cut-offs less than 25% at speeds over about 45mph.

The driver therefore had to learn to disregard its louder exhaust beat and rely more on feel and confirm this by checking the cut-off indicator. Because they could be run at shorter cut-offs, a wide open regulator where conditions allowed, was preferable.

In 1951 the final two LM Class 5s were built with a revised Caprotti gear having outside drive and the performance of these was reputed to be a vast improvement over their twenty predecessors. They were so strong and lively that some felt they should be in a higher power class. Whether true or otherwise, thirty BR Standard 5s were similarly fitted with apparently equally good results and, had steam continued rather longer, then this type of valve gear would probably have been in wider use.

Disposal of Black 5s has been dealt with in detail earlier and except for those later engines fitted with rocking grates it was just about as onerous as most other types.

What then made the Black 5 such an outstanding success immediately it was introduced despite the odd shortcomings?

First it came into being at exactly the right time, filling a long felt need on the LMS which was at that period sadly lacking in modern medium size mixed traffic locomotives. It then quickly proved to be vastly superior in every respect over previous types, not only in performance but also in terms of comfort and convenience for the crews. If this was not enough, it was capable of operating on just about every important line over the entire LMS network.

From the outset, the locomotive displayed no particular vices and as the design progressively improved so its remarkable versatility became more apparent. Finding they had so responsive an engine in their hands engendered such confidence that both drivers and firemen alike were prepared to tackle just about any turn and in due course Black 5s were called upon to do exactly this. Apart from the heaviest, long distance express passengers there can be few duties they were not rostered on. Duties which they invariably performed with equal competence. Good impressions are soon conveyed to colleagues who confirm this with their own experiences and then initial respect develops into forthright admiration.

I know of no other design which seemed to enjoy such universal acclaim from engine crews who could be rather critical at times. It was only when some of the BR Standard locomotives became 'accepted' in the late fifties that the aura surrounding them diminished somewhat. No one likes to see their favourites supplanted but even the most partisan adherents then began to grudgingly admit that Black 5s could be bested in terms of performance, servicing and creature comforts.

Until the advent of these BR designs I considered that they were the very best of their type for they had indeed become a legend in their own lifetime.

Chapter 12

B.R. Standard 4-6-0 Class 5MT

73000 Mixed Traffic Locomotive. Introduced 1951. Total 172.

TO REALLY understand the raison d'être for building the range of British Railways Standard Steam Locomotives one can probably do no better than study E.S. Cox's excellent book of that title. Heading the design team which brought them into being, he was able to provide the reasoning behind the twelve individual designs and also insights into the selection of standard fittings adopted and choice of technical features. I for one, was delighted that they pursued the course they did and despite a few understandable lapses the majority of enginemen of my acquaintance were either enthusiastic or at the very least, sympathetic to most of the range.

Should this statement cause the purists to raise an eyebrow, it must be remembered that locomen viewed a new deign from a somewhat different angle to the lay enthusiast brought up with fixed ideas on what the ideal engine should look like and tables of dimensions which often did not translate to theoretical performance and comfort on the road.

After all, a locomotive was many things to those who operated them. They were essentially a tool by which the men obtained their livelihood, but they could also be their travelling home for up to eighteen hours or more in one stint. A home that could be stationary for long periods or crashing along at 1½ miles per minute in a fury of sound and movement. It was difficult enough for the fireman to feed their voracious appetites and drivers to extract the desired performance when all was going well, let alone when adverse conditions prevailed, so it is perhaps not surprising that loco crews favoured engines that were reliable, comfortable and possessed the largest possible reserve capacity. In other words, they did not like anything that made an already hard job any harder.

The concept of standard locomotives or the standardisation of their various parts was practiced both in the days of individual railways and after the 1923 grouping. According to Cox, fears that problems would arise from locomotives not being accepted by one region if designed by another and difficulties with spares and servicing were allayed when during the period 1948-52 a number of LM Region types were constructed in other regional workshops in addition to those supplied from LM Works. Having gained this acceptance, it became somewhat easier to promote a proposed number of entirely new designs, plus new designs which were developments of existing types and finally some existing designs modified only in detail.

While Cox freely admits that the triumvirate of Riddles, Bond and himself were naturally influenced by their LMS background, they were not so steeped in that tradition as to close their eyes to what might be good on the other regions or for that matter other countries.

Not only were 'foreign' locomotives closely examined, but also their component parts and construction practices. The conclusion drawn was that however much the locomotives differed superficially and in details there was little to choose between the recent products of the regions.

Performance apart, it was apparent that under the guidance of H.G. Ivatt, the LMS had progressed rather further than the others in the direction of improved accessibility, maintenance, repair mileages and ease of servicing. This last aspect was much appreciated by loco crews for with the aid of those trans-atlantic features, rocking grates, hopper ashpans and self cleaning smokeboxes, the long and onerous work of disposal became but a few minutes of relatively light work.

Bearing the above in mind, the design brief was to follow the well-established principles of high superheat, robust long-travel valve gear, adequately proportioned boilers and the latest developments in draughting. However, the whole trend should be towards simplification so that a reduction in time required for repairs and servicing could be achieved.

The interchange trials of 1948 only served to confirm what had already been gathered from experience on the LMS, in as much that a properly designed steam locomotive would perform satisfactorily anywhere in the country on appropriate duties. They also showed that the simplest designs were at no disadvantage compared with the more complex, that multiple cylinders were not necessary other than when demanded by loading gauge restrictions and that small wheels were no bar to high speed. However, the need to provide a boiler of adequate capacity was as essential as it had always been.

With the benefit of hindsight, the design team realised that they had been misled by certain aspects of the trials and consequently wrong conclusions drawn, perhaps the most far reaching being that uncompensated 4-6-2 engines could be almost as sure footed as 4-6-0s. They had not appreciated at the time of the trials that it was the supreme expertise of those 'picked' drivers who coaxed seemingly reliable adhesion out of the various Pacific's but, with 'average' crews, they could become most uncertain starters.

Post war operating conditions were entirely different

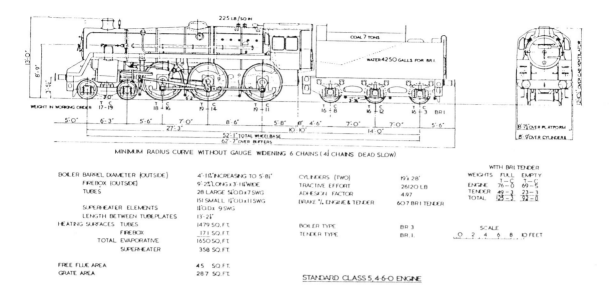

BOILER BARREL DIAMETER (OUTSIDE)	4'-11½"INCREASING TO 5'-8½"	CYLINDERS (TWO)	19"x 28"	WITH BRI TENDER

STANDARD CLASS 5, 4-6-0 ENGINE

to those of the late thirties and they imposed a number of constraints which influenced design philosophy. Acute shortages of skilled staff in all departments emphasised the need for maximum accessibility and the inclusion of long-life, low-maintenance components wherever practical. Low grade fuels were now the accepted standard and since skilled firemen were also at a premium, large fire grate areas which assured lower combustion rates in average working conditions seemed a desirable goal. As previously stated, H.G. Ivatt had shown the way and this desire to make very dirty and difficult jobs a little easier for the men involved was perpetuated by BR even to the extent of completely re-thinking the cab layout design.

The BR range of Standard locomotives was therefore conceived with somewhat different objectives in mind and more suited to prevailing conditions than those of pre-war construction.

Since all regions possessed sufficient first line express passenger and heavy freight locomotives for immediate needs it was decided to proceed first with three new deigns of mixed traffic engines which when finalised became Class 7, Class 6 and Class 5 in terms of power category.

The original proposal envisaged the Class 5 as a Pacific with an 18 ton axle load but since true Class 5 duties were being performed competently by numerous existing 4-6-0s which were some 11 tons lighter, any saving in lower running cost achieved by the greater thermal efficiency of a larger grate area would be off set by both increased initial and maintenance costs. If a locomotive was required which had a greater potential capacity

than present 4-6-0s but still with an acceptable axle load then it would be better to design this as a Class 6 in the first instance. Thus came into being the Class 7 MT 4-6-2 70000 (Britannias), the Class 6 MT 4-6-2 72000 (Clans) and the Class 5 MT 4-6-0 73000s.

It was intended from the outset that BR Standard Locomotives would share a common cab layout and use the same range of standard fittings and details. To deal with these latter items, two sub-committees were set up so as to select what was best in both practice and equipment from the former Railway Companies. When this had been accomplished, the various classes were allocated to specific design offices who not only issued the respective production drawings but also undertook the design of certain components on behalf of the whole standard series.

Doncaster was given overall responsibility for the Class 5 project, together with the wider one of designing all cylinders, slidebars, crossheads, coupling and connecting rods and valve gear. Derby was concerned with bogies, two-axle trucks, wheels, axles, axleboxes, springs and tenders. Brighton did sanding and brake gear and details for pipe, rod and lubrication layouts, while Swindon took over all boiler and ashpan mountings and details. Also, since Western Region men chaired both the Locomotive Standards Committee and also the sub-committee set up to select boiler mountings, it was hardly surprising that there was a trend to recommend Swindon fittings unless it could be demonstrated that there was a superior alternative. Hence all BR Standard locomotives were fitted with two of the excellent WR water gauges which I personally found both easier to read and also to fit replacement glasses when the need arose. As an added bonus, the more sophisticated WR gauge lamps were supplied with them and these also proved more reliable than the LMS version.

After a comprehensive series of tests involving both regional and proprietary instruments, Swindon designed live steam injectors showed a considerable superiority in range of working and maximum delivery capacity. These were adopted in three sizes to cover the proposed fleet giving maximum water deliveries of 34,800, 25,700 and 18,500lb per hour respectively. However, the WR top feed clack valve fitted at the point where the injector delivery entered the boiler was rejected. It had been used by the LMS since Stanier's time and had never proved entirely satisfactory since a tendency for leakage inside the boiler clothing had been an all too frequent occurence. On the other hand the very simple but effective Southern Railway unit had never been known to suffer from this problem and was therefore adopted in preference.

Exhaust steam injectors funtion at their best only under conditions of sustained running and it was at the time considered that the three Pacifics and the Class 5 4-6-0 were most likely to achieve this. The well-proven Davies and Metcalfe type were thus fitted to these locomotives and added a further small bonus to their overall efficiency.

The latest thinking was incorporated into the design of valves and cylinders, using large straight ports and passages together with piston valves of generous proportions. With Doncaster in charge of cylinders, slidebars and the rest of the motion, it was not entirely unexpected that the three-bar slidebar arrangement of the Gresley engines was adopted for the larger locomotives. It was not feasible though, to fit this system to those engines with pony trucks which had to pass the smaller L1 loading gauge, or where the rear end of the cylinders abutted on the leading coupled wheels. There was insufficient lateral clearance for the coupling rods to pass between wheels and slidebars and therefore the LMS pattern of one slidebar above and another below the crosshead was adopted.

The well tried, accurate and robust Walschaert valve gear was specified for the whole range of piston valve locomotives and on the larger engines an exceptionally long travel of 7¾in. in conjunction with $1^{11}/_{16}$in. steam lap, gave a starting cut-off of 78%. These generous valve events were one of the principal areas where the BR Class 5 and the Black 5 differed and a comparison can be made by noting their relevant dimensions.

On tender locomotives, an improvement on the reversing gear arrangement was also sought and in this respect a departure was made from the previous practice of a screw in the cab operating the weigh shaft via a long rod running alongside the boiler. By mounting the screw forward so that it acted directly upon the weigh shaft, it was thought that vibration and wear could be considerably reduced since the shaft running back to the cab would not be subjected to kick from the valve gear.

In keeping with the policy of low maintenance, roller bearing axle boxes were used extensively allowing carrying wheel sizes to be kept to a minimum. Tyre fastening was of the Bulleid form with two small lips and no ring, adopted in preference to the Gibson retaining ring.

Perhaps the most significant departure from previous practice was the attachment of the running plate and cab directly to the boiler instead of the main frames. The deeply valanced running plate provided a very rigid structure to which the various pipes and fittings were clipped, concealed from view but readily accessible from below. Mounted thus it was thought they should be free from differential vibration or expansion and therefore have less tendency for any loosening.

The foregoing is a brief review of some of the thinking and motivation that went into the design of the BR Standard locomotives. It must be reiterated that all out performance on the road was not the only objective. Changed conditions dictated other important requirements: simplicity in both construction and maintenance, visibility and accessibility of parts which would themselves be designed for long life service and aids to the crews so as to reduce and make less disagreeable the time required for disposal and preparation and also to ensure that operating the engines was rendered as comfortable and efficient as possible.

Let us see how well they succeeded by now comparing the Standard 5 with the Stanier 5.

When the decision was made to produce a Standard Class 5 4-6-0 locomotive, it seemed logical to base this on the highly successful Black 5 and incorporate its superb boiler. Between 1934 and 1951 the Black 5 had been developed albeit with many modifications, into an extremely useful engine and if quantity is a measure of desirability, then 842 examples must have placed it high on any shopping list. To add further weight, if any was needed, to this argument 852 Class 8F 2-8-0 which were closely related in many aspects, had also been manufactured.

As previously described even in its original form with only fourteen superheater flues the 3B boiler steamed adequately while the final twenty eight flue variant had proved to be truly excellent. Therefore, since both locomotives shared this major component it will be interesting to examine how they differed in other

Based around the excellent Black 5 3b boiler, steaming character-istics of the BR5s were very similar and although valve and cylinder design differed somewhat, overall performance of the two types was closely comparable. However, comfort, convenience and ride quality were in a totally different class, nor did the ride deteriorate with mileage at anything like the same rate.

While still maintaining Ivatt's visibility, accessibility, ease of maintenance theme, the BR designers managed to achieve a much more imposing, clean, streamlined exterior. It is a pity electric lighting was not adopted, but their other attributes coupled with ease of servicing made them a joy to work on.

respects and how these differences affected overall performance and general acceptance.

The maximum axle load of the Black 5 had risen throughout the years from 18 tons to 19½ tons and because during that period many routes had been up-graded, an axle load of 19¾ tons for the Standard 5 was now quite acceptable. In the event, although there were very obvious styling and some not so obvious engineer-ing differences, locomotive weight of the Standard 5 in working order exceeded that of its predecessor by less than three quarters of a ton.

Perhaps the most notable mechanical difference between the two engines was in the design and size of the steam chests and cylinders, the principal dimensions of which are given below.

	Stanier Black 5 in.	Standard 5 in.
Cyl. dia x stroke	18½ x 28	19 x 28
Clearance Volume as % of Piston Swept Volume	9.5	11.3
Piston Thrust lb.	60,500	63,794
Volume as a % of Piston Swept Volume	54	51.1
Piston Valves – Diameter	10	11
Steam Lap	1½	1¹¹/₁₆
Lead	¼	¼
Exhaust clearance	¹/₁₆	nil
Maximum Valve Travel	6.74	7.73
Maximum Forward Cut-Off %	76	78

Both used the very accurate and reliable Walschaerts Motion, but Standard 5s enjoyed a slightly larger coupled wheel diameter – 6ft. 2in. instead of 6ft. 0in. Even so, this still gave it an advantageous tractive effort which at 85% boiler pressure resulted in 26,120lbs compared to the Black 5's 25,455lbs.

The BR bogie followed the De Glenn-Churchward-Stanier tradition but had wheels 3½in. smaller at 3ft. 0in. diameter and at 6ft. 3in., a wheelbase 3in. shorter.

The coupled wheelbase was 2in. longer than the later Black 5s but because of the more compact BR tender design the total wheelbase was nearly 1ft. 6in. less.

As indicated in a previous chapter, frame fractures had been a source of concern throughout the lives of Black 5s despite progressive increases in plate thickness to 1⅛in. With this in mind an attempt was made to avoid past errors by using 1¼in. plate, the maximum permissible within weight limitations, while at the same time paying careful attention to the design and manufacture of the hornstays.

Most of the other mechanical differences were in respect of fittings and details as outlined earlier although mention should be made as to why external rodding was used for the regulator. Being aware that Pacifics had a greater tendency for slipping when rail conditions were bad, it was decided to provide a more sensitive control for these engines by fitting the superheater company's multiple valve regulator incorporated in the superheater header. Because the operation of this unit called for external rodding and a regulator handle in the cab working in a fore and aft direction, it was agreed for the sake of uniformity to retain this means of operation for all the other standard engines, even though they retained the normal slide type regulator valve in the dome.

Although the boiler was clearly derived from the Black 5, the rest of the locomotive's appearance differed considerably. During the war years there had been a growing trend towards transatlantic lineaments for the various practical reasons outlined earlier and H.G. Ivatt had expressed this rather starkly with his 4MT 2-6-0s. BR designs perpetuated these principles but the high running plate with its smooth, steep slope at the front blending into an efficient 'streamlined' cab at the rear gave, to my mind, a pleasing harmony suggestive of power and speed.

To many the cab is the centre of interest on a locomotive and it was possibly this feature which showed the most obvious improvement over the Black 5. Access was gained via steps attached to the tender and in the case of BR1 versions thence through unsprung cab doors fitted to the engine.

On viewing the footplate for the first time probably the most notable innovation was an absence of the movable fall plate between engine and tender front, providing a very stable platform to fire from. This was a feature I for one greatly appreciated, particularly when the engine was running at high speeds. Hand rails ran up to the roof on both sides of the door opening which gave an additional convenience when struggling on board with equipment.

The boiler face was impressively uncluttered and the few exposed pipes were clipped in neat runs giving the appearance of well thought out tidiness. One of the reasons for this being that the main steam manifold was now placed outside the front of the cab.

Ergonomically, the general layout was a vast improvement over previous practice since all the driver's controls were sighted around him within easy reach from a very comfortable padded seat complete with back rest. To add to this unaccustomed luxury, a partition behind the seat rose to the roof and incorporated a window which gave further protection from the elements when running tender first.

The regulator with its fore and aft movement was relatively unobtrusive and likewise the end on positioning of the reversing screw occupied less lateral space. Operation of these controls proved, as the designers had envisaged, more natural to the human form than the traditional arrangement.

At knee height and bracketed to the cab side at the left of the driver was the very effective steam operated cylinder drain cocks valve while directly to his front above the reversing screw were the large and the small ejector valves. These were the latest SSJ Gresham and Craven instruments and according to E.S. Cox were chosen in preference to regional types after comparative testing at Swindon.

The driver's operating handle for the combined vacuum and steam brake system was mounted horizontally on a pedestal convenient to the driver's right hand, while above this was located a separate independent steam brake. The pedestal formed an anti-glare shield and also housed the blower and sanding valves.

On the other side of the cab the fireman also enjoyed a padded seat, albeit without a back rest, and a rather lower partition minus a window was installed behind it. The absence of a window here was not because it was thought that the fireman did not merit such protection, but because it would have obstructed the withdrawal of fire-irons from the tender tunnel.

As with the driver, all relevant controls were positioned within easy reach around him and he could if need be, enjoy the benefit of operating both injectors and the damper controls without leaving his seat. Even the whistle could be reached from either side without having to get up and grope under the roof, which was a considerable improvement on most previous locations.

The Western type water gauges were far easier to read in poor light, whilst the accompanying gauge lamp was more sophisticated and reliable than the former LMS pattern. Instrumentation too, was not only clearer and

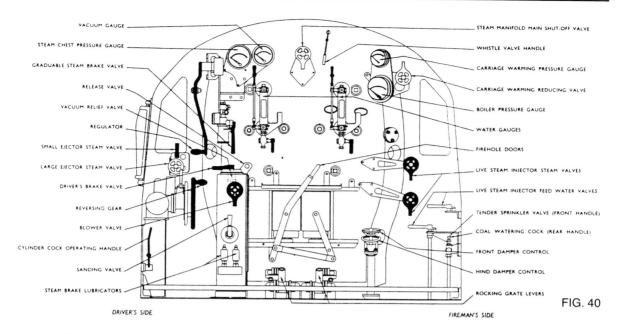

VACUUM GAUGE
STEAM CHEST PRESSURE GAUGE
GRADUABLE STEAM BRAKE VALVE
RELEASE VALVE
VACUUM RELIEF VALVE
REGULATOR
SMALL EJECTOR STEAM VALVE
LARGE EJECTOR STEAM VALVE
DRIVER'S BRAKE VALVE
REVERSING GEAR
BLOWER VALVE
CYLINDER COCK OPERATING HANDLE
SANDING VALVE
STEAM BRAKE LUBRICATORS

STEAM MANIFOLD MAIN SHUT-OFF VALVE
WHISTLE VALVE HANDLE
CARRIAGE WARMING PRESSURE GAUGE
CARRIAGE WARMING REDUCING VALVE
BOILER PRESSURE GAUGE
WATER GAUGES
FIREHOLE DOORS
LIVE STEAM INJECTOR STEAM VALVES
LIVE STEAM INJECTOR FEED WATER VALVES
TENDER SPRINKLER VALVE (FRONT HANDLE)
COAL WATERING COCK (REAR HANDLE)
FRONT DAMPER CONTROL
HIND DAMPER CONTROL
ROCKING GRATE LEVERS

DRIVER'S SIDE

FIREMAN'S SIDE

FIG. 40

more logically orientated but also more comprehensive. For the first time, a steam chest pressure gauge was provided for drivers who were interested in such matters, while a matching speedometer registered the results and did much to banish guesswork at permanent way slacks and other speed restrictions. Although both boiler pressure and carriage warming apparatus gauges were located as usual on the fireman's side their faces were angled towards the driver so that he could read them more easily.

The cab weather boards were also angled, which not only presented a pleasing effect but also did much to eliminate reflections at night. Positioned below the sliding firehole doors were the usual rocking grate catches while their portable operating lever could be seen neatly clipped to the right of these on the boiler face. Above, a generously sized sliding cab roof ventilator secured by twin locking handles, was both effective and convenient to use.

Perhaps it is not widely appreciated but tenders or at least their layout, is of considerable concern to firemen for many reasons. If the shovelling plate is at an awkward height or angle, or open tender doors, hand brake handle or any other item impedes him when firing, then it makes a physically demanding job more difficult. Even the ease of climbing on to the tank top and the degree of safety when once there have to be considered, while the more obvious ones of access to the coal space, ability to get coal forward and operate the scoop go without saying.

In the case of the BR Standard locomotives, several variations of tenders were fitted to suit different operational needs on the regions.

The original series of tender engines were fitted with one of three basic sizes of tender, all having inset coal bunkers to improve vision when running backwards. However, loco crews were more appreciative of having extra coal at the front of the tender than this feature and in any event it became apparent that greater capacity would be required for some of the longer runs. Therefore, the two larger tenders were redesigned with flush sides curved in at the top in a similar style to Stanier 4,000 gallon tenders. The partition marking the end of the coal space could be brought forward so as to give 7 tons instead of 9 tons capacity when desirable.

These types are listed below:-

Type	Coal tons	Water galls	Weight tons W/O
1 inset	7	4250	49.15
1B Flush	7	4750	51.25
1C Flush	9	4750	53.25
1D Flush	9	4750	54-50
			(steam coal pusher)
1F Flush	7	5625	55-5
			(no scoop)
1G Inset	7	5000	52-5
			(no scoop)
1H Inset	7	4250	49.15

In many respects the BR tenders were a considerable improvement over their Stanier forebears although as with most new designs, modifications had to be made. Extending up to the cab roof, the BR tender front plate gave a neat, flush appearance with only the hand brake and water scoop handles and the shovelling plate projecting into the cab. The former were rather smaller and less obtrusive than the Stanier pattern, while the shovelling plate possessed a tapered lip at its leading edge. This lip tended to restrain small coal from shaking on to the footplate while at the same time being less hostile to the crew's shins. Locker space was more generous than before since another compartment occupied the area above the coal access doors and with curved sided tenders a further locker was incorporated on the fireman's side since the fire iron tunnel had then been moved across as per Stanier types.

How, then, did these many apparent improvements over the Black 5 actually translate out on the road?

Possessing the same two outside cylinder configuration and Walschaerts Motion as the Black 5, preparation as far as it concerned the driver was basically similar. However, since even greater use of grease lubrication was made for the multitude of pin joints to be found in the motion, suspension and brake system, the task of oiling was rendered somewhat easier. So too was the driver's inspection, due to the emphasis placed at the design stage on visibility and accessibility. For the fireman it was again very similar to that of a Black 5.

The mechanical lubricators for cylinders and axle boxes along with the sand box filler tubes were at a higher level and therefore entailed slightly more climbing. On the other hand, footplates were usually more tidy because the profiled shovelling plate retained coal where it should be – in the tender. Following Ivatt practice a single ladder at the rear of the tender gave easy access to the top, although once there, one felt the sense of insecurity always experienced with inset tenders of this type. Later, substantial foot blocks were added but although an improvement, one never felt quite as confident as when standing in the well of a flush sided version. On all BR types the rear mounted ladder was offset from the centre line towards the driver's side, this being the more usual side from which water was taken.

My experience of these locomotives was almost entirely with passenger work which, because of the harder working and speeds involved, tended to emphasise any differences.

With essentially the same 3B boiler and possessing a very similar eight-section rocker grate as the later Black 5s, one would expect to achieve comparable results using identical techniques. This proved to be so as far as the production of steam was concerned relative to coal and water consumed. Although most engine crews were

unaware of it at the time, following trials at the Rugby Testing Plant on an early example, it was found to be deficient in terms of smokebox vacuum and unable to burn Blidworth coal efficiently at high outputs. Decreasing the blastpipe cap diameter from $5\frac{1}{8}$in. to $4\frac{7}{8}$in. coupled with an increase in air space through the bars by 5% improved the maximum evaporation of steam from 18,000lbs per hour to 24,000lbs. All locomotives already built were quickly fitted with these modifications, so I must assume that the engines I worked on were thus equipped. Certainly the exhaust had a somewhat sharper bark than a Black 5s throughout the normal working range of cut-off. Firing these engines was therefore to all intents and purposes exactly the same, but from the comfort and convenience point of view, the BR engine was incomparably better.

All new engines feel taut, are relatively quiet and ride well, but these BR 5s, with cabs attached to the boiler and having a continuous floor, provided a stability of ride I had hitherto only experienced on passenger tank locomotives. Nor did this seem to deteriorate markedly when higher mileages were attained which was not the case with Stanier engines. Perhaps I was lucky, but I cannot recall ever having a 'rough' BR locomotive in the true sense of the word, even though many had been in service long enough for a regional type to become distinctly uncomfortable. One can but speculate that this was due to improved design, materials and lubrication and so one can only applaud the Riddles' team for achieving exactly what they set out to do.

Because of the ride quality, it was quite an enjoyable experience to actually be able to sit comfortably on a padded seat between bouts of firing. Furthermore, both live and exhaust steam injectors which proved powerful and reliable could be easily operated while still 'in situ'. On the Stanier engines one had to stand up in order to reach the injector steam valves and in the case of the live steam one, walk over to the water regulator valve located behind the driver's seat.

The damper controls were similar to those used on Ivatt 4MT 2-6-0s, being a hand wheel operating on a threaded rod through its centre. These could be very finely set and likewise adjusted while still seated. Damper controls on Stanier engines whether they be of the umbrella or quadrant type were often a source of annoyance particularly on higher mileage engines when they tended to shake shut and could only be propped open with the aid of a spanner. The tri-tone whistle fitted behind the chimney on the initial batch of Standard 5s caused quite a stir. Since this delightful instrument could again be reached while seated from either side of the cab it was used equally by staid old drivers and young firemen at the least excuse with great enthusiasm. We were told that being cable operated they tended to stick open and to everyones regret they were eventually replaced with standard whistles located in front of the cab.

Daylight vision ahead was similar to that of the Black 5 but at night, the angled spectacles really did reduce reflections and were much appreciated by drivers and firemen alike. Also appreciated were the padded side window arm rests which were far more comfortable than the wooden Stanier version. However, when peering ahead from these side windows I found that the elegantly profiled but slimmer windshield did not offer quite so much protection as did the wider Stanier type.

Improved creature comforts also extended to the tender which not only provided considerably more shelter from the elements when running tender first but could readily accommodate all one's personal effects (including extra clothing) in its commodious lockers. Both hand brake and water scoop handles, being somewhat smaller than on Stanier tenders, seemed lower geared and with the latter, one had to remember to start extracting the scoop rather earlier if overfilling was to be avoided. To some extent though, the near flush fitting tank gauge helped in this respect since it was much more visible particularly at night. The tapered lip at the leading edge of the shovelling plate required a slightly different angle of attack with the shovel but one quickly adjusted and considering its other advantages, one wonders why such a simple feature had not been introduced before.

Driving the Standard 5 was also a new experience in many respects, for while the fore-and-aft regulator movement had been encountered on 4MT 2-6-0s, the end on reversing wheel lay at 90° to what was usual. Most drivers were non-commital over this new disposition, although all agreed that it was less obtrusive and therefore less likely to make painful contact with carelessly placed knees on a dark night. The winding action was normally light and smooth with fine adjustments being registered on an easily read drum scale. As with all types , of locomotives, occasionally a non-typical example turned up with a very stiff reverser which then brought condemnation down on the whole class. It is a reflection on human nature that if out of say 50 engines, there is one below par, then it is that single engine which is remembered and reviled, the other 49 being merely taken for granted.

Moving light engine or working non-fitted trains was more simple, economical and quieter than with the Black 5 or other engines fitted with the Standard LMS vacuum controlled steam brake, since there was no need

to use the small ejector to hold the brake off. Being on a simple ratchet, the independent Gresham and Craven unit was a delight to use and allowed additional braking techniques to be indulged in. It was also much appreciated on, for example, stopping passenger trains when the train could be held stationary in the platform on any gradient while at the same time creating a vacuum in the train pipe. Steam operated cylinder drain cocks proved effective and trouble free and when closed brought into use the mechanical cylinder lubricator steam atomiser.

Most of what has been said regarding the fireman applied to the driver who even more so, appreciated having all controls to hand and be able to view the road ahead at night without seeing little except for a reflection of his own features. The keener types were, for the first time, able to relate regulator openings to steam chest pressure and then experiment with precise alternative settings of cut-off whereas before it had been mainly a matter of guesswork. For those who wished to take the trouble, this instrument alone was able to engender a far higher consistency of driving over any given section.

However, as with the Black 5, they were extremely tolerant as to the driving methods adopted and gave a good showing whether worked with a partially open regulator and longish cut-off or fully open with the shortest practical cut-off. It was noticeable though, as drivers became familiar with them, that the latter method was used more frequently than with Black 5s. Apart from seeing the results of wire-drawn steam on the steam chest pressure gauge, the BR engines did not knock and rattle anything like as much when linked up. Indeed they were so smooth and comfortable that often 10 to 15% would be used when conditions allowed, whereas only the newest of Black 5s would be worked at less than 15-20%.

Despite the alterations in cylinder design, the 2in. increase in coupled wheel diameter and the slight advantage in tractive effort, there was in all honesty, little detectable difference in performance on the road and what has been said about the Black 5 applies equally to the BR engine.

Choice was therefore influenced principally by comfort and convenience and in this respect the BR5 was most certainly superior. From the fireman's point of view I would unhesitatingly opt for one every time, although it must be said that some drivers initially regarded them with less enthusiasm. Natural conservatism apart, it is human nature to feel secure and comfortable with what is well tried and familiar, therefore some genuine complaints were soon to arise. A draughty environment has always been part of loco-

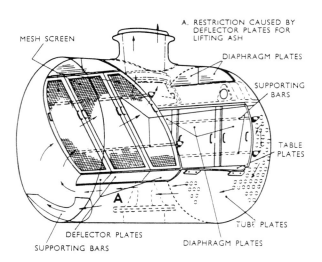

FIG. 41   TYPICAL SELF-CLEANING SMOKEBOX

motive footplate life, a condition often most welcome in high summer, but not so in winter. Being usually involved in energetic physical work, the fireman was not too discomforted, but the poor driver had no such labours to keep him warm and moreover often had to thrust his head out into an icy slipstream.

Older engines with unlagged boiler back plates radiated a considerable amount of heat, which frequently more than compensated for the reduced protection of their smaller cabs. Modern locomotives on the other hand had well insulated boiler faces and apart from being seated further from the firehole, an anti-glare shield was usually interposed. This, of course, applied equally well to both the Stanier and BR5s but because of the entirely new layout, draughts attacked the driver from different and unexpected directions which quickly brought them to his notice. Bellows were then fitted between engine and tender and these did ameliorate the effect to some degree; however a redesign on later versions returned to the use of a fall plate but now adjacent to the tender front. This still left the fireman with a continuous floor to fire from and in conjunction with a flush sided tender the grievance finally disappeared.

The other complaint rapidly to rear its head was that of fore and aft oscillations being transmitted to the trains. Two cylinder engines are balanced so as to give an acceptable hammer blow at the rail but the reduction is at the expense of a certain amount of fore and aft vibration. This compromise balance averaged around 50% which was the figure for the BR5 and indeed for many Black 5s; however, after ensuing tests the rear drawbar spring was found to be amplifying rather than damping these unwanted vibrations but by modifying the spring rates this problem was laid to rest.

Another noticeable oddity common to the larger BR tender locomotives was that when in motion, contact with less well aligned rail joints tended to set up a sympathetic drumming noise in the cab. It was in no way unpleasant and only apparent when working with a breath of steam, in fact it was simply because progression was abnormally smooth and quiet that one became aware of it at all.

I much regret that I never had the opportunity of working on one of the thirty examples fitted with the latest type outside drive line Caprotti valve gear. Rumours filtering through the railway grapevine indicated that without any of the previous vices attributed to them, they were now the fastest and most economical 5s yet. Without doubt the Caprotti arrangement blended far more pleasingly into the overall design than it did on the earlier Black 5s which were generally thought to be rather ugly.

With basically the same rocking grate, hopper ashpan and self cleaning smokebox, disposal of the BR5 was no different than dealing with the later series of Black 5s except that drivers found their inspection a little easier for the reasons previously mentioned.

As with all the BR series a very quick turn round on shed could be achieved if it suited the parties involved and union rules were not allowed to interfere, which is what had been hoped for at the outset.

At one time I would have thought it difficult to improve on a Black 5 but in just about every aspect the BR engine matched or bettered it. These excellent locomotives should have been able to carry steam forward for many years until diesels were reliable and the main lines had been electrified but such is the folly and greed of vested interest that this was not to be and withdrawal commenced in 1964.

Examples   preserved
73050,   73082,   73129 (Caprotti).

Express Passenger Engines. Introduced 1934. Total 191.

ALTHOUGH the designs of the 5XP and Black 5 ran concurrently and the former entered service a few months before the mixed traffic engine, the circumstances that brought it into being were rather different.

The Midland Railway policy of running frequent services with relatively light trains hauled by small engines worked quite well until a certain density of traffic was reached. The block system only allows a finite number of trains to occupy a length of track between two destinations at any given time and each train is kept to its allocated section by that block signalling system. The problem arises when more passengers wish to travel than can be accommodated within the limited load these small engines are able to haul. One answer is to increase train size and use two locomotives double headed and this is exactly what the Midland, and later, the LMS did. However, such a method is far from economic and could not continue indefinitely, therefore it was conceded that the alternative solution of using a single more powerful locomotive would have to be adopted.

The performance of the ex-LNWR Claughton class had not been particularly satisfactory and furthermore it had proved very expensive to maintain. Various modifications including larger boilers pressed to 200 psi and Caprotti valve gear had given some improvements but repair and running costs had remained unpleasantly high. The hurried but nevertheless highly successful introduction of seventy Royal Scots in 1927 filled the immediate requirement for a top link express locomotive but there still existed a need for a new second division express with a wider route availability than the Scots.

The idea of matching the enlarged Claughton boiler with a Scot's chassis germinated at Derby and thus the Patriot Class came into being. They were in effect a scaled down or 'Baby' Scot and soon proved not only superior to the Claughtons on the road but also over a period showed considerable savings in maintenance costs.

When Stanier took up the office of CME in 1932 he approved the building of further Patriots, albeit with minor changes pending preparation of designs for his own version. These were duly completed in time to fit taper boilers on existing frames of the last five already on order to produce the first of what were to become known as the Jubilees.

However as indicated in a previous chapter, the well tried Swindon principles of domeless boiler with low superheat did not transfer at all successfully to LMS conditions, particularly when mated to a three cylinder layout.

Initially they were considerably inferior to the Patriots as far as steaming was concerned, while superheat temperatures some 100°F lower, produced a detrimental loss in thermal efficiency with consequential higher fuel consumption. As previously discussed, a most intensive investigation was put in hand and many design changes were made to boiler and draughting arrangements as a result of numerous comparative trials. Improvements obtained with the Jubilee's 3A boiler were also applied to the similar Black 5 3B boiler although this had always been more satisfactory from the outset.

Without benefit of a modern stationary testing plant all this took some considerable time, but eventually by May 1936, Jubilees were being constructed with twenty four element sloping throatplate domed boilers with separate top feed. Trials the following year in this form indicated that they were at last showing their true potential and the resulting figures obtained were now superior to those recorded for Patriots. However, more was yet to come and by increasing the valve lead from a quarter to five sixteenths of an inch an improvement in steam distribution and mean effective pressure ensued. This modification incidentally was also applied to Royal Scots and Patriots with apparently equal success.

After a rather shaky start then, the Jubilees were at last able to take up the reigns and become the mainstay of accelerated passenger services on the Midland Division and elsewhere up to the outbreak of hostilities in 1939.

Although possessing a similarly sized boiler, albeit with a slightly larger firebox, the 6ft. 9in. diameter wheels capped by neat separate splashers conveyed the impression that it was a bigger engine than the Black 5. When coupled to their intended four thousand gallon tenders, Jubilees presented a beautifully balanced appearance of lithe agility rather than the brute power of Scots and Princess Royals.

Other than these larger coupled wheels with splashers and a reversing rod with intermediate support bracketed from the running plate, external details were similar to the Black 5s; but of course one major difference not so obvious at a casual glance was the inside cylinder and accompanying motion. This cylinder was set well forward and drove the leading coupled axle via a short connecting rod. The Jubilees 17in. x 26in. cylinders varied from other Stanier main line engine designs by having a stroke two inches shorter because of the crank axle and its clearances. Three separate sets of Walschaerts gear actuated piston valves of 10⅝in. diameter which at 62.7% of the cylinder bore gave one of the largest ratios ever used in British practice. The inside set was driven by a single eccentric on the right hand side of the crank axle giving a maximum travel of 6⅛in. which was ¼in. less than that obtained on the outside valves.

Unfortunately the inside big end proved to be a source of weakness on the Jubilees and this was never completely overcome despite modifications. 'Stink bombs' were incorporated into holes in the crank pin which when overheated released a strong smell of garlic to warn drivers of the problem. However, it frequently passed unnoticed until the big end actually disintegrated which then often caused substantial damage to the cylinder. On the other hand, cracked frames were never such a problem as they were with Black 5s and with incidences running at only just over a third of those for the two cylinder engine, they were classified as 'fair'. Admittedly at 1¹⁄₁₆in. (NBL engines were 1³⁄₃₂in.) their frame plates were slightly thicker than the initial batches of Black 5s but it was thought that the three-cylinder configuration gave a smoother torque and therefore subjected their frames to lower racking stresses from piston thrusts. For the same reasons axle-box wear on Jubilees was also somewhat reduced.

As with the Black 5s, they also benefitted in due course from improved frame stays, Horwich type horn-stays, stiffer hornblocks and manganese steel liners on the coupled axlebox faces and flanges. Not only did these features do much to reduce maintenance costs but also helped preserve the riding qualities of these engines over greater mileages.

With so many similarities with regard to fittings and cab layout, all that has been said about the Black 5 applies equally to the Jubilee and it would be pointless to repeat them. Whether it was mainly psychological or not, one always gained the impression that they were a true Express Passenger engine and more suited to this work than their two-cylinder stablemate. For example,

the firebox appeared considerably larger although in actual fact it was only just over nine inches longer than the Black 5s. Also the 6ft. 9in. coupled wheels gave it a lengthier stride and with six exhaust beats to each revolution there was always an added sense of urgency in its voice. There is no doubting the Jubilee's ability to run freely on suitable stretches with reasonable loads and many instances of speeds with maxima in the mid nineties have been recorded. Whilst this is only a few mph higher than that attained by some Black 5s, crews justifiably felt more comfortable at this pace with a Jubilee which after all had been designed for such duties.

Oiling a Jubilee during preparation was much more difficult, since not only did it possess a third set of Walschaerts motion, this additional set, invariably covered with filth, was inaccessibly located in those dark confines between the frames. For drivers then, preparation took far longer and was much dirtier and more tedious than with a Black 5 which in its later forms possessed numerous grease points apart from having only two sets of highly visible valve gear. On the other hand, firemen were not inconvenienced by this third cylinder and for them, preparation was exactly the same as with the mixed traffic engine. By the 1950s, Jubilees had dispensed with their Gresham and Craven drivers' brake valves and like the Black 5s, all were then equipped with LMS Standard Vacuum Controlled Steam Brake Units.

Getting under way was again a very similar procedure to that used with a Black 5 but having 1,155lbs more tractive effort gave it a theoretical 4½% extra pull. Jubilees certainly felt more energetic when opened up but some of this was no doubt attributable to the sharper and more rapid exhaust beat.

It might be expected that as Express Passenger engines they were maintained to higher standards than their mixed traffic brethren, but this was not normally the case. They too had set mileages to run between intermediate and general shoppings and like the Black 5s quite a dramatic deterioration of ride quality and comfort made itself felt once a certain degree of wear had taken place. In fact I experienced both extremes with Jubilees, the finest ever ride with a 4-6-0 was with No. 45699 *Galatea* and the worst with No. 45660 *Rooke*. Indeed it was difficult to believe they belonged to the same class of locomotive.

As with the Black 5, drivers were encouraged to use a wide open regulator and the shortest practical cut-off wherever possible. Lowish mileage engines responded to this method extremely well and when loaded within their capacity ran effortlessly in the eighties on level track even over relatively short stretches at around 15% cut-off. At these settings, they gave a good ride and were economical on both coal and water; however, they still performed very well when a partially open regulator was used although cut-offs would be longer at perhaps 20-25%, causing a slight increase in water consumption. With more run down examples it was necessary to reduce knock as much as possible and on occasions, prudence precluded notching up much beyond 40%; even so they still performed adequately if not too economically. Although fleet of foot, Jubilees could pull well on banks and provided the driver was prepared to 'drop her down the rack' and turn a deaf ear to the fearful cacophony this produced, they could be thrashed unmercifully to great effect. This technique was often employed when lifting a heavy train up a steep incline without losing time and although these all out attacks were of relatively short duration, quite extended efforts were possible by mortgaging the boiler and drawing on the reserve capacity of energy in the firebed. Jubilees in fact seemed to revel on runs where there was a mixture of fast stretches interspersed with sharp gradients of no more than fifteen minutes duration.

As with Black 5s it was recommended that when coasting 45% cut-off should be employed with the regulator just 'cracked' to give a breath of steam so as to reduce suction down the blast pipe. Whilst most drivers of my acquaintance used the 'drift' position of 45% very few gave them a breath of steam. However, Jubilees never suffered so badly as Black 5s from dirty valves and ports due to the balanced suction of its three cylinder configuration.

Firing a Jubilee was similar in principle to firing a Black 5 except that it required a more powerful swing of the shovel to reach the front of the grate which seemed much further away than the extra nine inches would indicate. Partly because of the nature of the work they were employed upon and partly because their extra exhaust beats and sharper blast tended to 'throw fire', a somewhat thicker firebed was normally carried. When a really prolonged effort was anticipated the rear of the firebox would be filled so as only to just permit the passage of a shovelful of coal between the top of the fire and the baffle plate. Also, because the forward sections of grate carried an increased depth, a much flatter trajectory was needed for coal to reach right to the front, hence the disproportionate amount of energy required to accomplish this.

Normally just the back damper open would admit sufficient primary air, but when carrying thicker fires I found it advantageous to use a partially open front damper as well. However, the fireman needed to be very diligent in the accurate placement of coal so as to maintain a uniform depth of fire over the whole grate area. Any neglect of this aspect of firing would soon result in holes being torn in it when the engine was being heavily worked for the reasons discussed above.

Even when carrying a thick firebed, enthusiastically driven Jubilees could be a spectacular sight at night and probably more responsible than most for lineside fires which proliferated during dry spells in late summer. At high speed, individual exhaust beats merged to produce a most exhilirating ferocious tearing roar which set the pulses racing and goaded the fireman to even greater efforts. The spark arresting capability of self cleaning smokebox equipment would have been most beneficial on these engines apart from easier servicing but sadly none were so fitted.

Generally speaking then, the fireman had to expend rather more energy than with a Black 5, but since they were usually rostered on tight schedules and allowed somewhat heavier loads this was only to be expected.

As far as steaming was concerned, I cannot recall having the slightest problem with any of them. In fact the finest example of perfect steaming in my experience was with No. 45699 *Galatea* on a run from Gloucester to Birmingham on a heavily loaded night mail in 1955. Despite the most brutal working imaginable which often required the use of both injectors to maintain boiler water level the pressure gauge needle hardly left the red line for the duration of the run. This run is described in detail in the author's previous book 'Saltley Firing Days' and following this superb performance, it was difficult to conceive that Jubilees had a steaming problem when first introduced.

Disposal of a Jubilee followed the same technique used for a Black 5 and since none were equipped with rocking grates or self cleaning smokeboxes, could involve anything up to an hour of very hard, hot and dirty work. Because of their tendency to draw cinders through the firetubes, their smokeboxes would often be filled with char, although on the other hand fires could be reasonably clean no doubt due to this same fierce blast coupled to invariable use of best quality 'passenger' coal.

As a second division Express Passenger locomotive, Jubilees were therefore excellent and once over their earlier problems, settled down to prove this for thirty years or so competently handling duties within their Class loading. Fast and economical, they could be thrashed up gradients for reasonable periods without becoming short of breath and in their designated capacity served both the LMS and BR very well indeed, while no one will deny they certainly looked the part.

Chapter 14
Stanier 2-8-0 Class 8F

Introduced 1935. Total 852.

FROM its formation in 1923, the LMS had been aware of the need for a large locomotive to replace the uneconomic working of heavy Toton to Brent coal trains by double headed 0-6-0s, a policy doggedly pursued by the Midland Railway for very many years. However, the solution at that time was not particularly simple since the route contained many severe loading restrictions although over the years, trials had been conducted with a number of types.

These included such obvious choices as the Somerset and Dorset 2-8-0 and LNWR 0-8-0 plus some not so obvious ones, the 0-10-0 Lickey Banking Engine perhaps being the most unlikely contender of all. Both Hughes and Fowler had proposed different forms of 2-8-2s but after a period of vacillation the 2-6-0 + 0-6-2 Garratt type was selected and three prototypes were constructed at Beyer Peacock in 1927, followed by a further thirty examples three years later. These enormous locomotives, nearly 88 feet in length and weighing over 155 tons managed to perform the work of two 0-6-0s, albeit using the same amount of coal; but at least they saved the cost of a driver and fireman. Having to a degree eased the Toton to Brent problem over the Midland line, there still remained on the LMS a growing requirement for mineral engines more powerful than 4Fs. The LNWR G1 and G2 class 0-8-0s seemed to possess the basic attributes and in due course Derby produced its own version which appeared in 1929. Using well designed cylinders, long-travel long-lap valves and Walschaerts gear these 7Fs showed a great improvement in economy but, like the Garratts, they too were shod with the inadequate 4F axleboxes. These proved so troublesome that only abysmally low mileages were possible between repairs and with such a fundamental limitation further expansion of the class was deemed undesirable.

Therefore, when Stanier became CME in 1932 the LMS was still deficient of an effective modern heavy mineral locomotive. As mentioned in the section dealing with Black 5s, initial priority was given to passenger and mixed traffic locomotives but the cancellation of an order for more 0-8-0 7Fs in 1934 presented him with the opportunity to introduce a 2-8-0 locomotive for assessment. The following year twelve engines duly appeared based as might be expected, around a modi-fied form of the Black 5s straight throatplate domeless 3B boiler. Originally it had been intended to use exactly the same boiler but it was then found necessary to shorten the barrel by one foot in order to move the firebox forward so that an acceptable weight distribution could be achieved. One advantage of following the 5 and 5X into production was that they benefitted from development work already in progress on the 3A and 3B boilers so that only the first batch possessed the early fourteen superheater element type. Thereafter sloping throatplate, 21 element domed versions were fitted and these proved excellent producers of steam.

In keeping with Black 5s, they slipped quietly into work without fuss or trouble almost unnoticed in the shadow of their more glamorous express passenger cousins. Gradually they multiplied, taking over the more arduous freight duties as their numbers grew, but even so only 126 had been produced by 1939 despite having in the meantime earned an excellent reputation. Then came the dramatic changes brought about by World War Two, when with a complete reversal of peacetime policy, major emphasis was placed on the movement of goods traffic. Being the most eligible contender, 8Fs were chosen by the War Department for mass production as their standard heavy freight locomotive and measures were put in hand for their construction to be undertaken not only in the workshops of all four main line companies but also by private manufacturers as well. From now on the history of 8Fs became very complex since in addition to modified versions produced to WD specification, the Railway Companies constructed them for their own use and for each other. 8Fs therefore enjoyed the distinction of operating on every line in this country and eventually in Europe and many Middle Eastern areas too. Although not all of the 8Fs produced were returned, the LMS in due course found themselves with a vast fleet of modern heavy freight locomotives which proved an invaluable asset after the war when the bulk of mineral traffic was still being conveyed by rail. Having such ample provision in the heavyweight division, enabled subsequent construction to be concentrated on the long needed replacement of elderly Class 2, 3 and 4 0-6-0s together with satisfying an ever growing demand for Black 5s. However, a requirement became identified to run larger loads at fitted speeds and it was felt that the extra tractive power of 8Fs would show to advantage over certain routes. In order that they could perform these duties without shaking themselves or the track to pieces a number of engines were modified so that they had 50% of the reciprocating weights balanced instead of the previous 66%. This was to reduce hammer blow at high rotational speeds and engines so converted displayed a five pointed star on the cab side.

Later, this requirement for heavy fast freights was more than adequately filled by the incomparable 9Fs and so these modified 8Fs were really only a stop-gap measure of doubtful success. Although surpassed in every way by the BR 2-10-0s, 8Fs continued to perform their allotted tasks efficiently and economically, even if not too comfortably, through to the end of steam.

The general appearance of 8Fs was very similar to that of Black 5s and in keeping with Stanier's other locomotives it presented a modern design of well balanced proportions. Of course its wheels were smaller and the running plate lower, but these features only served to emphasise the impression of powerful efficiency. The difference in size of 7in. less length and 224lbs weight passed unnoticed and the description of the Black 5s boiler, cab, fittings and tender serve equally well for 8Fs and do not require repetition. Some obvious minor variations occurred such as a straight reversing rod instead of the original one which curved downwards at the weigh shaft end, but on the whole, 8Fs did not deviate too much from their initial specification and certainly not to the extent experienced by Black 5s.

Although both locomotives shared the same cylinder and valve dimensions, it is interesting to note that the valve port width on 8Fs was ⅛in. narrower, but in respect of lap, lead and valve travel they were the same. Presumably it was thought that the 2-8-0 would be worked at longer cut-offs and at slower piston speed than the mixed traffic engine.

For the driver, preparation was virtually the same except for an extra set of coupled wheels with their attendant brake gear and when compared to later Black 5s, less grease lubrication was used, but even so the extra work occupied but a few minutes. On the other hand, firemen found the lower running plate made things slightly easier when filling its six sandboxes although judging how full the four forward ones were was just as difficult as with the 4-6-0. Steam sanding delivered to the front of the leading and third coupled wheels and to the rear of the latter and in general it was commendably effective.

The cab and its layout were identical even to the extent of possessing those excellent folding windshields mounted ahead of the opening side windows. It also possessed all the same advantages and disadvantages, although one became far more aware of the latter with a 8F. The chronic congestion which was so much part of the railway scene during the fifties often meant, as far as freight working was concerned, hours of waiting between movements of relatively short duration. With their airy cabs and fully lagged boiler faces 8Fs were not the warmest of engines and since night was most favoured for freight work, conditions when static especially if 'wrong way to the weather' could be very unpleasant indeed. It was at these times that the shortcomings of their wooden tip-up seats and the appeal of an old 3Fs generous locker lid were most felt!

Moving an 8F light engine soon demonstrated that possessing a third more tractive effort and coupled wheels only 4ft. 8½in. in diameter gave it a definite edge over the Black 5 in terms of initial acceleration and if in good condition they would run sweetly at 60mph or so. Unfortunately, few seemed to be in prime shape and with most, extreme discomfort would be felt long before this speed was reached. However, it must be born in mind that 60mph gives an equivalent piston speed of 80mph with a Black 5 and many of the latter became unbearably rough at that pace. The majority of heavy freights were rarely called upon to exceed 30mph and because most were run at longish cut-offs, excessive knocks in both motion and axleboxes could be kept to tolerable levels.

As with other Stanier designs though, quite a rapid deterioration seemed to take place in these bearings once the halfway point between repairs had been passed, although of course, this was to some extent dependent on the type of work and level of maintenance each locomotive had enjoyed.

Level of maintenance is the key to all locomotive performance, given that other things are equal, and certain defects are more serious to some locomotive types than others. For example, 8Fs had excellent boilers but they were rarely called upon to steam at anything more than very modest rates for much of the time. If the boiler was not always quite up to scratch it would often pass unnoticed. Likewise if valves and pistons were overdue for attention it is doubtful whether this would affect a leisurely crawl along the goods line, and only the crew are likely to suffer the effects of worn bearings. But because adhesion, particularly when starting heavy loads or climbing steep inclines is so important to a freight locomotive, anything which affects this can be very detrimental and of course greasy rails amplify the problem tenfold.

Wear and fatigue in the coupled wheel springs

unbalance the engine's weight distribution which in turn leads to a serious loss of adhesion and consequent excessive slipping. Unfortunately laminated spring performance was not very good on the LMS and frequent repairs and replacements were required between successive visits to workshops. Moreover, facilities and expertise varied widely from depot to depot and the situation was not rendered any easier by the difficulty in adjusting nuts and cotters seized by corrosion and fretting. Badly worn tyres was perhaps the second most serious cause of inadequate grip and not infrequently went hand in glove with worn everything else. Of course these detrimental effects could be considerbly reduced providing the sanding gear worked efficiently but regrettably our notorious British damp climate did not favour free running dry sand and unclogging sand traps was a routine occupation. The haulage capacity of 8Fs could therefore vary considerably but even so an engine in average condition handled heavy freight far more competently than any other on the system until 1954 when 9Fs appeared.

Furthermore like the Black 5s, they instilled a high degree of confidence in their crews since they tended to flatter the less skilled while at the same time allowing exceptional performance to be extracted by the proficient.

Driving methods were, as always, adapted to the circumstances at the time and perhaps the best way of illustrating this is to describe some of the duties allocated to 8Fs at Saltley MPD Birmingham.

Many 8Fs were perpetually occupied with the transfer of goods traffic between the LM and the old Great Western via Bordesley Junction on the Camp Hill line. Because this traffic was almost continuous, involving maximum loose coupled trains of around fifty wagons, a bevy of 8Fs was rostered and for convenience were allotted 'trip' numbers, although each trip covered exactly the same six mile round journey. Rather like buses on a circular route, time tables or delays were not too significant because what got left behind by one was invariably collected by the next.

Trains usually departed from Washwood Heath Junction and being nearly 1,000 tons gross weight, a certain amount of delicacy was needed to make progress on the 1:326/315 adverse gradient particularly if rail conditions were poor. Once on the move a steady 5-7mph could be maintained along the goods line using two thirds of the regulator's first valve at about 60% cut-off. A bank pilot was always requested at the West End Sidings which then provided rear end assistance to Bordesley Junction. These 'trippers' were inevitably brought to a stand at Duddeston Road where they might

wait upwards of an hour until the Western was ready to receive them. They therefore had to make a cold start on a 1:172 gradient albeit with the aid of a banker, but it was prudent to ensure that the sanding gear operated satisfactorily.

Once under way, provided the distant signals showed clear, it was usual to open the regulator to full first valve and try and build up as much momentum as quickly as possible before too much of the train ran onto the following 1:105 approaching Brickyard Crossing. If adhesion was good then the regulator could be fully opened with confidence while cut-off would be reduced to about 60% in order to achieve a run at the 1:62 section up to St. Andrews Junction.

If speed dropped noticeably here, a reversion to full gear would be quickly made because this was the most common place for the train to stick. Beyond St. Andrews, the gradient eased slightly to 1:85 and after a further half mile, over which the regulator was usually brought back to full first valve and the reverser notched up to 55%, the engine could be eased for a controlled entry into Bordesley.

It was interesting to note that providing the Class 3F banking engine was doing its share, then the 8F would be hauling two thirds of the train i.e. 34 wagons the remaining sixteen wagons being pushed by the pilot.

Firing 8Fs required the same techniques as used with Black 5s; they steamed just as readily and possessed a similar thermal reserve. With such 'stop-go' working as encountered with Bordesley trip duties, it was not necessary or desirable to carry a heavy fire and the only time it would be built up to a reasonable depth was just prior to the one and a half mile assault on the bank proper which entailed only ten minutes of continuous working.

After a period of shunting in Bordesley, a train of empties or mixed goods would then be taken back to Washwood Heath, when the whole operation started over again. In complete contrast to these leisurely trip duties moving heavy trains over short distances, was another involving the Western Region, only on this occasion it entailed much deeper penetration into that foreign territory.

The Long Marston was a Class A non-fitted mixed freight which because it was run over former Great Western metals, carried a prestige out of all proportion to the actual importance of the train and indeed gave the link its name.

It ran daily from Washwood Heath West End via Bordesley Junction to Long Marston, the MOD establishment some five miles south west of Stratford-upon-Avon. The route contained some notable banks upon

For many years any heavy, arduous or special work seemed to be invariably allocated to 8Fs, such was the fine reputation they steadily acquired. With the attributes of long endurance, spacious crew accommodation, high tractive effort and good adhesion, they were the obvious choice for snow ploughing duties. Mounted below the front buffer beam, as shown in this picture of 8703, these small ploughs were very effective and when conditions were particularly difficult, two such 8Fs would be coupled back to back.

which many Western 'vacuum' trains struggled for steam, but the Midland crews felt duty bound to fly the flag and delighted in demonstrating their superiority whenever possible. This competitive spirit must also have pervaded the upper echelons, since the best available 8F was always provided to assist in this attempt at 'one-upmanship'.

Unlike the trip turns, everything concerned with the Long Marston moved with great alacrity and no sooner had the engine been coupled to its train than it was called out of the yard. Signals cleared like magic, invariably giving an uninterrupted run on to the Western which, in turn, went to remarkable lengths to ensure it was not found lacking and often allowed the train to occupy paths allocated to its own vacuum fitteds. With so much effort focussed to eliminate delays, every day on this turn proved an exciting and enjoyable adventure.

Although trains were usually a substantial 40 to 50 wagons, half of which could be coal, drivers strove to gain as much speed as safety permitted by Duddeston Road and once past this Junction a wide open regulator and between 50 to 65% cut-off would maintain a steady 20mph up to Bordesley, provided the pilot played its

part. Of course with the prospect of some 30 miles of continuous hard work, the fire needed to be well built up prior to departure, a process which commenced before leaving the shed.

Fairly light running at 45% and a breath of steam sufficed for the short distance to Tyseley Junction from where the seven mile haul to Earleswood Lakes began. This was an undulating climb of gradients varying between 1:502 to 1:159 and was usually tackled on full first valve with the reverser being moved around in the 45-60% band. Twelve shovels of coal fired at 30 to 60 second intervals and continued use of the exhaust injector normally kept a full head of steam and water an inch from the top of the gauge class. With the prospect of a ten mile descent to Brearly West Junction following Earlswood Lakes summit, the fire was allowed gradually to run down over the final mile or so, the aim being to commence this lengthy period of coasting with full steam pressure for maximum braking effort, a thin fire and plenty of room in the boiler to avoid blowing off.

As ever, it was recommended that when coasting, the reversing screw should be in the 'drift' position of 45% cut-off and the regulator just cracked open. Whilst most Midland drivers habitually used the former, few could bring themselves to give the engine a breath of steam while so doing.

On long descents it was customary to apply the hand brake so as to reduce surging by keeping the train buffered up during intermittent use of the steam brake and this was invariably pursued especially over the 4½ mile drop of 1:150 following Wood End Tunnel. Despite some short rises it was not necessary to carry a thick fire for the rest of the run, since gradients were mainly favourable enabling 35-40mph to be maintained on a partially opened regulator and 25-40% cut-off. At these speeds the average 8F did not demand any particular balancing feats from the fireman while the driver could remain seated in reasonable comfort.

Although the homeward journey normally only involved returning with a full train of empty wagons it was run with the same sense of urgency and because of the challenge presented by sixteen miles of virtually continuous uphill slogging, it proved more demanding.

Five miles of easy running to Stratford served to prepare the fire ready for the arduous climb back up to the Lakes summit, a climb which commenced in earnest some three quarters of a mile from Wooton Wawen. A surprising amount of effort is required to lift 50 empty wagons up a 1:150 gradient particularly if a cross wind is blowing which was often the case here. However, full regulator and around 40% cut-off would suffice to maintain speed in the thirties for that ten mile haul, a continuous output 8Fs could produce with no undue stress. Steaming was usually very reliable even with 'goods quality' coal, although the firing rate would probably be in the order of 3,000lbs per hour or more.

Of course the majority of freight workings were not of such high order and while individual engines could be booked on runs of perhaps a hundred miles, much of it was covered at a more modest pace.

To operate loose coupled trains efficiently and safely it was not only necessary to have adequate hauling power, it was even more important to be able to stop. Fortunately the 8F possessed extremely effective brakes which engendered a high degree of confidence and were in fact considerably more powerful pro-rata than those of, for example, a 4F. I was exceedingly grateful for this attribute when attempting my first descent of the Lickey Incline with a non-fitted train. With the 8F I managed to halt dead on target at the water column, but had the engine been an older 0-6-0 it may not have resulted with such success.

Occasionally 8Fs were called upon to head passenger trains and although I did not experience this personally, we did at one period work a number of empty coach specials with them. During high summer a great deal of coaching stock moved South and West at weekends on Holiday Specials from Northern towns. Naturally these had to be returned as soon as possible for other duties and this was economically achieved by combining two such ten coach sets and running them behind an 8F. These were the only occasions I was able to experience their behaviour at higher speeds and fortunately 8Fs in good condition were normally chosen for the specials.

Bringing these impressive quarter mile long trains back from Bristol was not particularly demanding because despite a 650 ton load, the twenty bogies ran far more freely than an equivalent weight of freight wagons and point-to-point timmings were in any case relatively lenient. Even so, speeds of around 60mph could be achieved on many stretches which as previously mentioned is equivalent to about 80mph with a Black 5. I must confess to being amazed how smoothly the engine ran at this pace on my first trip, but then it had just been recently shopped and was still in absolutely prime condition.

With a partially open regulator and around 25% cut-off, progression at peak speed was remarkably quiet with no knocks or rattles, while the ride was very stable and free from lateral oscillations. Strangely enough the only time that we had a rough journey was with one of the specially balanced 'starred' 8Fs. This particular locomotive had obviously covered a fair mileage since last visiting works and despite running it at no shorter cut-off than about 40%, the bearings thumped like a steam hammer while it swayed and lurched in a most uncomfortable manner. As a result we came to the conclusion that when run down, the starred versions were just as bad as the others and a low mileage engine was preferred whatever the type.

Back on shed, disposal of 8Fs followed the same procedure as used with Black 5s, although generally their fires were in a worse state. Being normally fuelled with indifferent 'goods quality' coal produced a higher ratio of ash and clinker, while being confined to congested goods line led to long hours out in service with scant attention being paid to the cleaning of fires. Bordesley 'Trippers', for example, were rostered to be out for 24 hours covered by three sets of crews, but it was often more like 30 hours before returning to the shed and by this time the fire would be in a deplorable condition. Like the earlier Black 5s they were not fitted with rocking grates and self-cleaning smokeboxes retrospectively, which is a pity since not only would they have maintained a higher state of efficiency while on the road, they would also have enjoyed a faster turn round at depots.

From the foregoing it should be apparent that 8Fs were allocated a wide range of duties which they handled quietly and competently to the end of steam. Their many attributes endeared them to their crews who felt secure and confident that there was nothing better in their class at the time. Fortunately a number can still be seen gently trundling about doing light duties on preserved lines, but never again will their distinctive full throated exhaust be heard pounding up an incline with a heavy train of coal wagons which was, after all, what they were designed for.

Introduced 1927 Total 33.

THE circumstances and reasons for constructing a number of large articulated mineral locomotives to replace double headed 0-6-0s working Midland Toton-Brent heavy coal traffic has already been touched upon in the section dealing with 8F 2-8-0s. It will be recalled that the decision was made because severe weight and dimensional restrictions over these lines precluded the use of a conventional heavy mineral locomotive design. Hughes at Horwich had schemed four and later, three cylinder versions of a 2-8-2, but when these were dropped for the above reasons, thoughts turned to articulation.

Although Hughes had in mind a 2-6-0:0-6-2 layout, Beyer Peacock when confronted with specific requirements, recommended a 2-6-2:2-6-2 arrangement, and had they been allowed to proceed it would have incorporated all the latest principles which made the marque so successful on overseas railways. At approximately the same time Anderson, the forceful Motive Power Superintendent and former chief draughtsman at Derby, had been quite separately negotiating with Beyers for a 'Midlandised' Garratt.

Following Hughes' retirement in September 1925, design was transferred to Derby where Fowler had been appointed CME, but such was the dichotomy prevalent on the LMS at that time, Anderson rather than Fowler masterminded the Garratt development. Unfortunately insistence upon using cylinders and valve gear which he himself had developed for the Somerset and Dorset 2-8-0s resulted in a short valve travel of only 3¾in. Even worse, Beyer Peacock was not permitted to employ its normal generous size axleboxes and was obliged to use the very inadequate Midland pattern instead. No logic can be found in this short sighted obduracy, because Derby had already adopted long-travel, long-lap valves together with excellent axleboxes for the Horwich 2-6-0, 2-6-4 Tank and Royal Scot designs. One can only conclude that this insistence on using traditional and out-dated principles was motivated by nothing more than an unhealthy degree of arrogance and self aggrandisement. Therefore, when three prototype 2-6-0:0-6-2 Garratts appeared in 1927 only their Belpaire boiler and frames were of Beyer Peacock design, much of the remainder being strongly influenced by archaic Midland dogma.

However, with a tractive effort at 85% BP of 45,620lbs they were successfully able to perform the work of two 0-6-0s albeit at the same 17mph average speed and using a similar quantity of coal. They did, of course, save the expense of one set of enginemen, although the firemen naturally had to work twice as hard, but even this economy was to some extent eroded by the need for its undersized axleboxes to require shop repairs at lower than average mileages.

These three original locomotives had fixed seven ton capacity coal bunkers plus tanks at each end holding a total of 4,700 gallons, some 3,030 gallons of which was contained in the leading one. These were also the only examples of the class to be equipped with ejectors, train pipe and LMS vacuum controlled steam brake. Subsequent trials exposed a number of faults but even so a further 30 locomotives were delivered in 1930, although these did incorporate some minor changes. In order to try and obtain a free exhaust at reduced cut-offs while retaining a short valve travel, D.W. Sanford had developed a 'double exhaust valve'. These valves did give some improvement in economy but the results were much inferior to those produced by normal long travel gear and sometimes they were difficult to extract for servicing.

A more obvious change was the deletion of vacuum equipment, it no doubt being thought that these particular Garratts were not suitable for fast fitted trains. Also, one locomotive was supplied with a Beyer Peacock patent totally enclosed, self trimming rotating coal bunker of nine tons capacity. This overcame the objections of coal dust blowing into the cab when travelling bunker first and the problem of having to work coal forward at double the normal rate. It proved so successful that it was transferred to one of the original fixed bunker prototypes and the new batch of thirty all received ten ton versions.

No Garratts were stabled at Saltley and therefore my experience with them is far less comprehensive than with many other types, so apart from servicing duties on shed, it was confined to mainly relief of through freights. Even so, this could mean runs of up to fifty miles radius encompassing Gloucester, Derby and Toton and would embrace heavy mineral, mixed goods and empty wagon trains.

As was often the case, my first encounter with Garratts was on shed and there is no doubt about it, they appeared truly massive engines. Their size seemed even more awesome when stepping straight off one of our

Jinties, but with an overall length of 88 feet, they were very nearly three times as long and at 155.5 tons, well over three times as heavy as the 0-6-0 tank. We regarded parallel boiler Royal Scots as having very impressive boilers in terms of diameter but the Garratts was six inches greater and looked even more so because of its shorter barrel length.

One advantage of this particular articulated design is that a very large well proportioned boiler together with an equally large firebox and ashpan can be easily incorporated inside the loading gauge without compromising its performance in any way.

As may be imagined, a locomotive of these dimensions was something of a nuisance even at a depot as large as Saltley and at busy times they were often only coaled before being moved quickly to the nearby Bromford Sidings for disposal and preparation. Not that coaling rotary bunkers was a particularly speedy operation since it entailed climbing aloft armed with a coal pick before proceeding under the hopper. Three sets of double doors on top of the bunker needed to be opened and with each being secured by a long sturdy 'pin' which was more often bent than straight, a lot of persuasion with the coal pick was usually required. With steps all over the place and a liberal supply of hand holds, this climb was not too difficult and could be achieved from the cab or up the rear of the bunker unit.

Water filling holes were provided on both tanks, but firemen felt more secure when standing on the rear unit's flat platform, the front's curved upper shoulders warranting a measure of caution. In addition, a water scoop which could be used in either direction delivered to the front unit and when leading, could provide the crew with a very wet experience if allowed to over fill.

Being in effect two engines supplied from a single large boiler, Garratts consumed just as much fuel as the double headed 0-6-0s they replaced and at times this caused firemen to work at unaccustomed high rates. However, their labours were eased somewhat by fitting ten ton self trimming rotating bunkers which relieved them of the task of getting coal forward. This view of 4994 clearly shows the three sets of double doors in the top of the bunker through which it was filled.

Mounting the rather narrow steps to the footplate was quite a struggle if laden with equipment because, in addition to three steps instead of two, the doorway into the large twin side window cab was not particularly wide. However, once inside it offered the best of both worlds with the spaciousness of an 8F and the protection of tank engine all on one solid platform. The lagged boiler face was similar to that of a Crab in general arrangement but the absence of vacuum and steam heating equipment together with their gauges and pipework left its large area relatively uncluttered.

There were some controls unique to Garratts, its steam brake was but a simple valve, the handle of which operated in a 90° arc and both the rotary bunker gear and the arrangement for opening a section of grate was to be found nowhere else on the LMS. Forward vision around, over and past the vast boiler was bad enough but then the front unit added its obstruction, so that closing onto stock with buffers nearly sixty feet away could present problems. Rear view was somewhat better being less affected by steam obscuration but it was useful to have an alert fireman assisting as often as possible.

With having, in effect, two engines to deal with, drivers found preparation a very lengthy task made even more daunting by all the additoinal points not found on normal locomotives, but at least outside motion meant much was accessible. Neither did firemen have an easy time especially if the sandboxes required filling, for this alone could prove to be a monumental labour, while building up the fire took twice as long as usual.

Driving a Garratt was also a different experience because although controls were conventionally arranged, steam had a long way to travel to the cylinders and response to both regulator and brake was rather leisurely.

The enormous bulk demanded extreme care when manoeuvring on shed or in confined spaces, nor was this helped by numerous blows which in the fifties seemed to afflict most of the class. Being in the evening of their lives, possibly less maintenance was accorded them than in former days but with so much steam passing backwards and forwards along their length it was hardly surprising. In cold weather with the regulator open it was sometimes impossible to see much beyond the cab until travelling at 15-20mph and even then only by coasting could one's bearings be established. While working lightly, and this was a frequent occurrence with such a powerful machine when travelling slowly over easy roads, exhaust steam could roll down from the chimney further obscuring the driver's vision. Worst of all though, was dense fog, for even when not generating its own personal cloud the forward unit could be well past a stop signal by the time it became visible to the driver.

Encased in over 150 tons of metal, happenings at the outer extremities seemed rather remote, so that normal snatches and buffets felt by smaller engines when running loose coupled trains were far less noticeable. Therefore extra care had to be used when starting and stopping not only for the guard's comfort but also because it was that much easier to break a coupling. However, once under way Garratts slowly gained pace with the lack of fuss and inevitability of an ocean going liner, the exhaust making a soft, indistinct woofle somewhat reminiscent of the 0-10-0 Lickey Banker. Their trains, whether fully loaded or empty, seemed of no consequence to Garratts, who's ponderous progress was little hindered by such trivialities, nor did undulations of the track check their pace unduly once momentum had been built up.

Perhaps most difficult to come to terms with was the remoteness and isolation from what one was used to being part of. For example if the front unit slipped there would be no violent oscillations and crashes and bangs, the crew was so insulated by design and distance that it could almost pass unnoticed. The same applied if its motion bearings and axleboxes were worn; and one was not conscious either of the shouldering action of piston thrusts or the sharp bark of an exhaust which indicated valve event were in good order. Whilst all this detachment from the business end provided crews with a higher degree of comfort, it also equally removed sensitivity and that essential 'feel' a driver needs in order to obtain optimum results. However, it cannot be denied that the Garratts provided a really superb rock steady ride, at least up to 40mph which was about the fastest I ever travelled on one. There are, of course, many locomotives when new that will provide superb rides at this speed, but Garratts never seemed any different and one colleague enthusiastically extolled their virtues after a particularly hair-raising descent of Lickey.

Due to circumstances that were never quite clear, they departed from Blackwell with a heavy train of coal and pig iron of which only the front portion had the wagon brakes properly pinned down, and minus their guard who was unable to rejoin his own rapidly moving brake van.

Descending the 1:37 gradient at express speed, the driver was not a little alarmed to find that they were being diverted on to the slow line through Bromsgrove Station. Although the facing points here are probably about the best in the country, they carried a 40mph speed restriction and the Garratt was travelling at half as much again. To the crew's intense relief both it and the runaway train passed through without incident before finally coming to a halt three and a half miles down the line at Stoke Works Junction. It seems the Garratt behaved impeccably and rode like a coach all the way, which was just as well in the circumstances. This episode tends to confirm that there was nothing inherent in the Garratt principle to deter them from fast running and one can only speculate what might have developed on the LMS had they been equipped with long-travel long-lap valves and adequately shod.

Most of their lives though, were spent doing what they were designed for, trundling along at modest speeds with maximum length mineral trains in tow. For this they were driven in the manner of a 4F with a partially open regulator and longish cut-offs of certainly no less than 35%.

According to E.S. Cox, fitting double exhaust valves did effect some savings and tests over the Toton-Brent route showed reductions in coal consumption from an original 128.7lbs to 112.6lbs per mile and water consumption was likewise down from 88.3 to 84.6 gallons per mile.

Even with these improvements, it must be remembered that the firemen would still be working at nearly double the rate required by a 4F loaded pro-rata. Firing a Garratt could therefore be physically demanding and no doubt was, on long uninterrupted runs; however this was a rarity on the type of work generally assigned to them in the fifties when goods lines were moribund with congestion. Large engines were slow to warm up and equally slow to cool down and were therefore not so suited to 'stop-go' progression as smaller locomotives such as 3Fs, but fires still have to be maintained which inevitably led to a certain amount of wasted effort and wasted fuel.

Most firemen, particularly when coming from small Midland locomotives, gazed in awe on opening a Garratt's sliding firedoors and seeing for the first time its enormous firebox. With a grate area of 44.5 sq.ft. it was large by any standards but wide grates are usually shallow;; not so on the Garratt, however, for it was also far deeper than most. The generally accepted fire shape if any serious work was to be done was similar to that of 4Fs, although the flat grate did not demand it. The reason for filling the back of its firebox to mouthpiece level was primarily to ease the fireman's labours as the journey progressed. As can be visualised it required less effort to dump coal just inside the firehole and allow gravity and vibration to feed both front and sides than to fire it there with a thrust of the shovel. It was usual in these circumstances to open just the rear damper which tended to further concentrate activity at the back half of the grate. Should the situation arise when a lengthy halt was anticipated then a hole could be pushed in the thinner firebed at the front with a rake or clinker shovel. This would adequately control furnace temperature and prevent noisy blowing off through its four pop valves, although it was usual to maintain water level at only about two thirds of a glass which then allowed plenty of room to reduce boiler pressure with injected water.

Fire-irons were neatly located in a rack alongside the bunker but care had to be taken when obtaining and using these while in motion.

The fireman's main effort came when initially building up the fire since even one and a half tons of fuel shovelled on the grate would still leave room for more. Needless to say, any lumps of coal that would pass through the firehole were dropped in the rear of the firebox but because this was usually done 'against the clock', it raised more than an odd bead of perspiration. Of course he would still have to continue his labours under steady running conditions but this would then only require a firing rate of around one ton per hour which was quite reasonable.

The steam operated rotary bunker was a great boon to firemen as the fuel supply became used up and everyone enjoyed the novelty of being able to bring a couple of tons of coal to the shovelling plate by a few revolutions without the effort of working it forward with pick and shovel. Despite this labour-saving device, the enclosed cab could become quite warm, especially when travelling forward, but fortunately the roof was provided with two large ventilators which helped to keep temperatures tolerable.

Generally speaking, its large boiler steamed well, for although the exhaust sounded rather muffled it seemed to generate an adequate draught through the fire. Injector feed rates must have been matched to boiler capacity because either the exhaust steam or live steam injector could maintain boiler water level without difficulty under average working conditions. Therefore in spite of in effect, firing for two engines, the fireman at least benefitted from some aids in addition to enjoying a steady one piece platform upon which to stand and plenty of room to swing a long handled firing shovel.

Disposal did prove to be physically demanding and because of the engines' sheer size generally took far longer than usual. When Garratts arrived on shed for servicing they had normally been in traffic for many hours which would naturally equate with an empty bunker, a dirty fire and full ashpan and smokebox. Using a very thick firebed at the back of the firebox tended to increase clinker formation in this area so that often quantities were quite awesome. With commendable foresight the designers had arranged for a section of grate in the left front corner to swing down and through this aperture fire and dross could be dropped into the ashpan below. However, before this could take place, it was first necessary to clear the ashpan because any live fire dropping into it could cause severe buckling. With front and rear dampers wide open it was possible to do this from the trackside with a long ashpit rake using a pushing and pulling motion. Working first from the left and then from the right side it was in itself an exhausting task for the ashpan's capacity was colossal, but it had to be cleared completely before dropping the fire commenced. For this reason, it required two men working in unison, one on the footplate, the other raking out as before. Once this was completed attention could be turned to its smokebox which was just as vast as the rest of the engine but at least there was a large safe platform to shovel from.

Although Garratts managed for a time to do the job they were built for, they did so with no real improvement in efficiency or saving in cost other than a set of enginemen, one of whom had to work twice as hard. Moreover, their size made them a nuisance and maintenance costs were high. Had not Derby interfered with Beyer Peacock's original proposals it might have been a different story but that is a matter for conjecture; as it was 8Fs and later 9Fs performed their duties with far greater economy and less effort for their crews.

Chapter 16
B.R. Standard 2-10-0 Class 9F

Heavy Goods Locomotive. Introduced 1954. Total 251.

THE REASONS for building the range of British Railway's Standard Steam Locomotives together with the motivation and design philosophy that brought them in being has already been covered when dealing with BR Standard Class 5MTs. However, it may be useful to remind readers how original proposals for a heavy goods engine eventually evolved to become the 2-10-0 9Fs.

The original proposals envisaged a 2-8-2 with a sixteen and a half ton axle loading using the smaller of two boilers to be developed for new Pacifics in Class 5, 6 and 7 power categories, but owing to the release of numerous ex-WD 2-8-0s and Stanier 8Fs, there was no immediate requirement for such a locomotive. It was felt when the need did arise, some increase in running speed would be desirable and since this was limited by the small 4ft. 8½in. diameter wheels of current 2-8-0s, coupled wheels of 5ft. 3in. diameter would be more in keeping.

Apparently Riddles then took a hand, being somewhat unhappy over the 2-8-2 proposal for, as he pointed out, freight engines depended on adhesion and this layout offered little advantage over 2-8-0s. His wartime experience in designing and operating WD locomotives had impressed upon him the advantages of ten-coupled wheel arrangements and once he was satisfied that 5ft. 0in. diameter wheels could be accommodated under a

wide firebox within the L2 loading gauge, the decision was made to follow this path. However, placing the grate over its trailing coupled wheels pitched the boiler too high for the Pacific boiler to be utilised and still remain within the desired loading gauge. A new boiler therefore, had to be designed specifically for 9Fs with the maximum diameter reduced to 6ft. 1in., some 4½in. less than before, which unfortunately gave the slightly inferior free area ratio of 13.6%. This disadvantage may have possibly been redressed to some extent by the barrel length being 1ft. 9in. shorter while its grate area was only 1.8 sq.ft. less than the 4-6-2s. In any event it was felt that overall performance would not be adversely affected because of the lower steam demands made in general freight working. While a great deal of attention had been given to provide the Pacifics with an exceptionally large hopper ashpan, dimensional restrictions on the 9F prevented this component from being quite so generously proportioned, but it was sloped as steeply as space would allow.

Because of their superior adhesion, 9Fs were provided with normal slide type regulator valves in the dome instead of the more sensitive multiple valve regulators fitted to Pacifics. However, on some early 9F examples, slipping had caused their regulators to become locked in the open position due to high differential pressure between the valve faces. A solution was found by fitting

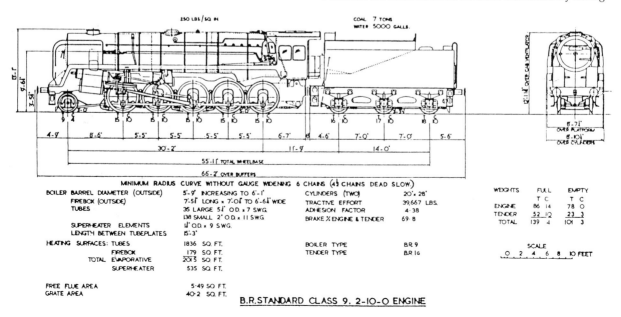

BOILER BARREL DIAMETER (OUTSIDE)	5'-9" INCREASING TO 6'-1"	CYLINDERS (TWO)	20" x 28"	
FIREBOX (OUTSIDE)	7'-5½" LONG x 7'-0½" TO 6'-6¼" WIDE	TRACTIVE EFFORT	39,667 LBS.	
TUBES	35 LARGE 5⅛" O.D. x 7 SWG	ADHESION FACTOR	4·38	
	138 SMALL 2" O.D. x 11 SWG	BRAKE % ENGINE & TENDER	69·8	
SUPERHEATER ELEMENTS	1⅛" O.D. x 9 SWG.			
LENGTH BETWEEN TUBEPLATES	15'-3"			
HEATING SURFACES: TUBES	1836 SQ. FT.	BOILER TYPE	BR.9	
FIREBOX	179 SQ. FT.	TENDER TYPE	BR.1G	
TOTAL EVAPORATIVE	2015 SQ. FT.			
SUPERHEATER	535 SQ. FT.			
FREE FLUE AREA	5·49 SQ. FT.			
GRATE AREA	40·2 SQ. FT.			

WEIGHTS	FULL		EMPTY	
	T C		T C	
ENGINE	86 14		78 0	
TENDER	52 12		23 3	
TOTAL	139 4		101 3	

SCALE
0 2 4 6 8 10 FEET

B.R. STANDARD CLASS 9. 2-10-0 ENGINE

the smaller valve from a Class 4 4-6-0 which gave a free area of only 22 sq.in. but despite this considerable restriction in its main steam circuit, no detrimental effect seemed to result in practice.

Although this decision to change the original proposal of a 2-8-2 to a 2-10-0 had enforced modifications which on paper compromised the final design somewhat, in practice these alterations proved most fortuitous.

Thus the last of BR's twelve types of Standard locomotives came into being and not only was it the most successful of the dozen but it proved to be just about the finest general purpose, do anything, mixed traffic engine ever produced in this country. Had the engineers set out to design such a machine in the first place it would have been a noteworthy achievement but having intended a heavy freight engine made the result even more remarkable. It naturally took time before BR realised just how magnificent and amazingly versatile this 9F could be, but it possessed all the right attributes in abundance.

The boiler produced steam in prodigious quantities even when using fuel of indifferent quality, demanding no great skill from firemen. The engine was extremely powerful yet ran like the wind and gave a beautiful ride at all speeds, while the fittings were thoughtfully positioned and worked well with good reliability. Furthermore the engine crew was able to appreciate all these features from the superb comfort and convenience provided by the BR cab and tender layout.

Although introduced in 1954, not many were initially seen in the Saltley area and in any case during the period 1955-56 I was enjoying life in the Passenger Links, so it was not until two years later that I was able to inspect one at close range. I was then in the top freight group booked with a very garrulous and conservative driver and it was when walking across the shed yard with him one day we spied a brand new example standing in a nearby siding. With me it was a case of love at first sight but he was nothing like so impressed, for on being asked what he thought, merely commented: "bloody great black thing – all boiler and wheels" – which I suppose summed it up pretty succinctly.

To a less jaundiced eye, though the 9F looked a most imposing engine, its large smoke deflectors emphasising the size of the massive boiler and wide firebox which blended smoothly into the streamlined BR cab, I imagine being conditioned over the years in associating this type of configuration with Pacific express passenger locomotives lent weight to the impression of power and speed. Adding in no small measure to the power aspect were the prominent cylinders and ten-coupled wheels which appeared rather smaller than they actually were because of the high level running plate. The rarity of this

ten-coupled arrangement tended to focus one's attention on them and I recall noticing the absence of a flange on the centre coupled wheels and reduced flanges on the second and fourth. This was, of course, to enable the exceptionally long 22ft. 0in. coupled wheelbase to negotiate normal six chain curves (four and a half dead slow) with no more difficulty than other engines. Just about all the features including tender variations already described for the Class 5 apply to 9Fs and even in the cab the main difference lay in the size and shape of the boiler back plate. Being higher and wider and devoid of carriage warming apparatus and speedometer it was even less cluttered, presenting a remarkably tidy appearance.

Opening the standard sliding firedoors revealed a large oval firehole through which could be seen its 40.2 sq.ft. rocking grate of almost square dimensions. Placing it over the rear coupled wheels reduced the firebox volume to a lower value then had been obtained with the Pacifics which in theory would lead to a slight disadvantage at high combustion levels. It also made for a rather more shallow grate than usual which was level over the rear half and then sloped gently towards the front. The firehole, in keeping with other BR types was at a convenient height for men of average size and lined up nicely with the tender shovelling plate.

Despite its size, drivers found preparation of 9Fs just as clean and straightforward as other BR Standard engines, which likewise were designed with maximum visibility and accessibility in mind. Liberal use of grease lubrication lightened the task considerably, while its small 5ft. 0in. wheels kept the motion at an easy height. With only the normal six sandboxes to fill, firemen also found no extra hardship except that a little extra care was needed when climbing up to and walking along its foot framing due to the wide boiler and smoke deflectors. As with Standard 5s, BR 1C full width tenders were preferred to the BR 1B inset type for exactly the same reasons as described earlier.

Driving 9Fs was a delightful experience difficult to describe for they seemed to possess every attribute ever desired in a locomotive and then managed to produce some pleasant surprises.

At Saltley many of our north bound freight workings departed from Water Orton Sidings some seven miles distant from the loco shed and travelling main line to this starting point gave crews an insight as to what they might expect from their engine. Easing open the light and sensitive regulator brought immediate response, so that its 140 ton bulk flowed into motion without apparent effort. Once on the main line with a clear road, 40psi steam chest pressure and the reverser notched fairly

There is no doubt whatsoever that 9Fs looked the quintessence of power and the ideal heavy mineral engine. What amazed everyone, including the design team, was its ability to run smoothly at express speeds while at the same time giving an impeccable ride. Once aware of these attributes, its potential was exploited to such effect that it was soon recognised as the finest mixed traffic engine ever produced in this country.

quickly back to 15% cut-off, speed built up rapidly into the fifties. At this pace the ride was as rock steady as any 2-6-4 tank engine, the only noticeable sound being the click of wheels on rail joints and a faint intermittent drumming from the cab roof ventilator. This may seem like the description of a brand new locomotive but although there are always exceptional examples in every class, the above is pretty typical of these engines as a whole.

My acquaintance with 9Fs did not really begin until 1957, by which time some of the earlier engines had covered sufficient mileage to be showing the effects of wear, but in all honesty I cannot recall any of them being much different and certainly there was never an incidence of knocking in motion bearings or axleboxes.

Every class has a star performer and within the scope of my own personal experience No. 92137 shone brighter than the rest. I had the pleasure of driving this Crewe-built 9F on what must have been just about its first road duty because not so much as a single smudge besmirched its gleaming paintwork and even the unmarked seats still gave off a smell of leather. A description of the run in question will perhaps enable the reader to gain some appreciation of a 9F at its best.

This particular night job ran from Water Orton to Toton under what we termed Class A lights (non-fitted express goods), but usually it was lightly ladened and almost seemed an excuse to get us and the locomotive to Toton for a return working. Travelling light engine to Water Orton revealed what a remarkable engine we had, the controls were light and as smooth as silk, there was no hint of noise or vibration and it ran like a greyhound with just a breath of steam. So turbine like was its progress at 60mph that it scarcely rippled the surface of my lid of tea standing on the brake pedestal; indeed had we been travelling in a Pullman Carriage we would not have experienced a better ride. Moreover, neither my mate nor the guard who had been engrossed in conversation while toasting themselves before the open firehole had the slightest notion of our rapid flight and were quite bewildered to find they had arrived so quickly.

Fate as fickle as ever gave us a train of only six vans which, together with the brakevan were piped to the engine so that we might run fully fitted and gain benefit from the additional brake power this provided.

We departed from Water Orton in our correct path and with only six vans No. 92137 required little more steam than when moving as a light engine and by the time we reached Kingsbury Junction we were romping along at less than 15% cut-off and 50 psi steam chest pressure. Such was our pace that by Wilncote we had caught up the train ahead, but despite being halted for a couple of minutes in Burton Station we were still slightly ahead of schedule at Stenson Junction. Once clear of the Junction we enjoyed an uninterrupted run

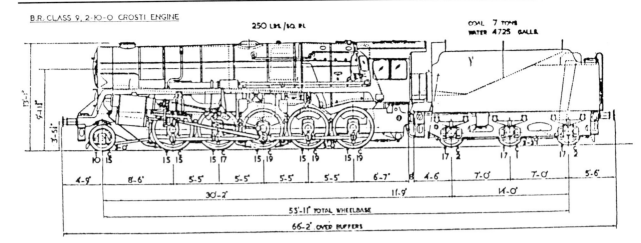

B.R. CLASS 9, 2-10-0 CROSTI ENGINE

and so taut was the regulator, I was able to ease it open to give us as little as 5 psi increases on the steam chest pressure gauge. Over the rising gradient to Weston on Trent this was showing only 70 psi at 15% cut-off and still with a clear road, I decided to experiment with gear settings. Now on the following gradient of 1:220 down to Castle Donnington I reduced the cut-off to just under 10% and increased steam pressure to 80 psi. No. 92137 hurtled along with an uncanny smoothness as quietly as ever in a night so dark that I was unable to see even the trackside. In fact, the only way to judge speed was by the sound of wheels on passing rail joints which now became almost continuous. Had it not been for this noise one might have easily imagined that we were not running on wheels at all but merely floating just above the tracks, so impeccable was the ride. Unfortunately, being so insulated from the normal buffets of footplate travel was very deceptive in total darkness and with our true speed difficult to judge, I was obliged to make some pretty hefty brake applications to check our pace for Sheet Stores Junction. Thankful for the extra brake power of the fitted vans it proved no problem and on checking the time as we rolled to a halt a little later in Trent Station I found that from start to stop we had covered the twelve and a half miles from Stenson in rather less than fifteen minutes.

This represented an average speed of 51 mph which indicated, taking acceleration and braking periods into account, we must have touched around 70 mph over the fastest section, somewhat quicker than permitted for a fully fitted let alone a Class A. It was a sobering thought to discover what one could unwittingly achieve with these 9Fs and it opened up new horizons for their use.

These possibilities were soon forthcoming because the operating people had gradually become aware that 9Fs were not only the finest heavy mineral to grace British Railways but were also a most powerful mixed traffic locomotive of immense potential.

Saltley's most prestigious duty was the 226 mile Birmingham to Carlisle express fitted freights run over the arduous Settle to Carlisle route. It was by far the most demanding for both men and machines, not only in duration which could involve seven to ten hours of continuous effort, but also because of the precipitous and wild nature of the high fells either side of Ais Gill.

For many years these trains had been competently handled by the best of Saltley's Black 5s and although only low mileage engines were used whenever possible they were often near their haulage limit with heavy loads in high winds on the 'long drag'. Nevertheless these Black 5s were much loved by top link drivers who considered them the best tool for a very difficult job. Therefore, in 1958 when their steadily increasing numbers allowed 9Fs to become more readily available and they were tentatively introduced to the Carlisle crews, some of the drivers viewed them with apprehension. It was bad enough having their well tried and favourite locomotives being usurped by another mixed traffic specifically designed for the job, but a heavy mineral engine with small wheels was something not easily digested. However, after sampling their outstanding power, comfort and conveniences on a number of runs, grudging acceptance often turned to open enthusiasm especially when they found that lost time could be recovered with staggering ease even on the steepest mountain sections.

I was very fortunate to join this elite link in 1958 and thereby able to partake in these pioneering changes which also included experiments with mechanical stoking. My driver, being conservative by nature, did not initially greet the 9Fs with favour but he was an excellent engineman who never used an ounce more steam than was necessary and after some notable runs, modified his views considerably. In fact it was with this driver who was the last I would have expected to go breaking records, that I travelled at the highest speed ever on a 9F or indeed any other class for that matter, over the Carlisle run. Strangely enough although the venue and situation was different, similar conditions of total darkness prevailed and that same incomparable engine No. 92137 deceived him just as completely as it had deceived me the previous year.

On this occasion we were working the 4.45pm Water Orton to Glasgow and departing dead on time we headed north with just about the heaviest train I can recall taking to Carlisle 48 (=52) wagons. After a week of exceptionally high temperatures, the atmosphere had now become very close and with the thermometer still in the high eighties, conditions on the footplate in front of a white hot furnace were almost unbearable. Although it was now some nine months since I had experienced that exhilirating trip to Toton, No. 92137, despite having lost its former shine, proved to be as mechanically superb as ever. 9Fs with over 56% more tractive effort were able to demonstrate their vast superiority over Black 5s with this type of load and because they could be worked on much shorter cut-offs they were relatively more economical. Of course some of this economy was due to the boiler being steamed well below its limit when compared to that of a Black 5 hauling a similar weight and was therefore able to operate at higher levels of efficiency. As will be seen from the accompanying log, No. 92137 was well able to handle this train and gained time at every opportunity with consummate ease in atrocious conditions.

The run was dogged by signal checks and then at Skipton we collected a linesman destined for Garsdale where violent thunderstorms had caused a block failure. In fact we ran into these storms at Hellifield and the torrential rain did not abate until approaching Appleby. With improving weather conditions we were able to increase our pace and after a final signal check at New Biggin set about regaining lost time. With a clear road before us at Lazonby the power was really turned on and with the steam chest pressure showing 180 psi and at around 20% cut-off our speed rapidly increased. In pitch black conditions on that beautifully riding 9F I am quite sure my mate had no idea just how quickly we were travelling, but the fact remains that the last fourteen and a half miles from Lazonby to a dead stand at Carlisle Petteril Bridge took just eleven minutes, an average speed of 78 mph. So incredible did this seem that I double checked the timings but they were quite definite and I could only come to the somewhat frightening

conclusion that we must have achieved a maximum of around 90 mph to have done so.

The fear arose because fitted freights were then limited to 55 mph and one could not help wondering how near to derailment the wagons may have been and how many other drivers on 9Fs could have been similarly deceived. There was absolutely no concern whatsoever regarding the engine for at no time did it seem any different from when travelling at half that rate, just a soft purr from the chimney, the rapid click of rail joints and the same silky, rock steady, effortless progression. Indeed no other tender locomotive I have experienced gave such a superlative and stable ride as these 9Fs and one can only speculate as to the reasons. Possibly it was a combination of many factors: the exceptionally long coupled wheelbase would appear to have eliminated lateral oscillations, the fact that only 40% of reciprocating masses were balanced may have kept their wheels more firmly on the rails at high revolutions and of course, the springing could have been near perfect. I never encountered a bad 9F but with No. 92137 all the plusses possible must have come together in that one incredible engine.

Firemen who had worked on Garratts did not find the 9Fs wide firebox too daunting since it was slightly smaller in area and not nearly as deep, but it was this lack of depth that demanded a change in technique.

9Fs steamed superbly and under normal running conditions they were not too sensitive regarding shape or profile of the firebed. It did not seem to matter whether it was conventional, haycock or saucer shape, providing normal firing rules were roughly adhered to and the area under its brick arch not choked. In fact it would stand terrible mismanagement even to the extent of having dead patches on the grate and still make steam and I know of no other locomotive that would behave quite that way. Of course, if really serious work was to performed over a long period then as with all other engines the fire had to be as near perfect as possible.

With so much power available, 9Fs could often be worked quite lightly for considerable stretches and when so doing I found that a very thin fire sufficed with primary air supplied only via the rear damper.

This tended to promote higher combustion rates over the grate nearest to the fireman but it was necessary to ensure that both back corners were always well filled. Although supplied with a large oval firehole to facilitate this, the shovel blade needed to be placed well inside which then brought the fireman's hands very close to that searing white heat generated under normal working conditions.

At first I wondered why I suffered so much from heat

4.45pm WATER ORTON to GLASGOW COLLEGE. Fully Fitted. Class 9F 92137 Load 48=52 Wagons.

		Booked Time	Actual Time	Remarks
Water Orton Stn. Junction		4.50	4.50	
Kingsbury Stn. Junction		4.55	4.55	
Tamworth		5.03	5.03	
Wichnor		5.13	5.12	
Leicester Junction		5.20	5.20	15mph PW restriction (Branston)
Burton Stn		5.21	5.21	Signal check
Repton		5.27	5.29	Signal check
Stenson Junction		5.30	5.33	Signal check
Melbourne Junction		5.35	5.37	Signal check
Derby – London Road		5.39	5.40	Signal check
Derby – Midland		5.40	5.41	
Derby – North Junction		5.41	5.42	
Ambergate		5.55	5.56	
Stretton		6.08	6.06	Signal check
Clay Cross		6.18	6.12‹6.20	Signal check
Horns Bridge		6.24	6.27	Signal check
Chesterfield Midland		6.25	6.28	Signal check
Tapton Junction		6.26	6.29	Signal check
Bronfield Colliery Sidings		6.18	6.41‹6.42	Signal check
Sheffield Midland	Arr.	6.48	6.54	Water
	Dept.	6.55	7.00	
Wincobank Station Junct.		7.03	7.08	
Cudworth		7.36	7.34	
Normanton North Yard		7.54	7.54	
Altofts Junction		7.56	7.55	
Stourton Junction		8.06	8.08	Signal check
Engine Shed Junction		8.10	8.12	Signal check
Whitehall		8.12	8.13	Signal check
Wortley Junction		8.13	8.15	Signal check
Shipley Leeds Junction		8.32	8.30	
Keighley		8.43	8.45	Signal check
Snaygill		8.56	9.00	Signal check
Skipton South Junction	Arr.	9.00	9.05	Examination & water
	Dept.	9.17	9.19	Collected linesman – block failure at Garsdale
Hellifield		9.40	9.40	Violent thunderstorms
Settle		9.45	9.50	Violent thunderstorms
Blea Moor		10.22	10.20	Violent thunderstorms
Ais Gill		10.41	10.40	Linesman set down at Garsdale
Kirkby Stephen West		10.49	10.50	20mph PW restriction Ormside
Appleby		11.01	11.10	Signal check
New Biggin		11.10	11.20	Signal check
Lazonby		11.21	11.29	
Carlisle Petteril		11.40	11.40	

radiation when firing 9Fs but upon reflection the answers were fairly obvious. The flat shallow grate brought the incandescent firebed much higher in relationship to the firehole than with deep narrow fireboxes. Being of larger area and nearly square in plan meant that a far greater proportion of that firebed was nearer to the fireman. Finally a larger firehole area obviously allowed more radiation to pass through it and because they steamed so well and the reduced free area over their grates required rather more secondary air to consume smoke, doors were set more open than for other types. However, it did not take too long to discover a way of greatly reducing this emission of unwelcome heat.

Before commencing a round of firing I always dropped two or three shovelsful just inside the firehole so that a small hump of dead coal was formed. This not only blanketed off much of the radiation, but also acted as a deflector, since by bouncing the shovel blade against this hump at the correct angle, coal could be shot into the back corners with the minimum of effort and without need to get too near. As with Class 5MTs, one live steam and one exhaust steam injector was provided, both of these had excellent flow rates, proved extremely reliable and could be operated whilst still seated.

It would be fair to say that the bulk of my experience with 9Fs, at least from a mileage point of view, was obtained working the Carlisles and it would be equally fair to say that this marathon run encompassed just about every working condition imaginable.

Not wishing to waste coal or my own energy I aimed to maintain the thinnest and hottest fire compatible with the situation and this, of course, required the 'little and often' method being used. It also payed handsomely to take advantage of a 9Fs rocking grate facility and operate it at regular intervals in its limited movement mode. Knowing the road was always of immeasurable help in fire management since it was then possible to build up the firebed prior to periods of heavy work and let it run down before a lengthy stretch of coasting.

For example, the fourteen miles of almost unbroken 1:100 from Settle to Blea Moor usually required the thickest practical depth of fire and both dampers open, but over the ten miles of undulating track leading to Ais Gill Summit it could be gradually run down in anticipation of the equally long descent to Ormside.

These Carlisle runs were therefore a mixture of light and heavy firing, but given reasonable coal and dedicated management the firebars were usually visible at the end of a run.

When both 9Fs and Black 5s were rostered to these runs it was interesting to make a comparison of relative fuel consumptions.

With lighter trains in good weather Black 5s were more economical because they too were running well within their capacity. With medium loads they broke about even, but with heavy trains particularly in wild conditions, 9Fs won hands down. However, if the run became unduly protracted by delays then with every passing hour the advantage began to swing back to Black 5s. This is not really surprising when one considers the grate areas involved, 28.65 sq.ft. as to 40.2 sq.ft. for the 9F, because even when standing the fire still has to be kept alight and the water boiling.

The most notable example of this occurred one day on the 11.45pm return working from Carlisle. Because it ran through the night it was often subject to delays by other freight trains and once out of the correct path things only became worse. On this occasion we actually took ten and a half hours instead of the booked seven hours ten minutes and as a result I fired the last shovel of coal approaching Water Orton, seven miles short of our destination. Fortunately we had a clear run and there was just sufficient capacity in the firebed and boiler for us to reach the shed but it was a very close run thing. Engines rostered for the Carlisles were always coaled to absolute capacity, way beyond standard loading gauge height so that instead of a nominal nine tons it was more like ten and a half tons. On this run the firing rate therefore averaged one ton per hour and since at least five tons had to be brought forward from the back of the tender in addition to breaking up innumerable large lumps of coal I had shovelled fifteen to sixteen tons during the night. Whilst this may sound daunting, 9Fs with their excellent BR1C tenders were relatively easy to fire. Being able to stand on a continuous stable footplate rather than perform perpetual balancing acts across a mobile fall plate with one foot on the tender and one on the engine each moving in several unpredictible directions at once, saved a lot of energy. Furthermore 9Fs possessed such a great reserve of energy in their large boilers they could run for miles when working lightly without need of firing or use of injectors. This ability, plus their high level of comfort and convenience even enabled firemen to snatch a quick sandwich at selected places which more than compensated for an extra ton of coal fired on the grate.

In the autumn of 1958 the first of three 9Fs specially modified and fitted with American Berkeley Mechanical Stokers arrived at Saltley. It was generally recognised that locomotive performance, irrespective of type was limited by the endurance of a single fireman to about 30,000 lbs of steam for one hour or 24,000 lbs per hour for several hours. Therefore this experiment with stokers was to explore what increased output would be obtainable and at what cost. Since the Birmingham to Carlisles were the longest and most arduous freight runs in the country, they were understandably selected for such trials.

The stoker arrangement was robust and simple, consisting of a main conveyor screw lying in a trough at the bottom of the tender coal space, driven by a small,

4.03pm Carlisle Durran Hill to Washwood Heath No. 2 Class 9F 92137 Load 45=48 Wagons.

		Booked Time	Actual Time	Remarks
Carlisle Durran Hill Depot		4.03	4.08	Violent thunderstorms
Lazonby		4.33	4.39	Block failure due to storm
New Biggin		4.48	4.53	
Appleby	Arr.	5.03	5.02	Water
	Dept.	5.08	5.08	
Kirkby Stephen West		5.36	5.20	Signals at Mallerstang due to woman being killed on line
Ais Gill		5.54	5.48	
Blea Moor		6.10	6.05	
Settle Junction		6.30	6.22	
Hellifield		6.35	6.28	
Skipton North		6.50	6.44	
Skipton	Arr.	6.52	6.45	Examination & water
	Dept.	7.12	6.55	
Snaygill		7.15	7.00	
Keighley		7.27	7.12	Signal check
Shipley Leeds Junction		7.38	7.25	
Wortley Junction		7.54	7.43	
Whitehall Junction		7.56	7.45	
Engine Shed		7.57	7.49‹51	Signal check
Stourton Junction		8.05	7.57	
Altofts Junction		8.17	8.07	
Normanton South Yard		8.19	8.09	
Cudworth Station		8.40	8.28	
Wath Road Junction		8.52	8.42	
Swinton Junction		8.54	8.44	
Rotherham Masboro'	Arr.	9.03	8.55	Water
	Dept.	9.10	9.03	
Masboro' South Sidings		9.14	9.05	
Beighton Junction		9.23	9.15	
Staveley		9.32	9.25	
Tapton Junction		9.37	9.30	
Chesterfield Midland		9.38	9.31	
Horns Bridge		9.39	9.32	
Clay Cross		9.46	9.38	20mph PW restriction through tunnel
Stretton		9.53	9.43	
Crich Junction		10.02	9.52	
Ambergate		10.03	9.53	
Derby North Junction		10.21	10.09	Diverted to goods line until LNW Junction
Derby Midland		10.24	10.12	
Derby London Road Junction		10.25	10.14	
Melbourne Junction		10.28	10.17	
Stenson Junction		10.33	10.25	
Repton & Willington		10.36	10.28	
Burton Station		10.42	10.32	15mph PW restriction at Branston
Leicester Junction		10.43	10.33	
Wichnor Junction		10.52	10.40	
Tamworth		11.05	11.00	Signal checks to Tamworth
Kingsbury Station Junction		11.13	11.10‹11	Signal checks
Warton Orton Station Junction		11.19	11.16	
Castle Bromwich Junction		11.23	11.20	
Washwood Heath Junction		11.28	11.23	
Washwood Heath No. 2		11.33	11.25	

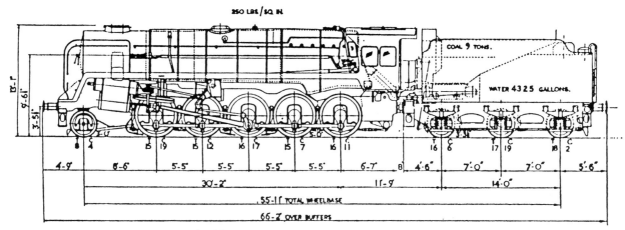

CLASS 9 2-10-0 FITTED WITH MECHANICAL STOKER

infinitely variable and reversible engine mounted on the tender front drag box. The screw worked on the Archimedean principle and forced coal through a crushing grid that broke down larger lumps to a usable size. Another screw, known as the raiser screw, delivered crushed coal on to a distributor plate set just inside the firehole. Four separate controllable steam jets fitted below the distributor plate were arranged to direct fuel to the front and back of the left and right hand sides of the firegate respectively. The controls to these steam jets were mounted on a panel in front of the fireman and the valves for the stoker engine somewhat lower, at seat level. Below the main steam pressure gauge, three others showed engine and jet pressures, black hands indicated pressures to the back corners of the grate, while red hands showed pressures to the front corners.

A standard size firehole was fitted above the raiser screw conduit, which was closed by manually operated butterfly-type firedoors. This arrangement permitted normal hand firing although in practice it was rendered extremely difficult for three reasons.

Firstly, the firehole was very much higher than normal, secondly the raiser screw conduit obstructed the fireman's usual stance and finally, because of a 'safety' barrier, coal did not drop on the shovelling plate, but had to be extracted from the tender piece by piece. Hand firing was officially recommended, indeed it was required, to initially prepare and build up a suitable firebed, but it was a slow, tedious back breaking process only to be indulged in when absolutely necessary.

The other departure from standard on these three engines was by way of improved draughting and the fitting of double chimneys. Subsequent testings at Rugby showed that no greater evaporation rate proved possible than with hand firing, for at 29,000 lbs of water

per hour, 6,000 lbs of coal was being consumed by the stoker in place of 4,750 lbs with hand firing. Much of this discrepancy was due to the production of fines by the crushing grid so that the jets then had to deal with both dust and pieces of coal up to 4 cm. across. Quite a percentage of dust tended to be carried out of the chimney unburned and was wasted, while to drive the stoker and jets consumed between 830 and 1,100 lbs of steam per hour.

It was planned to use these three 9Fs on local Bordesley trip duties for the dual purpose of running in and training Carlisle Link firemen in the operation of mechanical stoking. Since I was due to work the p.m. Carlisle run the following week, I had the honour of being selected for the first training session. The Firing Inspector in charge of tuition was already on board on No. 92165 when I arrived and he spent half an hour explaining the theory of Mechanical Stoking while demonstrating the various controls. He also pointed out that pending the arrival of special fuel, arrangements had been made to use passenger quality coal from the Coaling Plant. Because this contained numerous large lumps which could block the conveyor screw, it would be dropped into the tender in small amounts to be broken up by a gang of cleaners armed with coal picks. However, to reduce the possibility of blockages during our training period the tender was only partially coaled and if a jam occurred we should be able to clear it with a large crowbar provided for the purpose. Needless to say we were made very aware of the need to ensure that the screws' engine was shut down before attempting to use the crowbar otherwise serious mechanical damage would result. No mention was made regarding serious damage to firemen if they got their foot caught in the screw, but a small concession to safety had been made by attaching a three inch high steel strip transversely across the shovelling plate. Located just below the access doors it was intended to remind firemen of something nasty lurking beyond, but it turned out in fact to be a real nuisance by preventing coal from even a well filled tender falling on to the shovelling plate.

Before setting off I experienced the difficulty of building up the fire by hand, every shovel of coal had to be extracted over the safety strip, carried across the footplate, lifted above waist height and then, standing astride the raiser conduit, delivered as best one could.

Control of the stoker engine was quite sensitive so that the screw could be set to deliver anything from a fine trickle to a veritable avalanche, but unfortunately owing to the lumpy mixture of coal in use, the conveyor screw was never consistently loaded so that feed to the delivery plate was often intermittent. With a little experience it became possible to detect how well the screw was feeding by its sound, a muffled rumble accompanied by a graunching noise as coal was pulverised against the crushing·grid indicated all was well. When starved by a blockage the screw, relieved of any load, rotated at a greater speed giving off a higher pitched ringing sound. An inspection flap at the top of the raiser conduit enabled a visual check to be made on flow rates while a small peep hole in the firedoors proved useful in keeping an eye on just where the fuel was going.

It naturally took some practice to obtain the optimum setting for jet pressures with regard to balance and spread, mainly because of the disparity in particle size due to unsuitable coal. Fortunately once set, all jets could be controlled by the central stop valve so that by varying this, a fore and aft sweeping action could be obtained. This facility proved very useful when the locomotive changed to a period of heavy working and then back to lighter conditions. The strong blast tended to deposit a mass of small particles under the brickarch which then effectively reduced the active grate area, but by lowering overall jet pressure this tendency was to some extent ameliorated. I also found that a fully open front damper concentrated more primary air in the affected area, but even so, it was necessary to level the banked up 'slurry' with a rake from time to time.

Another problem not normally experienced on standard engines was that with such a thin firebed composed of very small particles it soon burned away and a few minutes standing found the grate covered with holes and dead patches. It was therefore necessary to operate the stoker in frequent short bursts just to keep the fire alight, but as is often the case there are ways around problems.

By running the conveyor screw with the jets shut off, a quantity of coal could be quickly dumped under the firehole. Although this initially buried jets and distributor plate alike it was of no consequence, since long before the coal ignited it could be spread by means of the firing shovel towards both back corners clearing the jets in so doing. By this means a reasonable body of partially burned fire could be maintained in the back of the firebox allowing for much greater peace of mind.

Local trip turns with their 'stop-go' movements, always called for wildly fluctuating demands which could not be met in the usual way with No. 92165 because of this inability to retain a substantial firebed. However, the short delays which inevitably occurred at times while the fire built up to full working temperature passed almost unnoticed, such was the immense reverse in 9Fs boilers.

At the end of the training period I felt sufficiently confident to take a Mechanical Stoker 9F on the Carlisle, but I was disturbed by the frequency of blockages experienced when large lumps of coal became jammed over the trough causing starvation of feed. The Firing Inspector assured me that greater attention would be given to this aspect when coaling the Carlisle engine particularly since he planned to accompany us on the maiden run as far as Leeds. I must confess to being rather enthusiastic over the project and resolved to do my utmost to make it a success because I found the prospect of having time to learn the road while seated comfortably relieved of physical effort, other than twiddling knobs, very appealing.

In the meantime No. 92166 had arrived and rather surprisingly this engine was selected for the first trial run to Carlisle. I say surprisingly because it had only covered a nominal mileage and it would have been more sensible to have used 92165 rather than retain it for further training sessions.

From external appearances the cleaning gang had done an excellent job, for the tender was filled with a mountain of well broken cobbles. Looking fit for a Royal Train we departed for Water Orton and during the seven mile journey to our start point the stoker worked perfectly, although on arrival one of the coupled axleboxes seemed a little warmer than the others. With a moderate load of thirty six equal to forty wagons we set off exactly on time for the long journey north.

Having manually built up a good firebed I was delighted to find the stoker well able to maintain it provided I used the spaying technique of varying the jet pressures. One advantage not available to normal engines was that the steam jets flattened firebox flames so that the whole grate area could be easily inspected

No. 92166 was the second of three 9Fs experimentally fitted with Berkeley Mechanical Stokers which were allocated to Saltley in the Autumn of 1958 for testing on the arduous, long distant Birmingham-Carlisle fitted freights. I was privileged to fire this engine on the 'maiden trip', but because of unsuitable coal causing frequent blockages of the feed screw, it did not result in the easy journey originally anticipated.

which, of course, was just as well in the circumstances.

The stoker worked perfectly until Tamworth when the first of innumerable blockages occurred, these spoilt what should have been a relatively effortless trip. With a full tender it was very difficult to insert the crowbar into tightly packed coal and both I and the Inspector found it extremely exhausting. In fact I was very pleased that he was there since one of us able to laboriously fire it by hand while the other equally laboriously prodded and heaved with the heavy crowbar.

At Sheffield the suspected axlebox had become very warm and it was thought that we may have to fail the engine at Leeds but following some lighter running it cooled again and we were able to continue.. I was sorry when the Firing Inspector left us at Leeds because I experienced more jams during the second half of the run, but at least as the coal supply became depleted they were progressively easier to clear. Happily over the long drag up to Blea Moor it functioned faultlessly and by way of experiment my mate worked the engine hard enough to regain several minutes of lost time. Although able to provide all the steam required on this spirited

climb, I gained the impression that No. 92166 did not steam quite as freely as normal 9Fs. Then followed another series of annoying blockages, but after passing New Biggin, the rest of the journey was trouble free and we arrived at Carlisle more or less on time.

The Carlisle lads seemed to have been rather more conscientious in preparing the coal since our return trip was a little better, but even so there were far too many jams.

Conclusions drawn from this maiden voyage were that in general the stoker performed quite well although at maximum effort the engine did not steam as freely, due in part to the fact that the firebed could not be maintained in the same perfect shape as with manual firing. Also it certainly consumed more fuel, but this was anticipated since a proportion of the fines passed unburned through the tubes as waste. With regard to physical effort, at least as much energy was used clearing jams as was used in normal firing, in fact it was more debilitating since different muscles were involved so that on balance nothing was gained in that direction while the coal supply remained uncertain.

This really was the gist of our subsequent report, because the trip two days later with No. 92165 followed much the same pattern as before and our colleagues fared no better either. Some weeks later this fuel problem came to a head despite genuine attempts to eliminate rogue lumps of coal entering the tender unseen.

The engine this time was the best of the trio No.

A further experiment with 9Fs was to modify ten examples to a Franco Crosti design incorporating a preheater drum. In their original form, steam exhausted from a long thin chimney mounted alongside the boiler just ahead of the firebox. Continually engulfed in fumes and with vision often totally obscured, this innovation was not at all popular with firemen. The experiment was not a success so the preheater drums were eventually removed and they reverted to normal draughting as depicted in this photograph of 92025.

92167, and once again appeared to have a beautifully coaled tender, but beneath its cosmetic exterior lay a slab of coal the size of a coffin poised just above the screw trough. Had it been engineered to cut off all fuel to this trough it could not have been more effective, because immediately after departing from Water Orton with an above average load it did exactly that and apart from a few minute respite at Leeds the feed remained immovably blocked until Blea Moor. Hand firing that 9F for nearly two hundred miles was an agony best forgotten and should never have been undertaken, but then, such is the optimism and stubborness of youth.

A quantity of suitable coal was eventually obtained specifically for Mechanical Stoker 9Fs but this was only sent to Durran Hill shed Carlisle. It was apparently used by Isle of Man Steamers and consisted of washed 1½in. diameter chips of high calorific value coal which, since it 'flowed' like dry sand could not cause any blockages and would have been ideal. Ironically after this coal arrived I never had another run with a stoker 9F to take advantage of it, but we were obliged to use these chips on standard engines for which they were totally unsuited.

The experiment merely proved what was already known i.e. for grate areas less than 50 sq.ft. Mechanical Stokers were not really necessary on the type of running encountered in this country. Moreover they were less economical on coal and water and in the case of a 9F could not improve on maximum steaming rates obtained by manual firing. If the correct fuel had been available from the beginning I am sure the experiment would have received some very enthusiastic support from the Carlisle link crews who, once certain of consistent operation, would have been prepared to push engines to the limit. In the event, the whole project seemed to have been treated in a half-hearted fashion as if just going through the motions, knowing full well that in 1958, minds had now been turned to Diesel and Electric Traction as a means of obtaining extra power.

However, it was an interesting little interlude in the history of BR steam traction and I was pleased to have been involved to the extent of making the pioneer run.

Of perhaps more significance, at least as far as costs and potential savings were concerned, was the batch of ten 9Fs modified to Franco Crosti design incorporating a preheater drum. The principle was fairly simple in as much that hot gases on leaving the tube bank of the boiler proper, reversed direction in the smokebox and passed through another set of tubes in the secondary drum before being ejected from a long thin chimney located alongside the main boiler just ahead of the firebox.

The secondary drum was used as a preheater for feed water so that water injected into the main boiler was only a few degrees lower than the water already there.

Some improvement in economy was obtained and this became better at higher outputs, but it by no means matched what the Crosti engineers had predicted. Unfortunately this saving was more than offset by increased maintenance costs arising largely from severe corrosion which attacked the smokebox and chimney in service.

I only worked Crostis on two or three occasions and while in general they steamed and behaved more or less as other 9Fs, having the chimney placed a few feet from the fireman's face was not at all popular. Apart from the physical obstruction of the chimney and on later versions a smoke deflector as well, the cab seemed to be perpetually engulfed in exhaust steam which made life very miserarble and reduced visibility on the fireman's side to zero.

No one was particularly sorry when their preheater drums were removed and they reverted to normal draughting albeit with the original smaller boilers. In this form they tended to be used on duties which did not call for high boiler output but this still allowed them plenty of scope.

Also tested on 9F No. 92250 was the Giesl ejector with the main objective of exploring the feasibility of being able to use low grade, low cost coal. Although it achieved lower blast pipe pressures for a given draught, the improvement was too small to justify extending the installation to other engines and moreover the efficient burning of low grade fuels was still not reliable.

From the foregoing, it may be deduced that the 9F was my favourite locomotive, well I would not deny that for I honestly believe that no other British steam engine possessed its incredible versatility. As a heavy mineral it was in a class of its own, offering immense brute power, inexhaustable steaming capacity, superb adhesion, remarkable economy and the highest level of comfort and convenience. For long distance express fitted freights, it was equally unbeatable since in addition to the above attributes it provided probably the most stable ride of any tender locomotive on a footplate so free from vibration and noise that it was positively uncanny. On stopping passenger trains it would out-accelerate all competition whatever the load, whilst even top expresses were handled in its stride, running smoothly at 90 mph and showing Britannias a clean pair of heels on banks.

What other locomotive could do all these things in such comfort with equal competence? Indeed if asked to operate a railway with just a single class of steam engine then there is only one possible answer – a 9F!

Further eulogy would be pointless because there are insufficient superlatives to do justice to this most remarkable of BR locomotives, it is just so sad that they were not allowed to live a little longer.

Fortunately there are two or three preserved examples still to be seen and perhaps dream of, thundering up to Ais Gill with a fully fitted express freight.

PART III

IT WILL BE recalled that in the introduction I explained the importance of being able to sample as many individual members of a class as possible working over the widest range of duties, in order to obtain a balanced judgement. This was because of the many variables encountered which affected a steam locomotive's day to day performance; experience gained by only an odd trip or two on a single engine could easily create entirely the wrong impression.

It is against this background that I now come to four locomotives which, although numerous and a common sight on British Railways in the fifties, I worked with on only a few occasions. However, because some readers may have a special interest in them I will state briefly what I found. The locomotives are: Riddles W.D. 8F 2-8-0, 2P 4-4-0, ex-LNWR G2 0-8-0 (Super D) and ex-LNER B1 4-6-0.

Chapter 17
Ministry of Supply WD 2-8-0

Introduced 1943. Total 935.

AS INDICATED earlier, Stanier 8Fs had been selected by the Ministry of Supply for construction as their standard heavy freight locomotive at the beginning of World War Two. With production spread over both railway and private workshops, output sufficed during the early war years, but when a second front in Europe was contemplated it became obvious that large numbers of locomotives would be needed. With many skilled men drafted into the services and other war work occupying factory space, the builders were finding great difficulty in meeting demands.

R.A. Riddles, formerly Stanier's principal assistant, had become Deputy Director General, Royal Engineer equipment and, well aware of the situation, developed a simplified form of Stanier's 8F which could be produced more quickly and easily. By avoiding sophisticated design features and replacing difficult to obtain items with more basic components, a substantial saving in the

weight of steel castings and forgings used, together with a 20% reduction in man hours was achieved. The principal changes included: Parallel boiler instead of Belpaire taper boiler. Replacement of all steel castings and some forgings by fabricated plate or cast iron. Use of cast iron in place of steel for wheel centres. Trimming feed to coupled axleboxes and displacement sight feed lubrication to cylinders instead of mechanical lubricators. Simplified cab and footplate layout and a large eight wheel tender.

Despite all emphasis being placed on austerity, accessibility and ease of maintenance, the overall appearance proved quite pleasing and included some features to become fashionable on later LMS and BR designs.

Although their boilers differed in shape, combined heating surface areas on the 8Fs and WDs were very similar and the WD grate, while possessing a slight

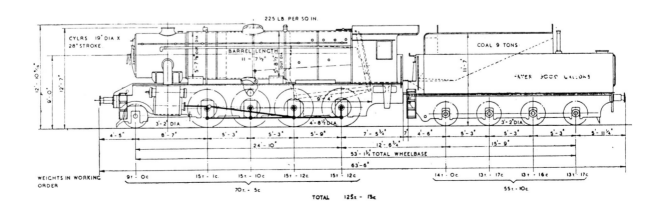

Despite being born in a period of severe austerity, Riddles WD 2-8-0s looked powerful and pleasing engines. However, appearances were deceptive and in service they proved not only far less efficient than Stanier 8Fs but also generally gave their crews a deplorable ride. With so much cost cutting built into their construction, this was perhaps, to be expected. However, some design features were considered worthwhile and did in fact become fashionable on later LMS and BR locomotives.

continuous slope, was also virtually the same size as that of the 8Fs. With an extra ½in. cylinder diameter the Austerity's tractive effort was theoretically 1,777lbs greater than the Stanier engine and yet it weighed a quarter ton less.

My acquaintance with these locomotives was quite brief, being confined to no more than half a dozen duties. None of these involved preparation or disposal, though on one occasion I recall the need to remove some heavy clinkering, en route. All were relief turns

experienced whilst in the Control Link during 1951-2 when maintenance admittedly was not at the highest level on BR; consequently and without exception, these locomotives seemed to be in a fairly run down condition.

How much of this roughness could be attributed to basic design and how much to wear is difficult to say but it must be borne in mind that these WD locomotives were not intended to have long lives. A more balanced judgement could perhaps be given if only a low mileage example had been sampled but unfortunately none came my way. I did not have the opportunity to drive any of them but the method adopted was similar to that used with an 8F and because of excessive motion bearings and axlebox knock in every case, long cut-offs were invariably employed. Regrettably all this wear and knocking did not help adhesion which in general seemed below par.

The cab and its layout was simple, austere and uncomfortable with none of the refinements found on Stanier engines such as windshields and arm rests which folded over side window runners. Indeed there was only one side window (instead of the usual two) which, together with the parallel boiler, hindered forward visibility. On the other hand having an inset bunker did improve the rearward view somewhat. Most of the jobs were west bound mineral or mixed freights which at least enabled us to test performance up the Camp Hill bank, and then after some miles of undulating track, a descent of the Lickey incline.

Using a fire which gradually sloped from being level with the bottom of the firehole to just a few inches thick at the front, the Austerities steamed adequately but not quite as freely as 8Fs. Although its exhaust did not seem to have the same 'bite' as the Stanier engine and there was only a single front damper, one became conscious of having to fire at a higher rate. Not that this posed any problems at low speed since the cab had sufficient space to use a long handled shovel from either side.

Unfortunately at around 20 mph the ride had deteriorated so much as to be distinctly uncomfortable and sitting down inadvisable. If forced to travel more quickly (because it would not be through choice!), then firing became very dependent on balancing skills since in addition to violent hammer blows, equally violent lateral and vertical twitching shook the footplate like a jelly, causing injectors and everything else to fly off. On most rough locomotives things become more tranquil when coasting, but not so the Austerities because the twitching continued and a horrendous fore-and-aft

buffeting started, giving the impression of weak intermediate springs. The only useful by-product of this alarming shock treatment was that it brought fuel forward to the shovelling plate more effectively than a coal pusher. Of course if the bunker was well filled to start with, a prolonged period of coasting would result in a footplate knee deep in coal.

In 1953 BR conducted comparative performance and efficiency trials with both 2-10-0 and 2-8-0 versions of WD locomotives and as would be expected, the larger boilered 2-10-0 was superior in terms of steam production. However, it is interesting to note that when the 2-8-0 was compared with Stanier's design it was deficient in this respect by 16% – maximum superheat temperature down 70°F and cylinder thermal efficiency 1.2% less. All this combined to lower the maximum horsepower available at the drawbar on the level by 22½%. This figure more or less confirms what we found in practical service and if ever there was a perfect illustration of the old saying 'you get what you pay for' then it was the WD 2-8-0.

The simplification in design and methods of production were no doubt necessary at that time, but the price had to be paid for in terms of performance, efficiency and comfort. As professional enginemen we could live with the first two, but the latter made life so intolerable that no matter how short the journey, we were only too glad to get off. I am sorry if the foregoing disappoints those enthusiasts who may have a place in their hearts for the WD 2-8-0s, but I know of no locomen who ever sang their praises.

Introduced 1928. Total 138.

2Ps were quite handsome little engines in their period and managed to cope with light passenger duties in a quiet, unruffled manner with commendable reliability. Although using the same G7S boiler as 4Fs, they seemed to steam more freely, but poor front end design limited their potential and by the fifties they had been completely eclipsed by new more vigorous contenders.

THE MIDLAND Railway Class 2 upon which this standard design was based performed in only a very mediocre way. This was recognised as being mainly due to poor front end design coupled with short travel valves causing severe strangulation of steam flow into and out of its cylinders and when it was decided to adopt this engine as a Standard LMS locomotive, some improvement was sought. However, at that time the battle over long and short travel valves was still being fought and unfortunately in this instance, the latter won the day. Once more Derby missed the opportunity to

bring about a significant advance, and like the Garratts and 3P 2-6-2 tanks, they never had the chance to fulfil their true potential.

However, some improvement was obtained by increasing boiler pressure from 160 to 180 psi enabling

19in. instead of 20in. cylinders to be used; but the valves remained in their original positon below them operated by the same Stephenson's Motion. In addition, the 7ft. ½in. diameter coupled wheels of the rebuilt MR engines was reduced to 6ft. 9in. for the new standard class, giving a slight increase in tractive effort. Whilst overall performance remained indifferent as they went about their light secondary duties, at least they were not over taxed and in terms of repair costs per mile, returned the lowest average figure of any of the LMS passenger types.

Apart from occasional local freight trip work at Saltley, one 2P was regularly booked as West Pilot in Birmingham New Street Station. This usually entailed nothing more than being on standby in case a westbound passenger train required assistance, plus executing a little shunting within station limits as the need arose. My experience of them was more or less confined to these duties and so I am unable to describe how they behaved on the light local passenger duties for which they were designed.

Since they shared the same G7S boiler, perhaps I can best describe them as being like a 4F placed on larger driving wheels, and yet their overall appearance was nicely balanced and pleasing. The cab and its layout were also very similar, although the fireman's seat-cum-locker was even more generous and much coveted as a place of repose. As with 4Fs, the 2P seemed to engender concern for the fireman's tuition and invitations to exchange sides so that 'station moves may be learned' were common place on West Pilots.

Preparation and disposal was usually a little easier than with 4Fs since they possessed fewer sandboxes to fill and normally consumed smaller quantities of what was already better (passenger grade) coal. Having a large stride, moving off seemed extremely leisurely; but if judging by sound alone as in darkness, its pace could be initially deceptive. Adhesion was rather uncertain, especially in greasy conditions, and when slipping, the side rods clanged in a most distinctive but not unpleasant tone.

Only on one occasion whilst working the West Pilot were we actually called upon to perform any piloting. This was when the Sheffield-Bristol night mail, headed by a Jubilee, arrived with part of its brick arch fallen in. Although the offending bricks had been extracted it was

feared that the rest might collapse and they requested our assistance until Gloucester where a relief engine was being prepared. It was a cold night of torrential rain and having been awoken from pleasant slumbers on the cosy warmth of the fireman's seat, my mate was far from delighted. By the time we had coupled to the front of the Jubilee I had rallied the fire somewhat and was as ready as we would ever be.

Up through the tunnel to Five Ways I could not hear whether we were working or not because of the fearful cacophony made by the Jubilee's exhaust just behind our tender. However, with regulator on full first valve and the fire a fierce white glare, I concluded that we must be doing our share. This was the first occasion I had fired a 2P that was working hard and was pleasantly surprised to find it steaming quite well, rather better than 4Fs in fact. Possibly blast pipe and chimney proportions were nearer the optimum with 2Ps but steam was no problem for the entire journey.

Once on the easier running between Kings Norton and Blackwell I became very aware of the 2Ps lively cavorting, possibly not helped by the probability that the Jubilee was pushing us as well as pulling its train. As a consequence the descent of Lickey felt a good deal more spritely than was actually the case; but it was over the generally falling gradients from Stoke Works to Eckington that the ride became nothing short of awesome. I do not know whether the Jubilee driver was trying to make up lost time or deliberately trying to frighten us but he certainly managed both. I doubt if that old 2P had travelled so fast in its life, for now both engine and tender were leaping about so frantically that it was most difficult to even stand let alone perform the act of firing. Nor was it made any more pleasant by sheets of rain which stung like bullets lashing around the cut-outs. Needless to say, we were both very glad to deposit the 2P on Gloucester shed after the most hectic ride of our lives, a journey which in the event, had not been necessary.

2Ps were therefore gentle, comfortable little engines if left to potter around on their light duties which they performed adequately if not impressively. They could however, have been a good deal more useful had they received a modern front end, but then so could other locomotives built at that time on the LMS.

First Introduced 1921.

THE LONDON and North Western Railway was the first railway to adopt 0-8-0s on a large scale and over the years from 1892 constructed no less than 572. In so doing it embraced eleven different classes which became very intermingled through rebuilding and then rebuilding again until finally being reduced to three closely related classes.

The G2 class was never rebuilt as such but they did receive, along with others, new Belpaire boilers in place of the original round topped type and it is in this form that I worked on them in the fifties. Fortunately this work was very brief, amounting to no more than two or three disposal experiences and a couple of relief turns out on the road, insufficient to give a comprehensive appraisal but quite enough to gain an insight into their shortcomings.

Old ex-LNWR drivers tended to eulogise over their hauling ability particularly when short of steam, which apparently was not an uncommon occurrence. Midland men however, viewed them with a jaundiced eye, feeling that if Crewe's design office had set out with awkwardness and discomfort in mind they could not have done a better job.

As a very junior fireman in the Shed Link I had made their acquaintance on the ashpit and discovered then that the flat, 7½ft. long grate was not the easiest to work

on. My driver had done most of the labouring and all the cursing while instructing me in technique, but what little I managed seemed very awkward and time consuming. Not until actually working a train, though, did the full horror of its footplate become apparent. Being somewhat more experienced by then, I must confess to an arousal of interest when being advised that we had a Super D. All ex-LNWR 0-8-0s were collectively known as Super Ds even though they were officially classified G1, G2 and G2A, a simplification much appreciated by the less informed. Fortunately it was daylight and I was able to explore this strange machine and discover what made it function more safely than had it been dark.

Unlike Dr. Who's Tardis, the miniscule cab was much smaller on the inside than it appeared from ground level and seemed to me no more than an afterthought squeezed betwixt firebox and tender when someone pointed out that there really ought to be somewhere for the crew to stand.

The footplate, if that is the correct term, was on two levels with high platforms either side of a narrow strip immediately in front of the firedoors. Attached to the cab sides above these platforms were semi-circular seats about the size of half a bar stool from which enginemen precariously dangled unless exceptionally long of shank. An unlagged boiler face protruded some distance from

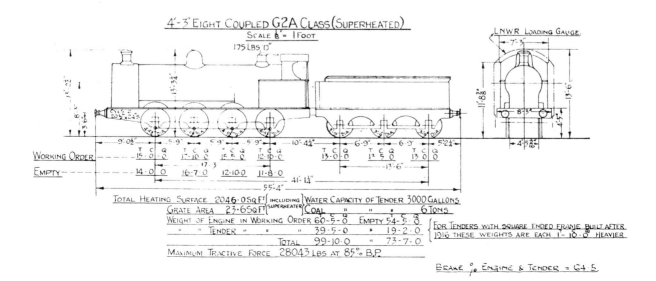

This photograph of 49173 portrays Super Ds as they are usually remembered, steadily wheezing along with their peculiar syncopated exhaust beat at the head of a long line of wagons. Although endowed with commendable hauling capacity they were afflicted with inadequate brakes, a miniscule cab and were perhaps the most awkward of all engines to work on.

the spectacle plate encroaching further into the limited area and was notable for having in its centre a regulator which worked opposite to normal i.e. pushed down to open and lifted to close. It does not require much imagination to visualise the chaos this innovation caused in the hands of a newcomer who instinctively opened the regulator every time he intended to close it. Adapting to this was as easy as driving a car equipped with an accelerator which closed when floored and opened to full throttle when released.

Not wishing firemen to escape without experiencing their fair share of difficulties, the designers had worked overtime and produced a few beauties. Unlike most locomotives, the flat grate was more 'active' at its front end and burned fuel at a higher rate under the brick arch than under the firehole. This seemed to be due to insufficient depth of ashpan and therefore volume of air at the rear, but it did mean that nearly every shovel of coal fired had to be swung vigorously in order to reach the front. Understanding designers usually place hand brake and water scoop handles either vertically or horizontally at the outside extremities of the tender where they are least obtrusive. Not so the Super D, for

some fiend had discovered that by using wheels instead of handles and by placing these close to the shovelling plate angled at 45° the chance of firemen striking them with their knuckles every swing could be guaranteed at nearly 100%.

Almost as successful in terms of awkwardness was the location of injector controls, with a steam valve practically in the roof high on the boiler face, a water control at virtually floor level and an overflow out of sight below; firemen were up and down like a fiddler's elbow every time an injector was used. Certainly this unwarranted exercise did not encourage frequent use, but as far as I can recall they worked with reasonable efficiency if somewhat noisily. To add to his frustration both platforms and the well between were finished with raised wooden blocks which effectively trapped coal dust and kept him continually busy with hand brush and slaking pipe. After the novelty of these strange new exercises had worn off on this frist trip I was then able to appreciate the lack of protection afforded by their diminutive cab when standing 'wrong road to the weather' in heavy rain.

On the credit side, the old Super D did manage to haul quite a substantial load in a sure footed if ponderous manner up the 1:157 gradient from Park Lane to Sutton Coldfield on our way to Walsall. Even at long cut-offs the exhaust had a peculiar syncopated beat with the emphasis on the second beat instead of the first and all the time accompanied by an asthmatic wheeze. The ride seemed reasonably stable but then at 15-20 mph most engines were usually docile – and at no time did we travel any faster. This was partly because the engine did not want to and partly because, with brakes no match for the locomotive's pulling capacity, *we* did not want to.

Despite the problems of trying to avoid all the obstructions, I managed to provide sufficient steam for the modest rate demanded. Had this been at a higher level I may not have fared so well; as it was I still contrived to painfully bark my knuckles a number of times in spite of wearing leather gloves.

For all their awkwardness they were rugged engines and many outlived the Derby 7F 0-8-0 which ironically had been introduced in 1929 to replace them.

As a machine for hauling mineral trains reliably but not very economically at slow speeds, they were satisfactory in their time, but by 1950, the Super Ds were, with their suspect braking, completely out of date and like many other classes, only still in harness because of a universal motive power shortage. All the Midland crews and most LNWR men agreed that they were the most awkward and uncomfortable engines of all to work on and it was generally conceded that in order to stand even half a chance of firing one correctly, one needed to carry a number of congenital deformities. Had I a wider experience of them perhaps I would have discovered some endearing features but as it was I felt in no way disadvantaged by being denied the opportunity.

Chapter 20

Ex LNER B1 4-6-0 Mixed Traffic

Introduced 1942. Total 410.

MY EXPERIENCE of these locomotives was unfortunately limited to only three occasions, all with the same late evening passenger duty working from Birmingham to Sheffield via Leicester. This was hardly enough to become familiar with them but I was sufficiently impressed to feel that they warranted a brief mention and in any case it serves to show that we did not have closed minds regarding 'foreign' engines.

When Edward Thompson succeeded Gresley in 1941 he was able to introduce his plans on locomotive standardisation and featured prominently in these was a 4-6-0 to perform similar duties to the highly successful LMS Black 5. Although visually different, many of the dimensions were very close, total heating surfaces and grate areas being virtually the same although of course the B1s used a parallel round topped boiler. Cylinder proportions corresponded less closely with B1s having at 20in. x 26in. a larger diameter but shorter stroke than Black 5s which gave them 1,423lbs greater tractive effort despite using 6ft. 2in. coupled wheels. With these two locomotives built for the same purpose coming from totally different backgrounds, comparisons are bound to be made and I shall endeavour to do this as far as possible.

I realise that beauty is in the eye of the beholder and perhaps I am biased towards taper boilers, but in my opinion they did not present the grace, balance and modern styling of Black 5s. Having said that, B1s certainly looked neat and cleanly functional although perhaps let down somewhat by a cab apparently borrowed from Gresley's B17s of 1928.

When engine crews are relieved en route, especially with passenger work, there is little time for the new crew to study much other than what immediately affects them with regard to carrying out their duties. The niceties of external design tend to take second place to the level of water in the boiler, steam pressure, condition of fire and, in the case of a 'foreign' engine, where the controls are and how they function.

Not having prepared or disposed of a B1, I can only speculate how difficult these tasks may have been, but sharing so many common features arranged in approximately the same places even to the extent of a rocking grate, leads me to suppose they would be similar to a Black 5. I will therefore confine my observations to the footplate, the working conditions found thereon and how the locomotive responded.

On first acquaintance, the cab appeared less spacious and somewhat more cluttered than Stanier cabs and yet the disposition of controls was more familiar than would be found on most other LNER types. Perhaps what made the footplate seem less commodious were the first things that caught my eye, two large luxurious padded bucket seats bracketed to the cab sides. Below and in front of these were raised platforms which not only acted as foot rests when seated but also enabled either crew member to look out through large curved spectacle glasses which followed the firebox contours.

When standing, these allowed a really excellent view over its parallel boiler although if seated, forward vision was restricted and best obtained by leaning out of the sliding side window. Effective vertical windshields here were up to LMS standard and so one could say that on balance it was a case of swings and roundabouts. The B1 allowed a better view across its boiler when standing which could be very useful for sighting signals on adverse curves, while Black 5s had the edge with regard to forward vision when seated. However, when it came to being seated B1s were incomparably better, providing the highest level of comfort I have experienced on any locomotive. The regulator and injectors were reminiscent of a Crab's, while the water gauges with their separate shut off cocks seemed rather archaic by our accustomed standards.

Boiler pressure, steam chest pressure and vacuum gauges were placed neatly in a row centrally over the boiler back plate and the carriage warming apparatus valve and gauge were conveniently mounted adjacent to the right hand injector. Most of the driver's controls were grouped around him, with a Gresham and Craven combination ejector located above a conventional reversing screw immediately in front. An excellent graduable steam brake valve and a steam sander valve were within easy reach, although the blower, mounted adjacent to the left hand injector, proved something of a stretch. Unfortunately the associated pipework for these fittings produced a plumber's nightmare which contrasted sharply with the neat appearance above the firebox. An umbrella type lever alongside the fireman's footrest controlled a single front damper while injector water regulators were again conventionally located behind the seats.

A hinged anti-glare shield was to us, a novel feature and so too the oven type fire doors which I had never encountered before. In the centre of this door was an

oval plate pivoted horizontally on its centre line which could be opened in steps to admit secondary air. I must confess that I did not like having to swing a large, hot piece of metal open every time I wished to fire and felt the whole arrangement was unnecessarily fussy, time consuming and not as efficient as sliding doors.

More than compensating for this though, was what I considered even more desirable than the superb bucket seats: a steam driven generator which provided power not only for electric running lights, but also comprehensive illumination in the cab as well. To be able to see any gauge and even the cut-off setting at the flick of a switch was a luxury beyond comprehension and I was very disappointed that this wonderful convenience did not carry over to BR Standard locomotives.

The 4,200 gallon tender was not so conveniently arranged or easy to shovel from as the Stanier unit and since BR tenders were closer to LMS rather than LNER styles I suspect that I was not alone in my opinion.

Although B1s looked neat and functional they did not, in my opinion, possess the modern, well balanced appearance of Black 5s. Perhaps their rather dated cab had something to do with it, but nevertheless, this cab contained the most luxurious seats I have ever encountered on a locomotive. B1s had their weaknesses of course, but in terms of overall performance on the road there was little to choose between them and our Black 5s.

Even so, a couple of lockers provided adequate space for personal effects and tools albeit at the expense of coal space doors which were rather on the small size. Behind these lay 7½ tons of coal in a self trimming bunker which did not self trim quite as well as it might and whilst this quantity of fuel should have been sufficient for most duties, the fireman would have spent a lot of time in the tender on a Birmingham to Carlisle trip.

Our trains were between eigth and ten bogies which the B1s started easily without undue slipping and accelerated briskly using full first valve and progressive notching up. We were fortunate in having 'moderate mileage engines' on all three journeys but even so they did not appear too happy on less than 25% cut-off whereas Black 5s in similar condition ran freely at less than 15%. Perhaps this had something to do with the impression of being somewhat busier and firing more coal than with the Stanier engine. However, at 25% and a partially open regulator, B1s soon settled down to easy running in the seventies if conditions allowed and at this speed the ride was quite good with no excessive knocking in bearings or axleboxes. Lateral stability was also well up to standard but there did seem a slight harshness vertically, although when seated one was so well insulated by thick padding, imperfections in the ride passed largely unnoticed.

The graduable steam brake proved extremely useful in holding the train secure while 'blowing the brakes off' (creating vacuum) when standing in a platform on a gradient; no such convenience was available on LMS locomotives but, of course, BR standards were so equipped.

Although the B1s grate was virtually the same area as a Black 5s, its slope followed early, rather than late versions of the LMS 3B boilers in that the rear half was level and the forward 50% sloped downwards. I found no difficulty in firing, using a firebed level with the bottom of the firehole and then thinning to about six inches at the front end. With the front damper fully open, the B1s crisp exhaust kept a good blast on the fire and, when the art of adjusting the secondary air flap had been mastered, consumed its smoke quite well. In fact I was delighted how freely the engines steamed and they seemed fully equal to Black 5s, although in all fairness, at no time were they extended to the limit for long periods and it would need a trip or two up the 'long drag' to Ais Gill in order to ascertain their true merit. Even at speed, firing required no special balancing acts or particular physical effort despite the oven door, and both injectors worked reliably and efficiently.

From the forgoing it will be deduced that I quite enjoyed my brief acquaintance with B1s but I appreciate this may have been biased by only working engines that were in good condition. Certainly their bucket seats and electric lighting were a revelation in luxury although some other aspects of their layout did not match those of Black 5s. As for performance, well there did not seem much to choose between them; perhaps the B1s acceleration at lower speeds was marginally better and the Black 5s held the advantage with freer running at shorter cut-offs when travelling fast. As a consequence B1s were possibly a little heavier on coal and water but the difference was not significant enough to be noticed in service.

Like the Black 5s, these ex-LNER engines proved to be thoroughly competent, versatile maids of all work and I did not really mind which type was rostered, but when the BR 5s appeared incorporating the best features from both classes and then some more, there was never any doubt, a BR 5 every time.